Toward a New Social Contract

Toward a New Social Contract

Taking On Distributional Tensions in Europe and Central Asia

Maurizio Bussolo, María E. Dávalos,
Vito Peragine, and Ramya Sundaram

Contents

Figures

Maps

Tables

Foreword

Rising inequality is among the most serious problems of our times. Economic progress has been remarkable in the last few decades, but not everyone has enjoyed the same gains, or even the same opportunities. The aggregate indicators, such as GDP growth or employment rate, paint a positive picture. Indeed, the setback of the global financial crisis of 2008 has been overcome, and most countries around the world have seen their income and employment not only return to the levels before the crisis but, in most cases, go beyond those and reach new heights.

However, a different picture comes into focus when one goes beyond the aggregates.

Technological change, globalization, and policy reforms have influenced industries, regions, and ultimately people in very different ways. Entire sectors have lost importance and many occupations are under threat of disappearing. In many countries, the labor share of total income has been declining, and given the accumulation of capital wealth in the hands of a minority, incomes are concentrating at the top of the distribution.

These changes have created opportunities, but the challenges cannot be overlooked. Services such as education and health care—key inputs to the accumulation of productive human capital—are becoming more expensive, and equal access to good-quality services is becoming an issue. Risk-sharing arrangements via targeted assistance or more general insurance have limitations. This uneven playing field generates inequality traps: without mobility and flexibility, technology- and globalization-driven opportunities become elusive, some groups are left behind, and distributional tensions arise.

In contrast to what populist proposals are promising, there is no quick fix. Curbing the trends—stopping trade or rejecting technologies—as well as passively compensating the losers have not worked in the past, and these measures will not work in the future. But inaction is not an option. The way societies adjust to distributional tensions and maintain social cohesion can make a big difference, not just in terms of equity but also in terms of future prosperity.

Given the long and varied experience with social welfare institutions, one would perhaps think that countries in Europe and Central Asia are well equipped to deal with distributional tensions. But, in fact, these institutions were designed for a very different economic environment. A key difference, even if not the only difference, is a rapidly transforming labor market where long-term wage employment is no longer the norm, especially not for the younger generations.

Instead of a quick fix, a long-term productive and stable solution requires (1) understanding better how inequality is evolving, and whether the growth process is or is not inclusive, and (2) rethinking the social contract—the shared principles used to regulate markets, define responsibilities and benefits, and redistribute incomes.

This report aims to offer contributions to these two requirements.

Inequality among individuals (or households), usually captured by inequality indexes such as the Gini, has shown a mixed pattern for the Europe and Central Asia region. Compared with the levels at the time of the fall of the Berlin Wall, this *vertical* inequality is, by the late 2010s, at higher levels. Also, it has been shown, that using tax data, the concentration of incomes at the top has increased. However, this report demonstrates that it is persistent unfairness and growing inequality between groups—rather than individuals—that are insidiously corroding social cohesion. Tensions between workers, between generations, and between regions have been increasing.

Insecurity, unfairness, and growing tensions among groups have also led to perceptions of increases in overall inequality and influence demands for corrective actions. Fissures in the social contract are becoming more evident. Losers from the distributional tensions—young cohorts, routine task-intensive and low-wage workers, inhabitants of lagging regions—choose to voice their discontent by supporting extreme political movements and parties or choose to exit the social and political dialogue altogether.

In terms of rethinking the social contract, rather than prescribing or even identifying a specific set of policies, the report proposes a set of three policy principles that, considered jointly, could help level the playing field and redesign a stable social contract. The principles consist of (1) moving toward *equal protection* of all workers, no matter their type of employment, while promoting labor markets' flexibility; (2) seeking *universality* in the provision of social assistance, social insurance, and basic quality services; and (3) supporting *progressivity* in a broad tax base that complements labor income taxation with the taxation of capital.

With its concerns for distribution and fairness and their implications for political stability and sustainable economic growth, this report continues the World Bank work in support of *paving the way toward shared prosperity* in Europe and Central Asia.[1]

Cyril Muller
Vice President, Europe and Central Asia Region
The World Bank

Note

1. This paraphrases the title of an earlier study in the same series: Bussolo, Maurizio, and Luis F. López-Calva. 2014. *Shared Prosperity: Paving the Way in Europe and Central Asia*. Washington, DC: World Bank.

About the Authors and Contributors

Maurizio Bussolo, Lead Economist in the Chief Economist Office for Europe and Central Asia, has been working on quantitative analyses of economic policy and development with research interests spanning both micro- and macroeconomic topics. He previously worked at the Organisation for Economic Co-operation and Development (OECD), the Overseas Development Institute in London, and Fedesarrollo and the University of Los Andes in Colombia. He has extensively published in peer-reviewed journals on trade, growth, poverty, and income distribution. He holds a PhD in economics from the University of Warwick.

María E. Dávalos is Senior Economist in the Poverty and Equity Global Practice. She joined the World Bank in 2010 and has worked in the Latin America and the Caribbean region, as well as the Europe and Central Asia region, on poverty, inequality, economic mobility, migration, and gender. She obtained a master's degree in economic policy management from the Centre for Studies and Research on International Development (France) and a PhD in economics from Fordham University.

Vito Peragine is Full Professor of Economics at the University of Bari. Previously, he was Lecturer in Economics at the University Carlos III of Madrid. He has published widely in the fields of inequality, poverty, and normative economics. He serves on the editorial boards of the *Journal of Economic Inequality* and the *Review of Income and Wealth*. He holds a PhD in economics from the University of York (U.K.).

Ramya Sundaram is Senior Economist in the Social Protection and Jobs Global Practice. She has extensive experience in advising governments on improving the effectiveness and coverage of social protection systems, on labor market and activation systems, on measurement and alleviation of poverty, and on inequality and inclusion. Ramya has a PhD in economics from the University of Pennsylvania and was Assistant Professor of Economics at the University of Arizona prior to joining the World Bank.

Aylin Isik-Dikmelik is Senior Economist in the Social Protection and Jobs Global Practice at the World Bank. Her work focuses on a wide range of topics on the social protection and labor spectrum, from designing and implementing effective social protection systems to improving labor markets and employability for inclusive growth. She holds a PhD in economics from the Johns Hopkins University.

Jonathan George Karver is a research analyst in the Poverty and Equity Global Practice for Europe and Central Asia, where he contributes to analytical work on poverty and inequality in the European Union. He has provided leadership and supporting roles for projects related to welfare measurement and fiscal policies, among others. He holds a master's degree in economics from the Instituto Tecnológico Autónomo de México.

Xinxin Lyu worked as a research analyst at the Poverty and Equity Global Practice for Europe and Central Asia, from 2016 to 2018. At the World Bank, she contributed to various pieces of analytical work done in the South Caucasus and Western Balkan countries, focusing on the measurement and analysis of poverty and the estimation of the impact of policies on poverty. She holds a bachelor's degree from the University of International Relations, China, and a master of science in economics from Tufts University. She is currently a PhD student in economics at Purdue University.

Mattia Makovec is an economist in the Social Protection and Jobs Global Practice at the World Bank. He works on various topics related to jobs and social protection in Europe and Central Asia, including minimum wages, migration, the integration of refugees, and the effectiveness of social protection systems. Previously, he held positions at Essex University, at the World Bank Country Office in Indonesia, at the University of Chile, and at the Ministry of Labor in Chile. Mattia holds a PhD in economics from Bocconi University and a master's in economics from University College London.

Iván Torre is an economist in the Office of the Chief Economist for Europe and Central Asia at the World Bank. His work focuses on inequality, income distribution, and the political economy of development. He previously worked as a consultant for the Inter-American Development Bank. He has a bachelor's degree in economics from Universidad de Buenos Aires and holds a PhD in economics from Sciences Po, Paris.

Mitchell Wiener is Senior Social Protection Specialist in the Eastern Europe and Central Asia region at the World Bank. He is a pension and social security actuary with more than 40 years of experience with public and private pension programs. He specializes in the design, financing, and administration of social security systems.

Soonhwa Yi works on identifying good policies to facilitate internal and international labor mobility in low- and middle-income countries. Prior to joining the Social Protection and Jobs Global Practice, she managed multi-institutional teams to take forward the global migration agenda of KNOMAD (Global Knowledge Partnership on Migration and Development) at the World Bank. Areas of her current research interest include labor policy responses to aging populations and jobs.

Acknowledgments

This regional flagship report is a joint product of ECA's Office of the Chief Economist, the Social Protection and Jobs Global Practice, and the Poverty and Equity Global Practice of the World Bank.

The work was carried out under the direction of Hans Timmer, Chief Economist of the Europe and Central Asia region, and with the guidance of Cyril Muller, Europe and Central Asia Regional Vice President; Michal Rutkowski, Senior Director of Social Protection and Jobs; and Carolina Sánchez-Páramo, Senior Director of the Poverty and Equity Global Practice.

This report was prepared by a team led by Maurizio Bussolo (Chief Economist Office for Europe and Central Asia), María E. Dávalos (Poverty and Equity Global Practice), Vito Peragine (University of Bari), and Ramya Sundaram (Social Protection and Jobs Global Practice), with support from Luís F. López-Calva, Practice Manager of the Poverty and Equity Global Practice, and Andy Mason and Cem Mete, Practice Managers of the Social Protection and Jobs Global Practice. The authorship of the chapters is as follows:

- The Overview was written by Maurizio Bussolo, María E. Dávalos, Vito Peragine, and Ramya Sundaram, with inputs from Iván Torre.
- Chapter 1 was written by Maurizio Bussolo, María E. Dávalos, Vito Peragine, and Ramya Sundaram, with inputs from Iván Torre.
- Chapter 2 was written by Maurizio Bussolo, María E. Dávalos, Jonathan George Karver, Xinxin Lyu, Vito Peragine, and Iván Torre, with inputs from Ignacio Apella, Damien Capelle (Princeton University), Lidia Ceriani (Georgetown University), Daniele Checchi (Università di Milano), Hai-Anh H. Dang, Ernest Dautovic, Carola Gruen, Tullio Jappelli (University of Naples Federico II and CSEF), Roberto Nisticò (University of Naples Federico II), Stefan Thewissen (OECD), Sailesh Tiwari, Hernan Winkler, and Gonzalo Zunino (CINVE).
- Chapter 3 was written by Maurizio Bussolo, Aylin Isik-Dikmelik, Mattia Makovec, Ramya Sundaram, Iván Torre, Mitchell Wiener, and Soonhwa Yi, with inputs from Florentin Philipp Kerschbaumer, Carla Krolage (CESifo), Laura Maratou-Kolias, Renata Mayer Gukovas, Atul Menon, María Laura Oliveri, Andreas Peichl (CESifo), Marc Stoeckli (CESifo), and Christian Wittneben (CESifo).
- Chapter 4 was written by Maurizio Bussolo and Iván Torre, with inputs from Esther Bartl, Ada Ferrer-i-Carbonell (IAE-CSIC), Anna Giolbas (GIGA Institute of African Affairs), Bingjie Hu, Jonathan George Karver, and Mathilde Lebrand.
- Chapter 5 was written by Maurizio Bussolo, María E. Dávalos, Vito Peragine, and Ramya Sundaram, with inputs from Joe Chrisp (University of Bath),

Mattia Makovec, Luke Martinelli (University of Bath), Mabel Martinez, Alice Scarduelli (CESifo), Marc Stoeckli (CESifo), Mitchell Wiener, and Jurgen De Wispelaere (University of Bath).

The report's advisory committee, comprising Francois Bourguignon, Francisco H. G. Ferreira, Marc Fleurbaey, and Ravi Kanbur, was a source of knowledge and inspiration. During multiple occasions—in long discussions at the authors' workshops, in bilateral communications, and at conferences and seminars—the advisors have been always available and generous in providing critical feedback that contributed to shaping the report.

We are grateful for invaluable comments from our reviewers, including Arup Banerji, Elena Ianchovichina, and Ana Revenga. The team also received useful comments at various stages from Margaret Ellen Grosh, Carl Patrick Hanlon, Ugo Gentilini, and Truman G. Packard.

We want to express gratitude to the wide range of participants at our authors' workshops, and at seminars and conferences in which we presented background research for the report. Feedback received at the 2016 OECD–World Bank high-level "The Squeezed Middle-Class in OECD and Emerging Countries" conference in Paris, the ECINEQ 2017 conference in New York, the 2017 Stanford-Cornell "Commodification and Inequality" conference in Palo Alto, the 2017 IBS Jobs Conference in Warsaw, the 2018 IZA–World Bank Jobs and Development Conference in Bogotá, and the 2018 IZA World Labor Conference in Berlin has been very useful in strengthening the report.

The team appreciates the writing skills, patience, and availability of William Shaw, who helped in the drafting and redrafting of all the chapters. Valuable contributions were offered by Mukaddas Kurbanova and Ekaterina Ushakova, who provided exceptional administrative support and oversaw the production of this report; Bruce Ross-Larson, who facilitated the development of the storyline through several hours of discussion among team members; and Robert Zimmerman and Thomas Cohen, who provided insightful comments and changes to the report and whose editing skills improved the report substantially. It also expresses gratitude to the communications team, including Carl Patrick Hanlon, Paul Clare, Artem Kolesnikov, John Mackedon, and Kym Smithies, for their support in preparing the outreach for and dissemination of the report, and the dedicated webpage.

Mary Fisk was the production editor for the report, working with acquisitions editor Jewel McFadden and production manager Aziz Gökdemir. Carlos Reyes designed the cover image, and Datapage International prepared the typeset pages. The team is grateful for their professionalism and expertise.

Abbreviations

CCT	conditional cash transfer
C-UCT	categorical unconditional cash transfer
EU	European Union
EU13	Bulgaria, Croatia, Cyprus, Czech Republic, Estonia, Hungary, Latvia, Lithuania, Malta, Poland, Romania, Slovak Republic, and Slovenia
EU15	Austria, Belgium, Denmark, Finland, France, Germany, Greece, Ireland, Italy, Luxembourg, the Netherlands, Portugal, Spain, Sweden, and the United Kingdom
EU28	the current full membership: Austria, Belgium, Bulgaria, Croatia, Cyprus, the Czech Republic, Denmark, Estonia, Finland, France, Germany, Greece, Hungary, Ireland, Italy, Latvia, Lithuania, Luxembourg, Malta, the Netherlands, Poland, Portugal, Romania, the Slovak Republic, Slovenia, Spain, Sweden, and the United Kingdom
GDP	gross domestic product
GMI	guaranteed minimum income
ISCO	International Standard Classification of Occupations (International Labour Organization)
LiTS	Life in Transition Survey
OECD	Organisation for Economic Co-operation and Development
PISA	Programme for International Student Assessment (OECD)
PPP	purchasing power parity
PPS	purchasing power standard
PRUBI	progressive realization of the coverage of universal basic income
PT-UCT	poverty-targeted unconditional cash transfer
PUBI	pure universal basic income
PUBI-AO	pure universal basic income for adults only
TUBI	tapered universal basic income or progressive realization of the coverage of the tapered universal basic income
UBI	universal basic income
UCT	unconditional cash transfer

Note: All dollar amounts are U.S. dollars (US$) unless otherwise indicated.

Regional Classifications Used in This Report

		European Union				Western Balkans
		Western Europe	**Southern Europe**	**Central Europe**	**Northern Europe**	
Europe and Central Asia	European Union and Western Balkans	Austria Belgium France Germany Ireland Luxembourg Netherlands United Kingdom	Greece Italy Portugal Spain Cyprus Malta	Bulgaria Croatia Czech Republic Hungary Poland Romania Slovak Republic Slovenia	Denmark Finland Sweden Estonia Latvia Lithuania	Albania Bosnia and Herzegovina Kosovo Macedonia, FYR Montenegro Serbia
		South Caucasus	**Central Asia**	**Russian Federation**	**Turkey**	**Other Eastern Europe**
	Eastern Europe and Central Asia	Armenia Azerbaijan Georgia	Kazakhstan Kyrgyz Republic Tajikistan Turkmenistan Uzbekistan			Belarus Moldova Ukraine

Other country groups mentioned in this report:

EU13: Bulgaria, Croatia, Cyprus, the Czech Republic, Estonia, Hungary, Latvia, Lithuania, Malta, Poland, Romania, the Slovak Republic, Slovenia

EU15: Austria, Belgium, Denmark, Finland, France, Germany, Greece, Ireland, Italy, Luxembourg, the Netherlands, Portugal, Spain, Sweden, the United Kingdom

EU28: Austria, Belgium, Bulgaria, Croatia, Cyprus, the Czech Republic, Denmark, Estonia, Finland, France, Germany, Greece, Hungary, Ireland, Italy, Latvia, Lithuania, Luxembourg, Malta, the Netherlands, Poland, Portugal, Romania, the Slovak Republic, Slovenia, Spain, Sweden, the United Kingdom

Overview

The Europe and Central Asia region stands out as the most equal region in the world. Of the 30 countries around the globe with the lowest Gini coefficient—a measure of income inequality whereby a lower coefficient corresponds to a more equal distribution—23 are in the region.[1] Compared with other regions, the countries in Europe and Central Asia redistribute income on a larger scale and have more extensive welfare systems, more progressive taxation, and more generous social protection. This reflects the strong preference of Europeans for egalitarian societies.

Yet, people in Europe and Central Asia are dissatisfied with the status quo and, as in regions that exhibit greater inequality, demand changes.[2] More people are either voting for populist parties that promise to get rid of current policies and establish a new social order, or they are not voting at all. Separatist movements are on the rise, while trust in political institutions is on the decline.

The primary goal of this report is to analyze changes in the distribution of incomes and resources that, even if not fully reflected in changes of inequality *among individuals and households*, are affecting people's security, aspirations, and sense of well-being and identity. When asked in opinion surveys, a large majority of people across all countries in the region expresses concerns about rising inequality. It is important to investigate the potential sources of these beliefs and views.

The report emphasizes the relevance of distributional tensions *among groups* and of unfairness. These reflect the economic drivers of the rising discontent with the political and social order in the region. The clash between these distributional tensions and the preferences for equity is posing a serious challenge to the social contract in Europe and Central Asia.

Distributional Tensions and the Need to Rethink the Social Contract

The weakening of the social contract is occurring in the context of a rapidly changing economic landscape. The entry of China, India, and the transition countries of Eastern Europe and Central Asia in the global market in the 1990s expanded the size of globally integrated labor markets from 1.5 billion workers to 2.9 billion workers, the "great doubling" as Freeman (2007, 55) calls it.[3] Recent technological progress is increasing the demand for advanced problem-solving and interpersonal skills, while the demand for less-advanced skills decreases as routine jobs become automated. Digital transformation allows new technologies and start-up firms to scale up quickly and is rapidly altering production patterns. These global forces continue to roil labor markets and cause uneven economic impacts throughout societies in Europe and Central Asia.

These pervasive changes are affecting specific groups differentially. Although some are benefiting from the transforming economic landscape, others are not. The report describes in detail the key distributional tensions among groups that are identified according to four criteria: birth cohort, occupation, place of residence, and, following the literature on inequality of opportunity, circumstances beyond the control of the individual, such as parental background and gender.

Horizontal inequality among groups—which affects young workers, people in vanishing occupations, individuals lacking good social networks, and people living in lagging regions—is not captured by the vertical inequality in income among individuals and households that is measured by the Gini coefficient. The changes in the Gini coefficient may even be at odds with the deepening distributional tensions. Widening horizontal inequality makes people feel they lack opportunity in an unfair system.

A shift to part-time, temporary, or gig jobs, such as driving for Uber, provides income, but not the benefits offered through full-time employment in this region. The value placed on noneconomic factors, such as autonomy and status, is also threatened by the rise of nonstandard forms of employment. This leaves workers more vulnerable to economic shocks and, regardless of income, perceptions that they are less well off.

Individuals who expected to join the middle class through educational attainment or through work experience find themselves instead struggling for financial stability and security. The steady size of the region's middle class masks the presence of considerable disappointment among working-age individuals who may still enjoy middle-class incomes but do not have middle-class economic security.

The report shows that government policies and institutions, which were designed in the twentieth century and had been working satisfactorily for quite some time, are not equipped to handle the emerging distributional tensions. This inadequate response clashes with the value that people place on equity and stability in the region and creates an imbalance. This imbalance—across markets, policies, and preferences in the distribution of resources—is a major reason for the appeal of populism and is exerting pressure on the social contract.

Based on an analysis of the rising distributional tensions in the region, this report calls for a fundamental rethinking of the principles behind the policies and institutions that regulate markets, define responsibilities and benefits, and redistribute incomes—a rethinking of the social contract where equity, progressivity, and universality are reevaluated.

Equity: A Key Aspiration in the Region

The desire for social equity is a characteristic of European civilizations dating back more than 2,000 years.

"There should exist . . . neither extreme poverty nor . . . excessive wealth, for both are productive of great evil," wrote Plato (Tanzi 2018, 302).

"An imbalance between rich and poor is the oldest and most fatal ailment of all republics," Plutarch later affirmed (Tanzi 2018, 302).

Following the Great Depression and the devastation of World War II, societies in Europe greatly expanded the welfare state. In Western Europe, free markets were combined with broad participation in education, social safety nets, and income redistribution, as well as universal access to health care. During the same period, countries in the eastern part of Europe and Central Asia featured state-controlled economic activity, alongside universal, state-provided access to services and to guaranteed work. While political, ideological, and economic perspectives differed significantly across countries, a common theme was the aspiration for equity and social cohesion.

Such a commitment to equity is not evident across all regions of the world. For example, in North America, the United States does not have a European-style welfare system because of different social preferences and degrees of aversion to inequality (Alesina, Glaeser, and Sacerdote 2001). About 70 percent of people in the United States believe the poor can help themselves to improve their situation. In Western Europe, only 40 percent of individuals believe that poor people have a chance to escape poverty on their own; in Eastern European transition countries, the share drops to 24 percent. As a result, a majority in Europe supports government policies to ensure well-being and redistribute income.

Balancing Markets, Policies, and Preferences

The term "social contract" originated in political philosophy in reference to the agreement of individuals to give up part of their freedom in return for protection provided by the state (for example, see Hobbes 2012; Locke 1988; Rousseau 1968). This report puts an economic interpretation on the concept. Individuals accept the broad outline of economic policies if the outcomes of these policies coincide with their preferences. This dynamic is similar, although not identical, to the approach of Binmore (1998), who sees the social contract as an equilibrium of a game between social entities and individuals, as well as the analytical approach proposed by Kanbur (1999) in the context of optimal taxation. It also resembles the recent effort to evaluate social progress, including distributional issues, by the International Panel on Social Progress (IPSP 2018). According to Rodrik (1999), well-functioning social contracts allow countries to manage shocks effectively and adapt to new, efficient equilibria. Countries that have unresolved distributional conflicts may experience inefficient outcomes because the losers do not trust the system, opt out, and resist the needed adjustments. Distributional tensions, if not balanced by corrective policies, institutional arrangements, or a shift of preferences on equity and fairness, can generate cracks in the social contract and stop or severely hinder economic growth.

Thus, a stable social contract finds a balance among the following (figure O.1):

- The market-generated distribution of resources and incomes
- Public policies, including taxes and transfers, regulation, and the provision of goods and services, that alter this distribution
- Individual and societal preferences for equity, perceptions of inequality, and the demand for the redistribution of opportunities and outcomes

Temporary deviations from an equilibrium among these three elements are normal and can be tolerated. However, a long-term imbalance risks generating ruptures in the social contract.

This conceptual framework is an organizing principle of the report. The report first describes the rise in horizontal inequality in the market-generated distribution of income and examines how policies (regulations, redistribution through taxes and transfers, and public expenditures) fail to fully address this. It also shows people's preferences for equity and the increasingly negative perceptions of the situation in income distribution and fairness. A main contribution of the report is the organization of a wealth of data and empirical research around the three elements shown in figure O.1.

This structure also highlights a growing imbalance between the distribution of income generated by the market and the policy regime in responding to the

FIGURE O.1
The social contract as a dynamic equilibrium

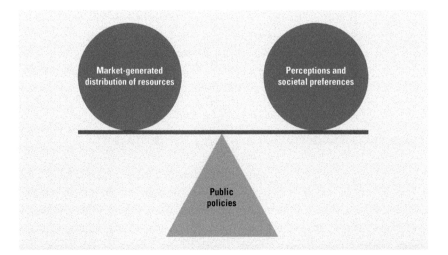

desires of individuals about equity. A failure to resolve this imbalance can undermine social cohesion and have serious implications for the stability of the social contract. The polarization in recent voting behavior in several countries of the region is a symptom of the discontent.

The final section of the report thus considers changes in the policy framework that could support a return to a long-term equilibrium and a renewed and stable social contract.

The Market-Generated Distribution of Incomes

The first part of the report considers four distributional tensions generated by the market:

- The intergenerational divide, or disparities between young and old generations
- Inequalities among workers engaged in different occupations, such as office clerks and machine operators versus nurse's aides, private security guards, or the more highly skilled engineers and scientists
- Inequality in access to economic opportunities based on geographical location
- Inequalities of opportunity based on gender, ethnicity, background, or other characteristics rather than individual effort (figure O.2)

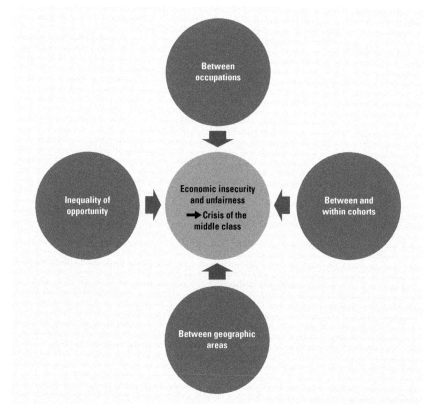

FIGURE O.2
Distributional tensions along four dimensions are explored

Some groups are on the losing side of more than one of these distributional tensions. Because it supports economic and political stability, the middle class is an important group. The first part of the report analyzes the extent to which the four distributional tensions are linked to the malaise of the middle class.

The four distributional tensions have emerged amid concerns and resentment over the falling share of labor relative to capital in total income and over the increasing concentration of top incomes and wealth. In the United Kingdom, the share of income held by the top 1 percent has risen by 7 percentage points in the past 25 years, reaching 14 percent in 2014. The number of billionaires in Western Europe rose from 90 in 1996 to 379 in 2017, and the number of Russian Federation billionaires rose from 8 in 2001 to 96 in 2017.

A Growing Intergenerational Divide

In Western Europe, relative to older cohorts, younger cohorts include a larger share of workers who are unemployed or in low-quality jobs. In 2015, temporary contracts represented close to 50 percent of employment among workers ages 15–24 in France and the Netherlands, compared with around 20 percent among the overall population in both countries. The young will likely have to work more years and will likely have less savings to finance retirement despite longer work histories compared with preceding generations. For these younger workers, lower earnings and fewer old-age income prospects imply a widening intergenerational divide, which is an important source of distributional tension even if it is masked by positive income trends more generally.

In addition, younger workers in Southern and Western Europe are facing higher income inequality at every point of the life cycle compared with older generations (figure O.3). For example, income inequality among Italians born in

FIGURE O.3
Income inequality is much higher among cohorts born in the 1980s

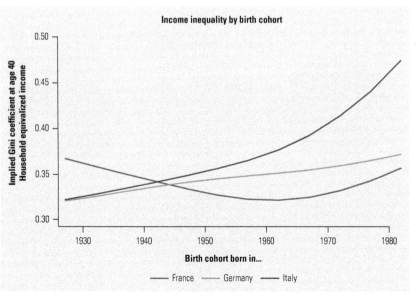

Source: Bussolo et al. 2018.

the 1930s was similar to that in (fairly equal) Japan (Gini coefficient of about 0.31). In contrast, income inequality among the cohorts born in the 1980s was at the level of (highly unequal) Chile (Gini coefficient of about 0.48). This greater income dispersion can be interpreted as a sign of greater insecurity and vulnerability.

Because inequality tends to rise as cohorts age, starting the life cycle with high inequality increases the likelihood of even greater inequality in the future. Together with slower growth, this creates more insecurity, along with the serious risk that populations in Europe and Central Asia will age ever more unequally (OECD 2017).

Polarization in Occupations

Occupational polarization has increased because economic transformation favors some sectors and occupations. More broadly, occupations intensive in routine tasks, typically in the middle of the wage spectrum, have shrunk across Europe: their share of employment has fallen by more than 10 percentage points in Southern and Western Europe and by close to 5 percentage points in Central and Eastern Europe (figure O.4). This has forced many middle-skilled workers into lower-skilled occupations, thereby reducing the incomes of low-skilled workers. At the same time, occupations at the top of the wage distribution—typically intensive in nonroutine cognitive tasks—have increased. This has been associated with an upward pull in incomes among highly skilled workers. Overall, the polarization of occupations in Europe has translated into greater labor income inequality: the Gini index of labor earnings rose by 8 points in Germany and Spain from the mid-1990s to 2013 and by about 5 points in Poland during the same period. More seriously affected by the occupational changes were workers already at the bottom of the income distribution, but workers in the middle also faced reductions in earnings growth and greater job insecurity because mid-income occupations are disappearing.

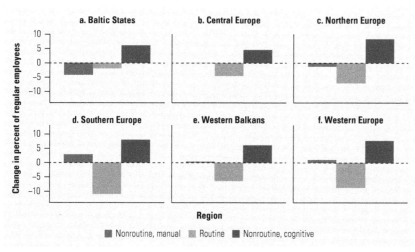

FIGURE O.4

The employment share of routine task-intensive occupations has fallen in Europe

Change in the share of employment, by occupation category, late 1990s to early 2010s

Source: World Bank calculations based on household surveys and labor force surveys.
Note: **Northern Europe:** Denmark, Finland, Norway, Sweden. **The Baltic States:** Estonia, Latvia, Lithuania.

FIGURE O.5

The share of employment, by occupational category, early 2000s to mid-2010s

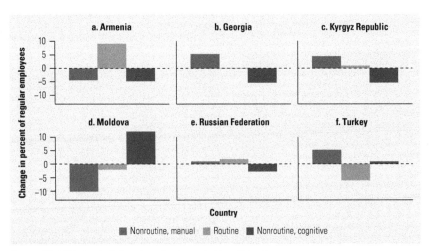

Source: World Bank calculations based on household and labor force surveys.

In the eastern part of Europe and Central Asia, particularly in the former Soviet Union economies, the picture is more nuanced. Occupational change has been less significant, and, with the exception of Moldova, this has meant a reduction in nonroutine cognitive task-intensive occupations. Highly skilled workers, usually prevalent in this occupation type, experienced an average decline of about 5 percentage points in their share of employment in Armenia, Georgia, the Kyrgyz Republic, and the Russian Federation (figure O.5). This occupational transformation in the former Soviet Union economies risks frustrating the aspirations of the well-educated younger cohorts that are entering the job market.

A Spatial Divide

Differences in income levels and poverty rates persist among regions in many countries of Europe and Central Asia, and, despite increases in average consumption among households over the past decade, inequalities between geographical areas have widened in several countries. In Armenia, for example, the difference in poverty rates between the less well-off and the more well-off regions rose from 25 percentage points to 38 percentage points between 2005 and 2014. In Romania, the poverty rate in the least well-off region was 2.5 times higher than the rate in the most well-off region. The poorest region in France had an at-risk-of-poverty rate three times higher than the rate in the richest region. In the European Union (EU), despite a reduction in country-level inequalities, differences in output across regions have been widening (figure O.6).

Differences in educational attainment are a key determinant of spatial gaps in welfare and undermine equality of opportunity. Across the region, in both the east and the west, there are gaps in the quality of education both between socioeconomic groups and between rural and urban areas. The spatial divide in learning between youth in urban areas and youth in rural areas in Bulgaria and Moldova is equivalent to around two years of schooling.

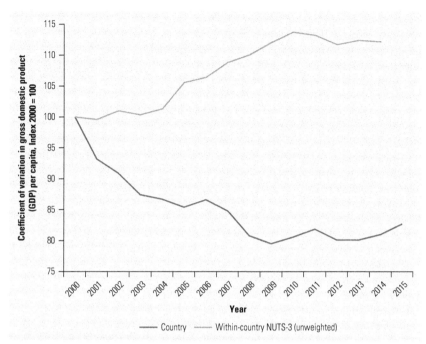

FIGURE O.6
Between-region spatial inequalities within countries have increased in the European Union

Source: Farole, Goga, and Ionescu-Heroiu 2018.
Note: Country refers to the coefficient of variation across European Union countries, signaling convergence in gross domestic product (GDP). The within-country coefficient of variation measure is at the Nomenclature of Territorial Units for Statistics–3 level (NUTS-3). GDP per capita is measured in Purchasing Power Standard (PPS).

Inequality of Opportunity

Inequality is often measured in outcomes, such as consumption, income, wealth, or even education, while fairness refers to the process generating these outcomes. Even in a context of stable income inequality, opportunity inequality—the proportion of the overall inequality deriving from circumstances beyond the control of individuals—may rise. Finding a good job—according to many, a crucial step in accessing a stable, middle-class standard of living—is becoming more difficult. It involves possessing favorable connections more than possessing ability or effort (Dávalos et al. 2016). Inequality of opportunity or changes in fairness may be emerging as key distributional tensions in the region.[4]

In Western Europe, the transmission of education privileges from parents to offspring has decreased (a result of the mass education effort), and the education premium in wages has also been trending downward. Together, these phenomena should have reduced overall inequality of opportunity. Instead, inequality of opportunity in incomes has been generally stable at high levels. Parental background still counts in explaining inequality in the earnings of offspring through a networking mechanism, analogous to the social separatism of the upper classes, as reflected in the growing importance of private education, private health plans, and private pensions (Milanović 2017). This means that networking among well-off parents buys better positions for the offspring in the income distribution, thereby achieving the same objectives promised by private education.

In Eastern Europe, by contrast, inequality of opportunity in education is increasing, which translates into greater inequality of opportunity in the labor market. Birth circumstances, especially parental background among individuals, are more important determinants of access to tertiary education among the generation that came of age in the early 2000s than among the generation that entered educational institutions before the subregion's transition to the market economy. Indeed, a large portion of inequality of opportunity in education among the youngest cohorts in Eastern Europe is explained solely by parental background: access to education has become more unfair over time because it is increasingly linked to parental educational achievement.

Increased Vulnerability in the Middle Class

Policies are often justified by reference to the needs of the middle class partly because a large, thriving middle class has been associated with political stability and sustained economic growth (for example, see Birdsall 2010; Birdsall, Graham, and Pettinato 2000; Easterly 2001).

Overall, the rise of distributional tensions and persistent unfair economic processes have altered the complexion of the region's middle class, reducing economic security and disappointing the expectations of many workers who had anticipated that they would be able to enjoy a middle-class lifestyle.

While the changes in the size of the middle class have been quite slow, there has been a pronounced deterioration in the sense of security and an expansion in the risk of dropping out of the middle class and into poverty. For example, the income necessary to guarantee a small probability of falling into poverty has risen from an average of US$34-a-day purchasing power parity (PPP) to an average of US$40-a-day PPP in the last decade (Bussolo, Karver, and López-Calva 2018) (figure O.7).[5] This additional US$6 can be interpreted as an increase in the insurance premium to mitigate the growing risk of falling into poverty. In some countries, the cost of the premium climbed by 100 percent or more. Thus, it rose from US$14 to US$32 in Bulgaria and from US$22 to US$44 in Latvia. This surge in vulnerability, linked to the changing profile of the middle class, is in line with the perception that the middle class is losing out. It has provoked heated policy debates and proposals for a full overhaul of taxation and social protection. It also has implications for the political platforms that can gain support from the middle class.

Public Policy Responses

Public policies are struggling to cope with rising inequality between groups in the region.

The significant progress in economic and social equality during the second half of the 20th century, mainly in Western Europe, was supported by mass education, labor unions, and substantial redistribution through taxation and public transfers (Atkinson 2016; Milanović 2017). Government policy and the welfare state were crucial in the effort to achieve equity and still deliver a considerable reduction in vertical inequality. For the 28 countries in the EU, the difference between the Gini

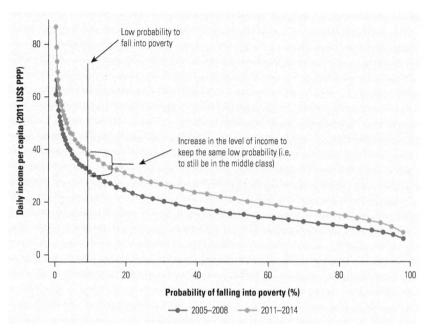

FIGURE O.7
The middle class in the European Union has become more vulnerable

Source: Calculations based on data of the Longitudinal–User Database of EU-SILC (European Union Statistics on Income and Living Conditions) (database), Eurostat, European Commission, Luxembourg, http://ec.europa.eu/eurostat/web/microdata/european-union-statistics-on-income-and-living-conditions. *Note:* The two curves in the figure have been obtained using pooled data for Austria, Belgium, Bulgaria, Cypress, Denmark, Estonia, France, Greece, Hungary, Iceland, Latvia, Lithuania, the Netherlands, Norway, Poland, the Slovak Republic, Slovenia, and Spain during the two periods indicated.

of market incomes and the Gini of disposable incomes averages the equivalent of 20 Gini points—an amazing feat.

However, the institutions and the policies face significant challenges in adapting to the profound global changes of the past few decades. The reaction of the welfare systems in most European countries to the emerging distributional tensions was partial and sometimes inconsistent. Losers were compensated by increases in transfers, but not by a significant decline in taxes. Several countries in Central and Eastern Europe introduced a flat tax on personal income, starting with Estonia in 1994 and followed by Bulgaria, the Czech Republic, Hungary, Latvia, Lithuania, Romania, and the Slovak Republic.[6]

These policies were largely regressive in terms of the vertical inequality of the income distribution. In Hungary, which was the last of the group of countries to institute the flat tax, in 2011, the average tax rate paid by the top three deciles of the income distribution fell by 2 percentage points between 2007 and 2014, while the rate paid by the bottom three deciles remained practically unchanged.

However, these and other policy changes had an even greater impact on horizontal inequality or inequality between groups. For instance, average tax rates in Bulgaria, Hungary, and Poland were reduced significantly for the winners of the shifts in occupations, while average tax rates were reduced by a smaller amount or remained unchanged for workers in occupations for which demand was falling. These changes accentuated the widening divide between the winners and losers of the changes in occupations. In Hungary, the distribution of income across age-groups was adversely affected. The average tax rate among tax-paying individuals ages 18–24 rose by more than 8 percentage points; among individuals ages 35–44, however, it dropped by 2 percentage points, and, among the 45–54 age-group, it did not change. In an already polarized society, these tax policy changes, on top of the initial disparities in market incomes and the reduced job security affecting younger workers, widened the intergenerational divide.[7]

Although most politicians pay lip service to the needs of the middle class, little has been done to protect vulnerable workers through changes in tax and transfer policies. Support has shrunk for households that rely on a single source of market income, and such households are facing a growing risk of falling into poverty. This contrasts with the support for households with several earners or pensioners, groups with greater economic security that rely on multiple sources of income or on steady public transfers. Dual earner households in Poland obtained a tax cut of close to 5 percentage points, a pattern similar to that in other Central and Eastern European countries. Similarly, in Belgium, Finland, and Sweden, households that were dependent on transfers and that enjoyed relatively high levels of income security also benefited from tax changes. In contrast, the economically insecure have not benefited from tax changes in any of these countries.

Preferences for Equity

Rising income inequality among groups runs counter to the strong preferences for equity and fairness in the region. If inequality in a country is not in line with the preferences of the population, there will be a demand for corrective action. The government may respond with changes in redistributive policies. However, if the policies do not address the dimensions of inequality that people care about and perceive as unfair, the policies are likely to fail.

The gap between perceptions of inequality and the inequality measures economists use is substantial and persistent. This may be because perceptions do not reflect reality, but it may also mean that individuals are concerned with types of inequality that are not readily or accurately measured by traditional objective indicators. In any case, perceptions matter.

"We suggest that most theories about political effects of inequality [demand for redistribution, the political participation of citizens, democratization] need to be reframed as theories about effects of perceived inequality," note Gimpelson and Treisman (2018, 27). Indeed, the demand for redistribution is much more closely correlated with the perceptions of individuals on inequality than with traditional measures of inequality (figures O.8 and O.9).

What Drives Perceptions?

People form their perceptions of inequality by considering the actual dispersion of incomes (or resources), as well as the process that generates this dispersion.

How much do people value the security afforded by stable employment, and how does this influence their views on inequality? When individuals are

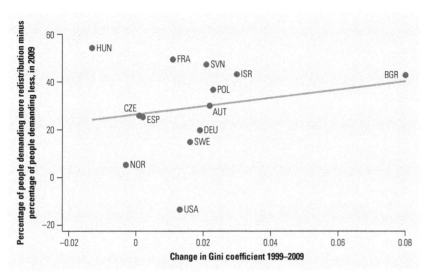

FIGURE O.8
Measured changes in inequality explain little of the demand for redistribution

Source: Bussolo, Ferrer-i-Carbonell, Giolbas, and Torre (2018).

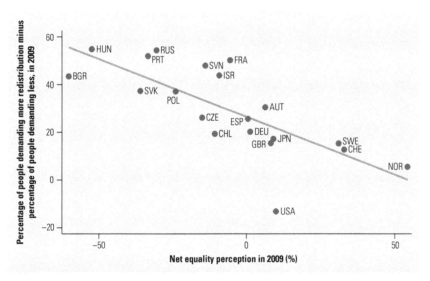

FIGURE O.9
Perceived inequality correlates strongly with the demand for redistribution

Source: Bussolo, Ferrer-i-Carbonell, Giolbas, and Torre (2018).
Note: Net equality perception is defined as the difference between the share of people believing their country is equal and the share of people believing their country is unequal.

asked to place themselves on a 10-step income ladder on which the bottom step represents the poorest 10 percent of the population and the top step the richest 10 percent, individuals who are not in stable, full-time employment are more likely to report that they feel poor (that is, that they belong to the lowest deciles or steps of the ladder) compared with those who have such employment (figure O.10). Declining job security is clearly an important source of dissatisfaction among middle-class workers. Similarly, for a given income, people reporting that they are in good health place themselves higher in the income distribution than do people who report they are in bad health.

FIGURE O.10
At any decile of consumption, individuals more likely feel poor when they are not in full-time employment

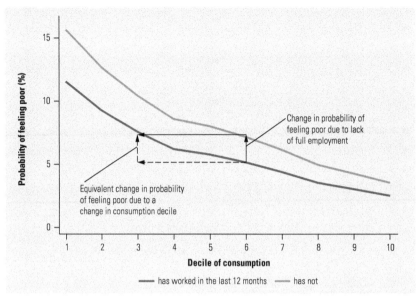

Source: Bussolo and Lebrand 2017.

Fissures in the Social Contract

Labor market regulations and redistribution systems in Europe and Central Asia have not been effective in protecting important segments of the population from the rise in social tensions driven by market forces. This means that societies are becoming less equitable, while people continue to value equity, which is evident from their preferences for fairness and their assessments of the impact on their welfare of the changes.

This imbalance may be reaching a critical level. Voting is becoming more polarized, and populist parties have achieved success in recent elections. Separatist movements have spread in Catalonia and Scotland. The 2018 appointment of a government led by the League and the Five Star Movement in Italy; the 30 percent of votes achieved by Marine Le Pen, an extreme right-wing candidate, in the runoff of the 2017 French presidential election; and the emergence of the euroskeptic Alternative for Germany in the 2017 German election are examples. Meanwhile, the already low level of trust in institutions has continued to trend downward. In 2015, only 11 percent of the respondents to the Life in Transition Survey expressed complete trust in their national government, and only 10 percent in their national parliament. This calls for a reexamination of the social contract with a focus on remedying the emerging distributional tensions and reestablishing social cohesion.

Analysis of recent data show that there is a direct correlation between these manifestations of the imbalance, or of the cracks in the social contract, and the emerging distributional tensions described above. For example, the group of workers penalized by recent shifts in the demand for skills appear to be voting more regularly for extremist parties. There is also evidence that polarization of the voting is related to regional welfare disparities. And younger generations are opting out of the system by not voting, as shown by their declining turnout at elections across Europe.

Looking Ahead: Public Policies for a Stable Social Contract

Market-driven inequalities, absent or delayed adjustments in public policy and institutions, and strong preferences for equity are contributing to instability in the social contract in the region.

The countries of Europe and Central Asia differ in many respects, and policy prescriptions ought to be context specific. Even so, three principles are relevant to any consideration of policy instruments to achieve people's aspirations for an equitable and cohesive society and to build a stable social contract:

- Promote labor market flexibility, while maintaining protection for all types of labor contracts
- Seek universality in the provision of social assistance, social insurance, and good-quality basic services
- Expand the tax base by complementing progressive taxation on labor incomes with taxation on capital

These principles can contribute to tackling the emerging distributional tensions affecting the stability of the social contract. Any approach should incorporate all three. Acting on one or two alone might exacerbate tensions.

Labor Market Flexibility and Protection

The dynamic labor markets of today call for greater efficiency in job matching that helps workers embrace better opportunities and assists firms in finding appropriate skills. This helps everyone in adapting and benefiting from the new world of work. The traditional employer-employee relationship has eroded in Europe over the last two decades. The erosion has been more dramatic in some countries, such as Poland. It has been accompanied by a proliferation in alternate types of contracts. Labor regulations should keep pace and avoid creating divisions among groups that may fuel distributional tensions and undermine the equality of opportunity.

Efforts to achieve flexibility cannot be undertaken only at the margin, which would result in protecting some workers, but not others. Partial reforms would mean that a majority of the people entering the labor market or starting new jobs will be active in nonstandard employment. In several countries, graduating from temporary to permanent employment is difficult. Some workers therefore experience greater economic insecurity, while others are in permanent employment with strong protections.

In the western part of the region, efforts to foster more flexibility should be aimed at closing the divide in protection across types of employment, thereby reducing labor market segmentation. The Jobs Act in Italy sought to reach this goal by simplifying the types of labor contracts and offering protection for all workers. In the eastern part of the region, informality is widespread in several countries, and a large share of the workforce does not benefit from the protections offered by labor regulations or by social insurance. If informality remains substantial, the key is to reform labor market institutions and other business regulations to promote greater formalization.

Social Assistance, Social Insurance, and Key Services

Social assistance is still an important policy arm in efforts to reduce poverty in many countries in the region. More nonpoor households are becoming vulnerable. This is incompatible with the aspiration to end poverty and vulnerability and promote a middle-class society. Extending the reach of social assistance programs ought to be a key feature of any new social contract among countries in the region.

The nature of the initiatives implemented to realize the objective of providing guaranteed minimum protection among the population will vary by country. Fiscal and political considerations are crucial. There are advantages and disadvantages to means testing and to universal approaches. Income-based targeted schemes, well established in many countries in the region, can be used to supply generous transfers by assisting the people most in need. However, that may leave many people unprotected, including the many nonpoor who are vulnerable. Complex eligibility rules, stigma effects, a lack of knowledge among potential beneficiaries, and the administrative burden of delivering and receiving the benefits are some of the obstacles. Universal approaches to social assistance may address some of these challenges.

The universal basic income (UBI) being discussed in many forums could provide broader protection and security to the population through greater coverage and take-up, and it would reduce disincentives to work. Yet, a UBI may be associated with other challenges. Depending on the design, it might entail a substantial fiscal burden, and the feasibility and equity impacts of implementing a UBI relative to other approaches must be weighed. A pure UBI—a minimum income transfer to all individuals—does not exist in the region, but categorical unconditional cash transfers are being provided as a benefit among population groups such as children and the elderly.

The emergence of distributional tensions represents a clear message: the growing economic insecurity affecting nonpoor households is a call for a review of the design and coverage of social assistance.

The changing nature of work is likewise a call for a reexamination of social insurance. In Europe and Central Asia, pension systems are the main channel for social insurance. However, the systems in many countries do not supply adequate protection in old age to individuals who have been active in nonstandard forms of employment or in informal work or who have been out of work. Aging populations threaten the sufficiency of the coverage and financial sustainability of the systems.

The poverty-preventing objective of social insurance among the elderly, chronically ill, unemployed, or disabled should be separate from the consumption-smoothing objective. Insurance against the catastrophic risk of illness, injury, job loss, and other shocks that could drive households into poverty could be provided directly by government in conjunction with income support for all people in need as part of a guaranteed minimum poverty prevention package. This minimum package could cover everyone and would be financed through general tax revenue, thereby avoiding reliance on employment relationships and mandatory payroll contributions. The decoupling of social insurance from employment could facilitate the expansion of coverage to all, reduce the adverse impact on work incentives and the labor demand of firms that is associated with the financing of social insurance through payroll taxes, and enhance the sustainability of social insurance systems. In a dynamic labor market, such an insurance scheme could encourage people to seek out and take on better jobs without fear of losing coverage. Meanwhile, a mandated insurance plan could address consumption-smoothing if the provider of the financing for program benefits is identified and the benefits are reasonable in relation to the contributions.

Public policies in Europe and Central Asia also need to aim at recognizing a universal right to quality services to ensure that everyone can build their human capital and access economic opportunities. Key services—water, sanitation, transportation, education, health care, childcare, and eldercare—are provided in most countries. Yet, these services are not available to all. Under a stable social contract, they should not be out of reach of segments of the population. Universal provision of these services as a premarket intervention could represent great progress in ensuring equal opportunity for all.

Education, in particular, has been a great equalizer. Education systems can help level the playing field by addressing the concern over the widening inequality of opportunity and the persistent spatial inequalities in many countries. However, simply expanding access to education no longer guarantees equal impacts. The focus should be not only universal access to schooling, but also universal access to learning as a key feature of a new social contract. Throughout education systems, learning should include the development of cognitive skills (numeracy and literacy) and socioemotional skills so that younger generations, regardless of their socioeconomic background or the location of their residence, leave school prepared to lead productive lives and able to adapt to the changing nature of work. Developing these skills starts early in life. So, the gaps in the access to early childhood education that affect the most disadvantaged need to be closed.

Education and training services accessible to all adults that allow for learning new skills or for upskilling require strong partnerships between public and private providers. Employers should be encouraged to participate, which may require incentives, especially if more flexible labor markets and shorter job tenure reduce the returns to investments by firms in employees. Firms could contribute to building training systems that are more flexible in responding to labor market demands and provide more work-based learning.

Progressive Tax Systems

Public policies need to expand the tax base, raise tax rates on top earners, and implement more progressive taxation that does not target only income. Higher taxes on capital income and higher taxes on wealth (for example, on inheritance or bequests) could underpin a more equitable fiscal system in the region. Because capital and the returns to capital are concentrated among a smaller share of the population, taxes on capital could enhance the progressivity of tax systems and reduce the inequalities between economic groups. They could also promote equality of opportunity among people whose lack of endowments mean that they do not start life on an equal footing. They can also supply a source of financing to expand and strengthen the social contract.

Increasing progressivity in the inheritance tax and in capital income taxation represent ways to promote equity and boost financing sources. In a globalized world where capital is highly mobile, capital taxation would be difficult to establish without coordination across countries. Recent proposals include global or regional taxes on capital (Atkinson 2016; Piketty 2014).

Conclusion

The widening economic fissures in the societies of Europe and Central Asia are affecting young workers, people in vanishing occupations, individuals lacking good networks, and residents of lagging regions, and they are threatening the sustainability of the social contract. Institutions that have achieved a remarkable degree of equity and prosperity over the course of several decades now face considerable difficulty in coping with the associated challenges. Surveys reveal growing concerns about the inequality of opportunity, while electoral results show a marked shift in favor of populist parties that offer radical solutions to voters dissatisfied with the status quo.

There is no single solution to all the ills in every country, and the response to these problems varies considerably across the region. However, this report proposes three broad policy principles:

- Promote labor market flexibility, while maintaining protection for all types of labor contracts.
- Seek universality in the provision of social assistance, social insurance, and basic quality services.
- Expand the tax base by complementing progressive labor income taxation with the taxation of capital.

These principles could guide the rethinking of the social contract and fulfill the aspirations for growth and equity among the peoples of Europe and Central Asia.

Notes

1. Calculations based on data in Milanović 2016; PovcalNet (online analysis tool), World Bank, Washington, DC, http://iresearch.worldbank.org/PovcalNet/.
2. Other World Bank reports have analyzed the need to adjust the social contract in other regions and have also provided evidence on the changing nature of intergenerational mobility (Ferreira et al. 2013; Narayan et al. 2018; World Bank 2015). The challenges of new distributional tensions seem even bigger in Europe and Central Asia given the limited tolerance for inequality in this region. Ridao-Cano and Bodewig (2018) analyze the impact of emerging inequalities on economic growth in the European Union (EU). The current report focuses on additional distributional tensions and challenges facing taxation and social protection systems.
3. Freeman (2007, 55), writing about the effect of this doubling on the United States, asserts that it "presents the U.S. economy with its greatest challenge since the Great Depression." He adds that, "if the country does not adjust well, the next several decades will exacerbate economic divisions . . . and risk turning much of the country against globalization."

4. Recent studies document this phenomenon in the United States. For example, Chetty et al. (2016) show that intergenerational mobility, a special case of equality of opportunity, has fallen dramatically in the last few decades. For a recent global perspective, see Narayan et al. (2018). Also see EqualChances.org (database), World Bank, Washington, DC, http://www.equalchances.org/. The database is the first online repository of internationally comparable information on inequality of opportunity and socioeconomic mobility.

5. For more on the definition of the middle-class income thresholds in terms of vulnerability, see López-Calva and Ortiz-Juárez (2014).

6. The Czech Republic and the Slovak Republic abandoned the scheme in 2013 after having introduced it in 2008 and 2004, respectively.

7. The estimates refer to 2007–14. This period is not long, but the trend observed is in line with the trajectory observed in the longer period, for example. in taxation. The data are based on EUROMOD (Tax-Benefit Microsimulation Model for the European Union) (database), Institute for Social and Economic Research, University of Essex, Colchester, UK, https://www.euromod.ac.uk/using-euromod/access; EU-SILC (European Union Statistics on Income and Living Conditions) (database), Eurostat, European Commission, Luxembourg, http://ec.europa.eu/eurostat/web/microdata/european-union-statistic son-income-and-living-conditions.

References

Alesina, Alberto F., Edward Glaeser, and Bruce I. Sacerdote. 2001. "Why Doesn't the United States Have a European-Style Welfare State?" Brookings Papers on Economic Activity 2: 187–254.

Atkinson, Anthony B. 2016. "How to Spread the Wealth: Practical Policies for Reducing Inequality." Foreign Affairs 95 (1): 29–33.

Binmore, Ken. 1998. Just Playing. Vol. 2 of Game Theory and the Social Contract. Economic Learning and Social Evolution Series. Cambridge, MA: MIT Press.

Birdsall, Nancy. 2010. "The (Indispensable) Middle Class in Developing Countries; or, The Rich and the Rest, Not the Poor and the Rest." Working Paper 207 (March), Center for Global Development, Washington, DC.

Birdsall, Nancy, Carol Graham, and Stefano Pettinato. 2000. "Stuck in the Tunnel: Is Globalization Muddling the Middle Class?" CSED Working Paper 14 (August), Center on Social and Economic Dynamics, Brookings Institution, Washington, DC.

Bussolo, Maurizio, Ada Ferrer-i-Carbonell, Anna Giolbas, and Iván Torre. 2018. "Perceptions, Reality and Demand for Redistribution." Background paper, World Bank. Washington, DC.

Bussolo, Maurizio, Tulio Jappelli, Roberto Nisticò, and Iván Torre. 2018. "Inequality across Generations in Europe." Background paper, World Bank, Washington, DC.

Bussolo, Maurizio, Jonathan Karver, and Luís F. López-Calva. 2018. "Is There a Middle-Class Crisis in Europe?" Future Development (blog), March 22 and forthcoming working paper.

Bussolo, Maurizio, and Mathilde Sylvie Maria Lebrand. 2017. "Feeling Poor, Feeling Rich, or Feeling Middle Class: An Empirical Investigation." Working paper (May 29), World Bank, Washington, DC.

Chetty, Raj, David Grusky, Maximilian Hell, Nathaniel Hendren, Robert Manduca, and Jimmy Narang. 2016. "The Fading American Dream: Trends in Absolute Income Mobility since 1940." NBER Working Paper 22910 (December), National Bureau of Economic Research, Cambridge, MA.

Dávalos, María E., Giorgia DeMarchi, Indhira V. Santos, Barbara Kits, and Isil Oral. 2016. "Voices of Europe and Central Asia: New Insights on Shared Prosperity and Jobs." World Bank, Washington, DC.

Easterly, William Russell. 2001. "The Middle Class Consensus and Economic Development." *Journal of Economic Growth* 6 (4): 317–36.

Farole, Thomas, Soraya Goga, and Marcel Ionescu-Heroiu. 2018. *Rethinking Lagging Regions: Using Cohesion Policy to Deliver on the Potential of Europe's Regions.* World Bank Report on the European Union. Washington, DC: World Bank.

Ferreira, Francisco. H. G., Julián Messina, Jamele Rigolini, Luís F. López-Calva, María Ana Lugo, and Renos Vakis. 2013. *Economic Mobility and the Rise of the Latin American Middle Class.* Washington, DC: World Bank.

Freeman, Richard B. 2007. "The Great Doubling: The Challenge of the New Global Labor Market." In *Ending Poverty in America: How to Restore the American Dream*, edited by John Edwards, Marion Crain, and Arne L. Kalleberg, 55–64. New York: New Press.

Gimpelson, Vladimir, and Daniel Treisman. 2018. "Misperceiving Inequality." *Economics and Politics* 30 (1): 27–54.

Hobbes, Thomas. 2012. *Leviathan.* Edited by Noel Malcolm. Clarendon Edition of the Works of Thomas Hobbes Series. New York: Oxford University Press. First published 1651.

IPSP (International Panel on Social Progress). 2018. *Rethinking Society for the 21st Century: Report of the International Panel on Social Progress.* 3 vols. Cambridge, UK: Cambridge University Press.

Kanbur, Ravi. 1999. "Comments." In *Economic Policy and Equity*, edited by Vito Tanzi, Ke-young Chu, and Sanjeev Gupta, 239–42. Washington, DC: International Monetary Fund.

Locke, John. 1988. *Two Treatises of Government*, 3rd ed. Edited by Peter Laslett. Cambridge Texts in the History of Political Thought Series. New York: Cambridge University Press. First published 1689.

López-Calva, Luís F., and Eduardo Ortiz-Juárez. 2014. "A Vulnerability Approach to the Definition of the Middle Class." *Journal of Economic Inequality* 12 (1): 23–47.

Milanović, Branko. 2016. *Global Inequality: A New Approach for the Age of Globalization.* Cambridge, MA: Harvard University Press.

———. 2017. "The Welfare State in the Age of Globalization." *globalinequality* (blog), March 26. http://glineq.blogspot.com/2017/03/the-welfare-state-in-age-of.html.

Narayan, Ambar, Roy van der Weide, Alexandru Cojocaru, Christoph Lakner, Silvia Redaelli, Daniel Gerszon Mahler, Rakesh Gupta N. Ramasubbaiah, and Stefan Thewissen. 2018. *Fair Progress? Economic Mobility across Generations around the World.* Washington, DC: World Bank.

OECD (Organisation for Economic Co-operation and Development). 2017. *Preventing Ageing Unequally.* Paris: OECD.

Piketty, Thomas. 2014. *Capital in the Twenty-First Century.* Cambridge, MA: Belknap Press.

Ridao-Cano, Cristobal, and Christian Bodewig. 2018. *Growing United: Upgrading Europe's Convergence Machine.* Washington, DC: World Bank.

Rodrik, Dani. 1999. "Where Did All the Growth Go? External Shocks, Social Conflict, and Growth Collapses." *Journal of Economic Growth* 4(4): 385–412.

Rousseau, Jean-Jacques. 1968. *The Social Contract.* Translated by Maurice Cranston. Penguin Books for Philosophy Series. London: Penguin Books. First published 1762.

Tanzi, Vito. 2018. *Termites of the State: Why Complexity Leads to Inequality.* New York: Cambridge University Press.

World Bank. 2015. "Towards a New Social Contract." MENA Economic Monitor (April), Middle East and North Africa Region, World Bank, Washington, DC.

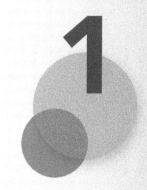

Introduction

Emerging Distributional Tensions in Europe and Central Asia

Globalization and technological change are altering the day-to-day lives of people across Europe and Central Asia. A large share of jobs is susceptible to automation in the region, including, for example, nearly 40 percent of jobs in Georgia and Tajikistan and around 60 percent in Croatia and Latvia (World Bank 2016). Different jobs requiring different skills are being created. Increasingly, workers are entering into nonstandard labor contracts or finding opportunities to become self-employed.

Changing opportunities generated by markets can lead to new distributional tensions. Those people who are ready to take advantage of emerging opportunities because of their skills, access to markets and digital technologies, and location will gain from these changes, while others may have fewer economic opportunities within reach. These dynamics create new divides that can affect social cohesion by making inequalities more salient across groups described by different skills and occupations, of different generations, living in different regions, or born to parents of different educational backgrounds.

Public policies play an important role in taming market-generated inequalities in Europe and Central Asia. Available evidence shows that the lower levels of inequality in the region relative to other regions around the world derive mostly from public redistribution systems. A look at market incomes shows that the countries of Europe and Central Asia exhibit inequality gaps similar to

those in Latin America, where the redistributive effect of taxes and transfers is more limited (Lustig 2017). In Europe and Central Asia, nonmarket income represents a substantial part of total household income, particularly among the poorest 40 percent of the population (the bottom 40) (Bussolo and López-Calva 2014).

The Potential Implications for the Social Contract

In a changing economic context that might be giving way to increasing distributional tensions, public policies may no longer be equipped to respond in line with people's preferences and perceptions about equality. Europe and Central Asia possesses some of the oldest and most developed models of the welfare state in the world. The preferences in the region seem to value economic security. Evidence from the eastern part of the region, for example, shows that people aspire to the stability provided by a full-time job, strongly associated with public sector jobs (Dávalos et al. 2016). These preferences seem to be at odds with the changing nature of employment. Moreover, many welfare state mechanisms were not designed to operate in the dynamic context of today's world nor to deal with potential distributional tensions that may be emerging. For instance, if more jobs are in temporary contracts or of shorter tenure than in the past, insurance systems tied to standard open-ended employment contracts might no longer be adequate. The result is that people across countries perceive that the playing field in access to economic opportunities is increasingly less level (EBRD 2018). Voice is being given more frequently to the word "unfairness," even if inequality across individuals and households is less in the region than in other parts of the world (Dávalos et al. 2016). Europe and Central Asia accounts for 23 of the 30 countries with the lowest Gini coefficient among 158 countries across the world (figure 1.1).

Underlying all stable societies is some form of social contract, an implicit agreement among the members of a society. This agreement is backed by institutional arrangements that influence how markets function, how responsibilities and benefits are defined, and how resources are redistributed (World Bank 2017). This report defines a stable social contract as one in which, in the context of a given distribution of resources generated by market forces, the way that distribution is affected by public policies (through the fiscal system, but also through rules and institutions that affect the functioning of the markets) is aligned with people's perceptions and preferences, a combination of people's beliefs and social values and norms (figure 1.2).[1] The elements that bring the social contract into equilibrium—the role of the market, public policies, and people's preferences—can be vastly different across countries. A mismatch between what the market delivers and what people expect and value can tear the social contract.

Despite different economic, social, and political paths, particularly between Western Europe and the countries of Eastern Europe and Central Asia, a drive for equity has underpinned the social contract in the region. The formation of the social contract in Europe and Central Asia has a long history, beginning with the Elizabethan Poor Relief Act of 1601 that created a Poor Law system in England and Wales. The major foundations for social contracts that prevail in most countries in

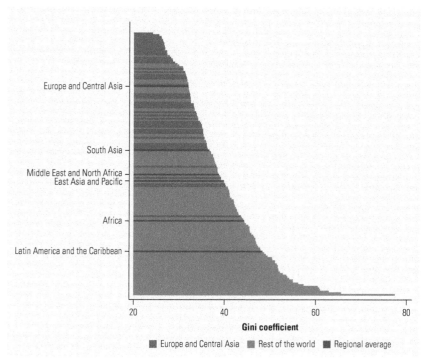

FIGURE 1.1
Income inequality is lower in Europe and Central Asia than in most of the rest of the world
Gini index of inequality, 2014 or latest year available

Sources: Calculations based on data in Milanovic 2016; PovcalNet (online analysis tool), World Bank, Washington, DC, http://iresearch.worldbank.org/PovcalNet/.
Note: The Gini index has been calculated on income whenever possible; alternatively, consumption is used. Rest of the world = all countries, including high-income countries. Europe and Central Asia includes Western Europe. Regional averages are unweighted averages of individual countries.

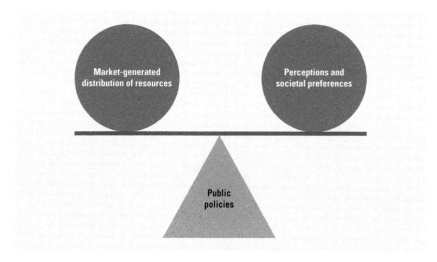

FIGURE 1.2
The social contract as a dynamic equilibrium

Europe and Central Asia developed following World War II, with a strong component of equity.

Countries behind the iron curtain had a system based on state ownership of many of the means of production, and state enterprises were the main suppliers of welfare services to the population. Western European economies have supported economic and social interventions to provide social justice within the framework of a capitalist economy and representative democracy.

The social contracts in Europe and Central Asia have faced serious challenges in recent decades. In Western Europe, the end of full employment in the 1970s led to changes and some retrenchment in the welfare state. The fall of the Berlin Wall and the varying speed in the transition experienced by the formerly centrally planned economies also drove a transformation in welfare systems; the social contract in some transition countries remains strongly influenced by the legacy of the arrangements under the Soviet system. Nonetheless, a preference for the fair distribution of incomes is at the core of the social contract and of societies in Europe and Central Asia (Alesina and Glaeser 2004; Alesina, Glaeser, and Sacerdote 2001).

Is a Rethinking of the Social Contract in the Region Warranted?

The report uses the three parts of a stable social contract—the distribution of resources by the market, public policies, and social preferences—as an organizing principle in exploring the equity dimension of social contracts in the region.

Chapter 2 focuses on market forces and analyzes four key areas of emerging distributional tension (figure 1.3). First, the chapter examines whether the labor

FIGURE 1.3
Distributional tensions along four dimensions are explored

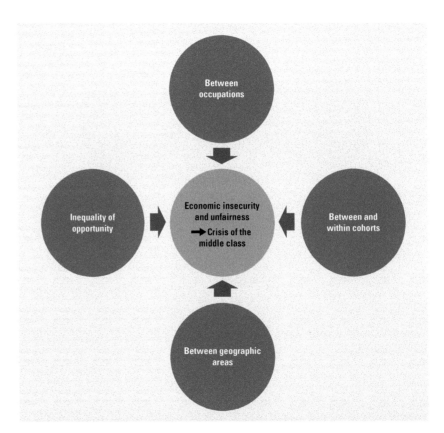

market engagement of certain occupations is changing more relative to other occupations (the distributional tensions between workers in different occupations); specifically, it looks at how technological progress is affecting the demand for different skills, altering the occupational structure of employment, and impacting the earnings and economic security of certain groups. Second, the chapter explores whether economic and institutional forces (for example, pension arrangements or the availability of new types of jobs) are reducing the earnings prospects of some cohorts compared with others (younger and older generations) and increasing the dispersion of incomes within the same cohort, potentially opening a generational divide (distributional tensions between and within cohorts). Third, the chapter examines whether people in certain geographical areas have more limited access to opportunities, including in building up their productivity through access to services; specifically, it looks at whether spatial inequalities exist, and whether they are persisting or widening (distributional tensions between geographic areas). Fourth, the chapter explores whether the share of total inequality that can be attributed to circumstances outside an individual's control is rising and how this affects the ability of workers to benefit from economic opportunities (distributional tensions from inequality of opportunity). Chapter 2 also considers how these four areas of distributional tension are related to a crisis of the middle class that has become more manifest in growing economic insecurity than in an actual reduction in the share of populations in the middle of the income distribution.

Chapter 3 examines the second element of the social contract and discusses the tax and benefit systems and labor market policies in the region. An array of policy instruments is assessed in the report, with the objective of understanding whether they are able to respond to emerging inequalities and contribute to economic security and equal access to opportunity for all. Performance and challenges in three policy areas that are particularly relevant to the distributional tensions are investigated. First is the evolution of labor market regulations, interventions, and institutions and their role in managing or influencing distributional tensions among workers. Second, what has been the impact of taxes and transfers in reducing inequality (not only across income groups, but also, for example, between groups of workers in different occupations) and in compensating for the growing vulnerabilities among some groups. Third, what has been the role of policies in facilitating labor mobility within countries. The report explores whether housing policies, for instance, are having an impact on labor mobility and thus access to economic opportunities among some groups, particularly groups in remote rural areas.[2]

Following the discussion of market and policy trends in the previous chapters, chapter 4 explores the third element of the social contract, people's perceptions of recent changes and societal preferences for equity. It looks at how the preferences of individuals are shaped and, more generally, the type of society in which they would like to live. An important dimension is introduced: people's perceptions of inequality and how these are associated with demands for redistribution. The chapter brings together the three elements of the social contract: market-driven inequality, public redistribution, and societal preferences for equity and shows that imbalances in the social contract may be emerging. Signs of these imbalances include polarization in voting and in the negative trends in the trust exhibited by individuals in public institutions. Voting for populist parties, lower turnouts in elections, and a substantial increase in distrust are strongly associated with those people who are on the losing end of distributional tensions, such as workers in more precarious positions, individuals in young cohorts, or people who have been cut off from economic opportunity.

Chapter 5 presents a rethinking of public policies to tackle the distributional tensions and strengthen the social contract. Although the policy agenda for strengthening the social contract is country specific in that it aligns with each country's markets, preferences, and policies, general policy principles are set forth that may contribute to the debate on a new social contract in the countries of Europe and Central Asia. These principles are focused on the balance between labor market flexibility and protection, the role of social assistance and social insurance in providing economic security, the provision of good-quality services, and tax policies that foster more equitable fiscal systems.

Notes

1. For a treatment of the social contract as a bargaining process between conflicting individuals and interests, see Binmore (1994, 1998). The text view of the social contract is related to the analytical approach proposed by Kanbur (1999) in the context of optimal taxation. Kanbur (1999) sets out a framework for thinking about optimal taxation that includes (a) the degree of inherent inequality as reflected in the extent of productivity distribution; (b) the incentive effects, captured in that model by the elasticity of labor supply; and (c) the degree of egalitarianism, captured by the inequality aversion parameter.
2. A somewhat different categorization of policies that affect the distribution of income is proposed by the International Panel on Social Progress (IPSP 2018), which distinguishes among premarket (for example, the provision of education), in-market (for instance, labor market regulation), and postmarket interventions (such as taxes and transfers).

References

Alesina, Alberto F., and Edward L. Glaeser. 2004. *Fighting Poverty in the US and Europe: A World of Difference*. Oxford, UK: Oxford University Press.

Alesina, Alberto F., Edward L. Glaeser, and Bruce I. Sacerdote. 2001. "Why Doesn't the United States Have a European-Style Welfare State?" *Brookings Papers on Economic Activity* 2: 187–277.

Binmore, Ken. 1994. *Playing Fair*. Vol. 1 of *Game Theory and the Social Contract*. Economic Learning and Social Evolution Series. Cambridge, MA: MIT Press.

———. 1998. *Just Playing*. Vol. 2 of *Game Theory and the Social Contract*. Economic Learning and Social Evolution Series. Cambridge, MA: MIT Press.

Bussolo, Maurizio, and Luis F. López-Calva. 2014. *Shared Prosperity: Paving the Way in Europe and Central Asia*. Europe and Central Asia Studies. Washington, DC: World Bank.

Dávalos, María Eugenia, Giorgia DeMarchi, Indhira V. Santos, Barbara Kits, and Isil Oral. 2016. "Voices of Europe and Central Asia: New Insights on Shared Prosperity and Jobs." World Bank, Washington, DC.

EBRD (European Bank for Reconstruction and Development and World Bank). 2018. *Transition Report 2017–18: Sustaining Growth*. London: EBRD.

IPSP (International Panel on Social Progress). 2018. *Rethinking Society for the 21st Century: Report of the International Panel on Social Progress*. 3 vols. Cambridge, UK: Cambridge University Press.

Kanbur, Ravi. 1999. "Comments." In *Economic Policy and Equity*, edited by Vito Tanzi, Ke-young Chu, and Sanjeev Gupta, 239–42. Washington, DC: International Monetary Fund.

Lustig, Nora C. 2017. "The Impact of the Tax System and Social Expenditure on the Distribution of Income and Poverty in Latin America: Argentina, Bolivia, Brazil, Chile, Colombia, Costa Rica, Ecuador, El Salvador, Guatemala, Honduras, Mexico, Nicaragua, Peru, Dominican Republic, Uruguay, and Venezuela." CGD Working Paper 450 (March), Center for Global Development, Washington, DC.

Milanovic, Branko. 2016. *Global Inequality: A New Approach for the Age of Globalization*. Cambridge, MA: Belknap Press: An Imprint of Harvard University Press.

World Bank. 2016. *World Development Report 2016: Digital Dividends*. Washington, DC: World Bank.

———. 2017. "Leveling the Playing Field: Rethinking the Social Contract in Europe and Central Asia (ECA)." ECA Concept Note (March), World Bank, Washington, DC.

Are Distributional Tensions Brewing in Europe and Central Asia?

This chapter first briefly assesses the inequality in the distribution of income and wealth *across individuals*. A rising inequality and a concentration of income and wealth for the top 1 percent of the population are important, especially when more economic power is accompanied by more political power, but those are also, by now, quite well-studied issues. In fact, focusing on this type of (vertical) inequality alone misses a lot. In Europe and Central Asia, inequality *between groups* (horizontal inequality) is growing. This, together with heightened economic insecurity and, at times, a more unfair process generating the distribution of incomes, is behind the brewing distributional tensions in the region.

The chapter identifies and considers in detail four key distributional tensions. First, in some countries, technological progress is boosting the returns to higher-level skills, but also driving complex changes in the distribution of skills. The polarization of occupations is forcing a large group of middle-skilled-level workers employed in occupations intensive in routine tasks into lower-skill jobs, thereby reducing economic security and the incomes of low-skilled workers. Second, economic and institutional forces (such as globalization, labor market regulations, and pension arrangements) are reducing the earnings prospects of young workers relative to older workers and retirees and increasing inequality among the young. These forces are driving a generational divide because many young workers may not be able to join or maintain themselves in the middle class. Third, spatial inequalities in Europe and Central Asia reduce the economic opportunities of groups living in lagging subregions and underserved rural areas. Fourth, inequality of opportunity—the share of total inequality that can be attributed to circumstances outside an individual's control—still represents an important share of total inequality. This share is rising in some countries in the region, reducing worker social mobility and adding to a perception of unfairness.

These four distributional tensions—among workers, across generations, among geographical areas, and in opportunity—are not necessarily highlighted when vertical inequality, or disparities across individual incomes, is considered. However, these tensions are relevant for the stability of the social contract. If individuals belonging to groups that are losing, or that are exposed to more intense economic insecurity, cannot move to other groups, then social cohesion suffers. The chapter concludes with an analysis of the situation of the middle class, a class that represents the bulk of Europe's population. The expansion of the middle class has slowed in most countries and even reversed in some. Even more importantly, however, decreasing economic security, rather than a shrinking population share, characterizes the "crisis" of the middle class. Many people still have middle-class incomes, but they are, or feel, vulnerable to fall into poverty, as their incomes are less stable and less secure. The analysis shows these vulnerable people belong to the groups that are on the losing side of the distributional tensions: younger cohorts, workers in middle-skilled occupations, residents in lagging regions. A society with a shrinking or vulnerable middle class is a symptom of a more polarized society and, in turn, a society with a lower support for the current social contract.

Inequality across Individuals in Europe and Central Asia

Inequality has increased worldwide in recent decades. In most countries, the inequality gap is widest today relative to the last 30 years. In the countries of the Organisation for Economic Co-operation and Development (OECD), the richest 10 percent of the population earn 9.6 times the income of the poorest 10 percent, a significant increase since the 1980s when the ratio was 7 to 1. In emerging countries, the income gaps are even greater. The Europe and Central Asia region is no exception. Income inequality in the region has risen during the last 25 years, although the trends and magnitudes vary across the region.[1]

Income inequality in the European Union (EU) widened during the 1990s, but has been relatively stable since then. Figure 2.1 illustrates trends in the average Gini index of per capita household income in various regions of the current EU. In 1988–98, income inequality widened across all regions. The biggest increases occurred in the Baltic States and Central Europe (with an average increase of 12 and 8 Gini index points, respectively). This change, associated with the transition from a planned to a market economy, was driven mostly by increased inequality in labor income.[2] Inequality also increased in continental Europe and Northern Europe, though the pattern was heterogeneous in the latter. Inequality remained roughly stable in Southern Europe in 1988–98 with the exception of Italy, where it increased. Income inequality presented a slight U shape in the case of the Baltic States.[3] The following period shows a more mixed pattern, with a stable trend in 2003–08, with the exception of the Baltic States, in which inequality narrowed, and

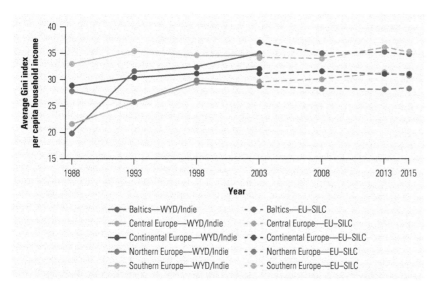

FIGURE 2.1
Trends in income inequality, European Union, 1988–2015

Sources: Data for 1988–98: independent databases and WYD (World Income Distribution Dataset), Stone Center on Socio-Economic Inequality, Graduate Center, City University of New York, New York, https://www.gc.cuny.edu/Page-Elements/Academics-Research-Centers-Initiatives/Centers-and -Institutes/Stone-Center-on-Socio-Economic-Inequality/Core-Faculty,-Team,-and-Affiliated-LIS-Scholars /Branko-Milanovic/Datasets. Data for 2003–15: EU-SILC (European Union Statistics on Income and Living Conditions) (database), Eurostat, European Commission, Luxembourg, http://ec.europa.eu /eurostat/web/microdata/european-union-statistics-on-income-and-living-conditions.
Note: The independent databases represent a collection of household surveys gathered by academic scholars for the study of income and wealth inequality. EU-SILC is a harmonized EU–based survey carried out annually since 2003 in most EU countries; Central Europe = Bulgaria, Croatia, Czech Republic, Hungary, Poland, Romania, Slovak Republic, and Slovenia; Northern Europe = Denmark, Finland, Norway, and Sweden; the Baltic States = Estonia, Latvia, and Lithuania; Continental Europe = Austria, Belgium, France, Germany, Ireland, Netherlands, Switzerland, and United Kingdom; Southern Europe = Cyprus, Greece, Italy, Malta, Portugal, and Spain.

a mild increase in inequality during the last recession (2008–13) only in Southern and Central Europe.

Inequality in the economies of the former Soviet Union, Turkey, and the Western Balkans has narrowed in the last decade after increasing during the transition. Data on household incomes from the initial years of transition in the former Soviet Union economies are scarce and, because of dramatic changes in relative prices, unreliable as a means of measuring household welfare. For this reason, estimates on inequality rely on household consumption information. Figure 2.2 shows that Central Asia saw a strong decrease in inequality between 1993 and 2003, although this is possibly a rebound from the transition period, on which there is limited data. Belarus, Moldova, the Russian Federation, and Ukraine saw a decline in the same period, particularly because of the strong performance of Russia. In the Western Balkans, which is only fully observed after 2003, inequality has shown a slight decrease. In the case of the South Caucasus, an initial decrease between 1998 and 2003 was later reversed, with an increase until 2013. Turkey experienced a long-term decline in inequality, albeit with relative stagnation during the 1990s and a slight increase in 2008–13.

FIGURE 2.2
Trends in consumption inequality, former Soviet Union economies, Turkey, and Western Balkans, 1988–2013

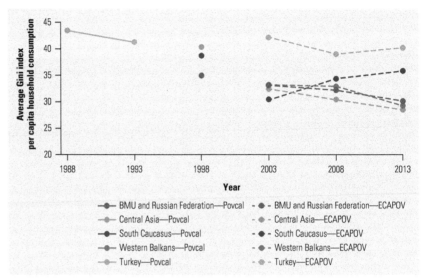

Sources: Household consumption, 2003–13: ECAPOV database harmonization as of April 2018, Europe and Central Asia Team for Statistical Development, World Bank, Washington, DC; 1988–98: PovcalNet (online analysis tool), World Bank, Washington, DC, http://iresearch.worldbank.org/PovcalNet/.
Note: Western Balkans = Albania, Bosnia and Herzegovina, the former Yugoslav Republic of Macedonia, Montenegro, and Serbia; Central Asia = Kazakhstan, Kyrgyz Republic, Tajikistan, and Uzbekistan; South Caucasus = Armenia, Azerbaijan, and Georgia; BMU and Russia = Belarus, Moldova, Russian Federation, and Ukraine.

FIGURE 2.3
Gini index adjusted for the top incomes, 2011

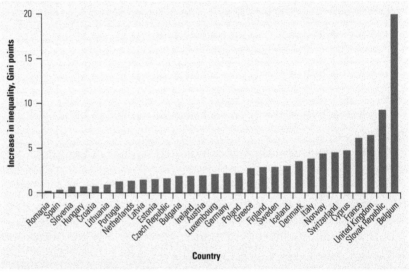

Source: Calculations based on Hlasny and Verme 2018.

This analysis, based on household surveys, may understate the level of inequality or overstate the recent decline in inequality because surveys typically do not include the income of the richest individuals in the region.[4] Increasing attention is being paid in the literature, in the media, and in many forums around the globe to income concentration among the richest. Indeed, accounting for top incomes in traditional household survey–based measures of inequality such as the Gini index reveal higher income inequality (figure 2.3).

Available evidence indicates that concentration of income is growing in many countries in the region.[5] Among the countries on which data are available, the income share of the top 1 percent of the population is highest in Russia and Turkey and has increased in many countries (table 2.1). The World Inequality Database provides estimates for the top 1 percent income share in 17 countries of Europe and Central Asia, mainly Western European countries, but including Hungary,

TABLE 2.1 Top 1 Percent Income Shares Vary Across the Region, but Have Risen in Many Countries

a. Top 1 percent income shares, latest available estimates

		Year	Top 1% income share
	Netherlands	2012	6.3%
Low	Denmark	2010	6.4%
	Finland	2009	7.5%
	Norway	2011	7.8%
	Spain	2012	8.6%
	Sweden	2013	8.7%
Medium Low	Italy	2009	9.4%
	Hungary	2008	9.6%
	Portugal	2005	9.8%
	Ireland	2009	10.5%
	France	2014	11.0%
Medium High	Germany	2011	13.0%
	Poland	2015	13.3%
	United Kingdom	2014	13.9%
High	Russian Federation	2015	20.2%
	Turkey	2016	23.4%

b. Average percentage point change in top 1 percent income shares, circa 1980–2014

	Change in top 1% income share
Netherlands	0.48
Denmark	0.94
Spain	0.95
France	2.00
Germany	2.26
Italy	2.48
Finland	3.14
Norway	3.20
Ireland	3.85
Sweden	4.60
Portugal	5.45
Hungary	7.01
United Kingdom	7.21
Poland	9.14
Russian Federation	16.78

Source: Based on data of WID (World Inequality Database), Paris School of Economics, Paris, https://wid.world/.
Note: Panel a: the population is comprised of individuals more than 20 years old. The base unit is the tax unit defined by national fiscal administrations for the measurement of personal income taxes. It may refer to individuals or be equally split across adults according to the available data in each country. Panel b: Denmark (1980–2010), Finland (1980–2009), France (1980–2014), Germany (1980–2011), Hungary (1980–2008), Ireland (1980–2009), Italy (1980–2009), Netherlands (1981–2012), Norway (1980–2011), Poland (1983–2015), Portugal (1980–2005), Russian Federation (1980–2015), Spain (1981–2012), Sweden (1980–2013), and United Kingdom (1981–2014).

Poland, Russia, and Turkey.[6] The top 1 percent income share has increased substantially in countries such as Poland and Russia and stands at around 20 percent in Russia and 23 percent in Turkey. This big expansion in the share of total income captured by top earners is related to the fact that, while, for the vast majority of individuals, wages are by far the largest component of income, a distinguishing feature of the incomes of top earners is the share of capital income. This share has grown in the last two decades. For instance, in France, the top 0.01 percent receives about 20 percent of their income from capital (OECD 2014). This suggests that income inequality may be related to inequality in capital holdings, that is, wealth inequality.

Wealth has also become more concentrated. Data on wealth are scarce, and the coverage of the World Inequality Database, the source of table 2.1, is limited. The Forbes list of billionaires indicates that the number of billionaires in Europe and Central Asia rose from 106 in 1996 to more than 500 in 2017 (figure 2.4). The number of billionaires in Western Europe increased from 90 in 1996 to 379 in 2017, and the number of Russian billionaires rose from 8 in 2001 to 96 in 2017. While 62 percent of the region's billionaires are concentrated in Western Europe, the billionaires in Eastern Europe are far richer: three to four times richer in the case of Russia because of high growth rates in net worth over the past decade and two to three times richer in the case of billionaires in other Eastern European countries. The sources of wealth vary across the region. There is a concentration in mining among Russian billionaires, the financial sector in other Eastern European countries, and manufacturing in Western Europe.

Labor income is losing ground as a share of total income. The labor share of income declined in Western Europe particularly during the 1980s, though it remained relatively stable thereafter. However, since the mid-1990s, a growing number of countries in the region, especially those that transitioned out of a planned economy, have witnessed declining labor income shares (figure 2.5). The largest decline in 1994–2014 occurred in Azerbaijan (−34 percentage points), followed by the former Yugoslav Republic of Macedonia and Serbia (−19 percentage points), Armenia and Tajikistan (−16 percentage points), Estonia (−12 percentage points), Luxembourg and Turkey (−11 percentage points), and Kazakhstan (−10 points). The current literature has been exploring various hypotheses to explain this, from advances in information technology and the decline of the relative price of investment goods, to automation, financial deregulation, and an increase in industry concentration, which allows incumbent superstar firms to exploit monopolistic rents (Autor et al. 2017; Eden and Gaggl 2015; Karabarbounis and Neiman 2014; and Stiglitz 2012).

The greater concentration of wealth and the decline in the share of labor income may result in widening income inequality. Piketty (2014) argues that the main driver of inequality is the tendency of returns on capital to exceed the rate of economic growth. As an economy expands, a larger share of gross domestic product (GDP) is represented by profits, while the share of GDP accounted for by worker wages shrinks. This may explain the parallel trends in wealth and income inequality.

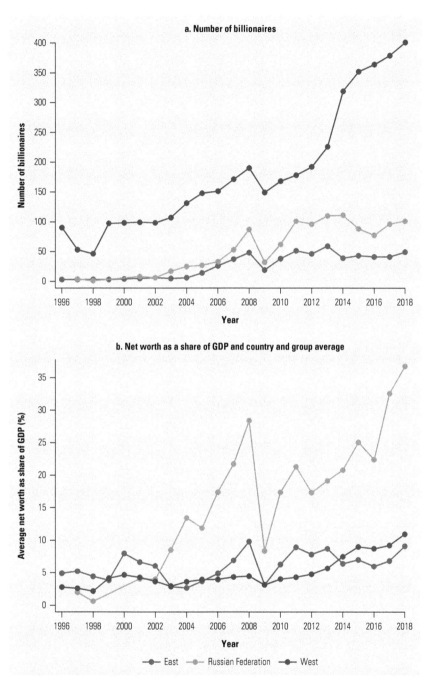

FIGURE 2.4
The number of billionaires and their net worth have increased

Source: Based on "The World's Billionaires," Forbes Media, Jersey City, NJ, https://www.forbes.com /billionaires/list/#version:static.
Note: West = Austria, Belgium, Czech Republic, Denmark, Finland, France, Germany, Greece, Iceland, Ireland, Italy, Lithuania, Netherlands, Norway, Poland, Portugal, Romania, Serbia, Spain, Sweden, and United Kingdom; East = Georgia, Kazakhstan, Turkey, and Ukraine. Panel b: east and west data reflect the group-level average of the country-level average of net worth as a share of GDP and can therefore be interpreted as the net worth of the average billionaire as a share of GDP in each group of countries. GDP = gross domestic product.

FIGURE 2.5
The declining share of labor income, particularly in transition economies

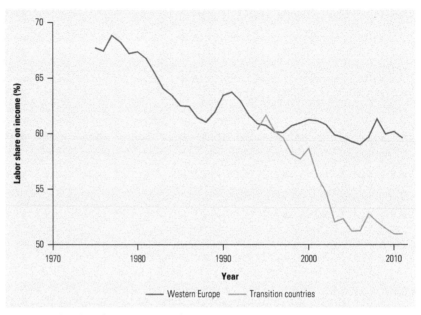

Source: Based on data of Karabarbounis and Neiman 2014.
Note: Western Europe = Austria, Belgium, Denmark, Finland, France, Germany, Greece, Ireland, Italy, Luxembourg, Netherlands, Norway, Portugal, Spain, Sweden, Switzerland, and United Kingdom; Transition countries = Central and Eastern Europe, the Baltic States, the Western Balkans, and the remaining economies of the former Soviet Union. Turkey, though not strictly a transition country, is also included in this last group.

While the previously mentioned measures of inequality across incomes of individuals reveal no reason for alarm in Europe and Central Asia, the adjustment showing the share of top incomes is more in line with people's perceptions that inequality is widening (chapter 4).[7]

Moreover, incomes may be clustering at the extremes of the distribution and, while vertical inequality may narrow, polarization may become more severe (Zhang and Kanbur 2001). So, a look at the polarization of distribution or, equivalently, at what is happening at the middle of the distribution may reveal that clustering is a relevant distributional shift.

While inequality across individuals or polarization are indeed important, most of the focus of this report is the distributional tensions that may arise because of between-group inequality, that is, horizontal inequality (box 2.1). This perspective is critical to social stability and, as highlighted by Stewart (2002, 4), is also a "precondition of economic development." This is because individuals within disadvantaged groups may not be able to contribute to society's prosperity if between-group inequality persists. For example, the children of parents in disadvantaged groups may not be able to accumulate sufficient human capital or, even if they can do so, may not have access to the most productive occupations. Inequality across occupation groups, generations, and regions and inequality of opportunity are the focus of this chapter.

BOX 2.1　Horizontal Inequality

Horizontal inequality refers to inequality between groups. These groups may be culturally defined (or constructed), such as racial, ethnic, or religious groups; they may be defined by situation, such as regional location or age; or they may be defined based on economic criteria, such as occupation. This is in contrast with vertical inequality, which is inequality across all households or individuals. Vertical inequality can be decomposed into between-group inequality (horizontal inequality) and within-group inequality. Within-group inequality typically accounts for a larger share of vertical inequality, but horizontal inequality may nonetheless be substantial.

Inequality can be measured along many dimensions, for example income, assets, life expectancy, health, educational attainment, opportunities for political participation, or access to public services. The classifications used to define groups should be meaningful and recognizable to the individuals so grouped and to society at large, and rapid movement from one such group to another should be difficult for individuals.

Horizontal inequality often endures, even for centuries, for example, inequality between blacks and whites in the United States. But horizontal inequality may also disappear within a few generations because, for instance, of the upward mobility of immigrant groups in some countries. The welfare cost of horizontal inequality tends to be high because people become trapped in deprivation.

This contrasts with vertical inequality, which may, at least partially, be characterized by churning, as households rise into or fall from the upper segments of the income distribution over time.

Horizontal inequality also matters because the members of the groups may identify with their groups, and the well-being of the group affects their identity. Likewise discrimination based on group identity can lower efficiency, and persistent horizontal inequality can undermine political stability.

The potential for economic policy to address horizontal inequality depends, in part, on the group involved. For example, governments can have a direct impact on the relative incomes across groups through policies on social protection, and governments can address regional inequality through public investment and service provision. By contrast, improving the position of racial or ethnic groups may require changes in norms, culture, and social relations to reduce boundaries between groups (for example, through intermarriage) or encourage greater acceptance of underprivileged groups.

Government policies can support or hinder such changes. Policies that prohibit discrimination against disadvantaged groups in the accumulation of assets (for example, in lending) or human capital (access to education) can eventually narrow horizontal inequality. Such policies may need to be supported by affirmative action in favor of underprivileged groups to counteract the effects of past discrimination. For example, educational admission policies based on competitive examinations will discriminate against young people from less well-educated backgrounds or those that do not speak the dominant language. However, there is a risk that affirmative action may add to the boundaries between groups, thereby discouraging the social acceptance of some groups.

Comprehensive programs may be necessary because deprived groups often suffer from privations across several dimensions. Thus, improving secondary schools that serve underprivileged groups may be of little help if households cannot survive without the full-time labor of their older children. Raising contacts with more privileged groups in an equal setting—for example, avoiding segregated schooling—can improve the opportunities of the less privileged. Strong group organizations can promote self-respect, provide mutual insurance, and strengthen the bargaining position of the group, but may also reduce beneficial contacts and, similar to affirmative action, may highlight group divisions.

Source: Stewart and Langer 2007.

Labor Market Polarization and the Shifting Demand for Skills

Technological change, globalization, and institutional or policy changes are transforming labor markets in Europe and Central Asia.[8] Advances in technology, including the Internet and various forms of mechanization, are reducing the demand for work that is intensive in routine tasks (Autor and Dorn 2013; Autor, Katz, and Kearney 2006, 2008; Autor, Levy, and Murnane 2003; Goos and Manning 2007; Goos, Manning, and Salomons 2014). For example, airline ticket agents are being replaced by websites, and assembly line workers are being replaced by robots. The rise of developing countries in the global economy has intensified the competition facing low- and mid-skilled workers in advanced countries who have traditionally relied on now-declining manufacturing industries. Many countries have eased regulatory restrictions on firing and reduced other worker protections to facilitate adjustment to shocks by making markets more flexible. However, in many cases, this has created dual labor markets, whereby only skilled and experienced workers continue to benefit from high levels of protection, while the rest face more vulnerable employment conditions (chapter 3). Many of the displaced jobs tend to be in medium-earning occupations, generating a shift into low-paid and, to a lesser extent, high-paid occupations. This polarization of occupations has implications for the distribution of earnings that may not be reflected in a rise in the Gini coefficient, but could still cause rifts.

Job polarization, understood as the simultaneous growth of occupations at the extremes of the wage spectrum and the hollowing out of mid-skill jobs, has driven significant changes in the distribution of wage income. A worker's occupation—not simply the skill level—has become an important determinant of labor market earnings in the United States in recent decades (Acemoglu and Autor 2011). What is the situation in Europe and Central Asia? Do countries in the region experience occupational and earnings polarization? The next two subsections address these issues, considering, first, occupational changes in the region and then diving deeper in country case studies. For these studies, a formal decomposition analysis aims at determining the importance of occupational changes in changes in the earnings distribution and, ultimately, income distribution. A brief outline of the main results paves the way for the detailed analysis.

Results: polarization in occupations. From the fall of the Berlin Wall to the early 2010s, the western part of the region experienced job polarization. Jobs in the middle of the distribution, intensive in routine tasks, are becoming less available. In the eastern part of the region and from about 2000 to 2010, the occupational transformation was more mixed. The share of jobs at the low end and in the middle of the distribution expanded. Routine biased technological change, automation, appears not to be widespread in the eastern part of the region, where occupational changes are more closely linked with the formalization of jobs (chapter 3). Especially in the lower half of the distribution, unpaid family work or self-employment was being replaced by more wage work. But this is likely to be a transitional effect, partially caused by the temporarily high growth rates. The shifts in the occupational structure meant that many workers had to move to different jobs or, especially in the east, enter the labor market in the expanding number of low-end occupations, which may not have been their aspiration.

Results: changes in the earnings distribution. The polarization of jobs in the western part of the region was not accompanied by polarization in earnings (as in the United States; see Acemoglu and Autor 2011). Instead, there was a regressive change in the distribution of earnings. Workers displaced in the middle occupations added to the supply of workers for jobs at the bottom more rapidly than the demand for such jobs, and the greater competition drove wages down. At the higher end, demand outstripped supply, and wages rose. The reverse occurred in the eastern part of the region. Wages at the bottom of the distribution rose, along with the number of jobs. A detailed decomposition analysis confirms that occupational change was especially relevant in the regressive change in the earnings distribution in the west, while other factors, such as demography and higher educational attainment, were at play in the east.[9]

Both halves of the region experienced increasing distributional tensions. In the west, deterioration in economic security and in the incomes of low-skilled workers put pressure on redistribution systems (chapter 3). One result was a growth in dual earner households as households boosted their participation in the labor market to offset the deterioration in incomes. In the east, the aspirations of the more well educated to obtain high-end jobs were frustrated, similar to the outcome in the Middle East (Arampatzi et al. 2015).

Trends in Occupational Change in the Region

Individuals are employed in occupations, and any given occupation can be understood as a bundle of tasks. Six tasks may be defined (box 2.2). Each occupation is intensive in each of these tasks, but in different ways. Changes in the labor market may be described in terms of how the intensity of each of these tasks is evolving in overall employment. This is the approach followed, for instance, by Hardy, Keister, and Lewandowski (2016). Overall employment may become more routine intensive because the occupational structure changes and occupations that are more intensive in routine tasks come to account for a larger share of total employment. An alternative approach, followed by Autor (2014), the World Bank (2016a), and this report, involves grouping occupations according to relative task intensity.[10] This allows the change in occupational structure to be examined directly rather than inferring the change according to the change in the average task content of employment. This is more useful in evaluating the distributional tensions in the labor market because individuals choose and employers demand occupations rather than tasks.[11] In this approach, occupations are classified based on the intensity of each task involved. For simplicity and given the high correlation that exists between some tasks, the classification used in this report groups occupations into three categories based on their intensity in routine tasks; nonroutine, cognitive tasks; and nonroutine, manual, physical tasks (box 2.2; see annex 2A).

Occupations can be classified into three groups based on the type of task involved. Occupations intensive in routine tasks may include either routine cognitive tasks, such as filling out forms or performing repetitive administrative assignments (an office clerk), or routine manual tasks, such as operating a machine in a factory (a metal molder). These occupations are typically found in the middle of the wage distribution in high-income countries (Goos, Manning, and Salomons 2014).

BOX 2.2 Construction of Occupational Categories

Grouping occupations according to task content implies making a decision on which task dimension to prioritize. Because the potential number of tasks characterizing an occupation may be large, this report relies on task content indexes formulated by the Institute for Structural Research that originate from O*NET and follow Acemoglu and Autor (2011).[a] There are six task content indexes: (a) nonroutine, cognitive, analytical; (b) nonroutine, cognitive, personal; (c) routine, cognitive; (d) routine, manual; (e) nonroutine, manual, physical; and (f) nonroutine, manual, personal. Additionally, indexes (c) and (d) can be combined into a routine-task intensity index based on Autor, Levy, and Murnane (2003). Each occupation at the 4-digit level (unit group titles) of the International Standard Classification of Occupations (ISCO) 88 has a value in every task content index.[b] For the purpose of this work, occupations are aggregated at the ISCO 88 2-digit level (submajor group titles) by taking a simple average of the indexes of the unit groups included in the corresponding submajor group. This is done to have a common aggregation level across countries because not all surveys record occupations at the 4-digit level.

There are 27 submajor occupation groups in the ISCO 88 classification. These are divided into three groups as follows. First, the 27 groups are ranked according to the routine-task intensity index. The first category—occupations intensive in routine tasks—includes the top third of the groups

(9 groups) with the highest index value. The remaining 18 submajor occupation groups are divided into two groups according to their value on the nonroutine, cognitive, analytical index.[c] The half with the highest values on the nonroutine, cognitive, analytical index is included in the second category, occupations intensive in nonroutine, cognitive tasks. The bottom half is included in the third category, occupations intensive in nonroutine, manual tasks. Annex 2A, table 2A.1 presents a statistical summary of the categories. The categorization of occupations is based on the relative intensity of some tasks. Thus, nonroutine, manual, physical task content is high in both the first and third groups, but the first group also exhibits high routine-task intensity, whereas the third group shows a low value for routine tasks. In this sense, the first group is relatively more routine-intensive than the third group, which is relatively more intensive in nonroutine, manual, physical tasks.

This classification is possible if occupation data are available at the ISCO 2-digit level. In some instances, the relevant data are available only at the ISCO 1-digit level (major groups). In this case, the first occupation category (occupations intensive in routine tasks) includes ISCO major groups 4, 7, and 8; the second occupation category (occupations intensive in nonroutine, cognitive tasks) includes ISCO major groups 1, 2, and 3; and the third occupation category includes ISCO major groups 5, 6, and 9.

a. A caveat involved in using O*NET data is the assumption that the task content of each occupation is the same across all countries and that it is the same as the content for each occupation in the United States, for which O*NET was specifically constructed. There is evidence that the tasks performed in a same occupation, for example, an office clerk, differ across countries (Dicarlo et al. 2016). See Occupation Classifications Crosswalks: From O*NET-SOC to ISCO (database), Institute for Structural Research, Warsaw, April 6, 2016, http://ibs.org.pl/en/resources/occupation-classifications-crosswalks-from-onet-soc-to-isco/; O*NET OnLine (database), Employment and Training Administration, U.S. Department of Labor, Washington, DC, https://www.onetonline.org/.
b. The current version of the classification is ISCO 08, and most of the surveys undertaken after 2010 have used this classification instead of ISCO 88. The categorization here is based on ISCO 88; correspondence tables allow ISCO 08 occupations to be mapped onto this categorization.
c. Results practically do not change if the nonroutine, cognitive, personal index is used.

Occupations intensive in nonroutine manual tasks involve low-skilled work, for example, work as a nurse's aide or private security guard, that cannot easily be replicated by a machine. These jobs are among the lowest paid in modern economies.[12] By contrast, occupations intensive in nonroutine cognitive tasks require high-skilled professionals, such as scientists, engineers, or managers, and are usually the highest paid in modern economies. In the literature on job polarization, the second and third categories are referred to, respectively, as lousy and lovely jobs (Goos and Manning 2007).

Technological progress has sharply reduced the share of jobs involving routine tasks, usually middle-paid jobs, in Europe over the last two decades (figure 2.6). The share of routine-task–intensive occupations in total wage employment fell from an average of around 40 percent in 1995 (ranging from 23 percent in Albania to 50 percent in Italy) to around 33 percent in 2013 (ranging from 23 percent in Montenegro to 41 percent in the Czech Republic).[13] The decline in the share of routine-task–intensive occupations was as high as 11 percentage points in Southern Europe and as low as 2 percentage points in the Baltic States.

By contrast, the employment share of nonroutine cognitive-task–intensive occupations, usually well-paying jobs, has risen substantially. The share of these occupations in employment grew from an average of 25 percent in 1995—though in countries such as Italy and Portugal, this share was below 20 percent—to 32 percent in 2013; several countries, such as Luxembourg, Norway, and Switzerland, had shares above 40 percent. The increase in the share across regions ranged from 8.0 percentage points in Scandinavia and Southern Europe to 4.5 percentage points in Central Europe, and the employment share in 2013 ranged from almost 38 percent in Northern Europe to around 26 percent in Southern Europe.

Changes in the share of employment in occupations intensive in nonroutine, manual tasks, usually low-paying jobs, have varied across Europe. The employment share of these occupations rose from 35 percent in 1995 to 38 percent in 2013 in Southern Europe and from 31 percent to 32 percent in Western Europe. Thus, these subregions experienced a rise in both kinds of nonroutine tasks at the expense of routine tasks. The employment share of nonroutine, manual tasks remained stable at 33 percent in Central Europe and 37 percent in the Western

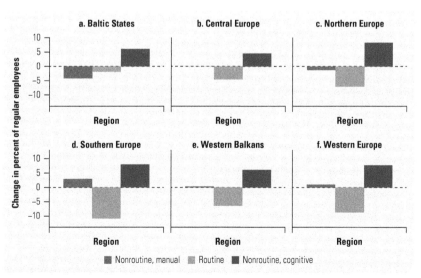

FIGURE 2.6
The employment share in routine task-intensive occupations has fallen in Europe
Change in the share of employment, by occupation category, late 1990s to early 2010s

Source: World Bank calculations based on household surveys and labor force surveys.

Balkans over this period, while this share fell from close to 38 percent to 35 percent in the Baltic States and from 35 percent to 34 percent in Northern Europe.

Overall, these data illustrate significant shifts in occupational structure in Europe, as well as job polarization in some subregions. All European subregions experienced a fall in the employment share of routine-task–intensive occupations and a rise in the share of nonroutine cognitive-task–intensive occupations. In countries where nonroutine cognitive-task–intensive occupations are the only ones to enjoy a rise in demand, high-skilled workers already at the top of the distribution may experience a greater increase in wages relative to low-skilled workers. However, this tendency to greater inequality could be addressed by expanding the supply of high-skilled workers through education and training. However, in Southern and Western Europe, the employment share of both rose in the most highly paid occupations (involving nonroutine, cognitive tasks) and the least well-paid occupations (involving nonroutine, manual tasks). This job polarization can drive greater distributional tensions because many middle-paid workers who perform routine tasks may be displaced to less well-paid jobs.[14]

The eastern part of Europe and Central Asia—the former Soviet Union economies and Turkey—did not experience the job polarization seen in Western and Southern Europe. The employment share of nonroutine cognitive-task–intensive occupations fell by an average of 5 percentage points from the early 2000s to the mid-2010s, with declines in all countries on which there are consistent data, except Moldova and Turkey (figure 2.7).[15] The expansion in wage employment at the expense of unpaid family work or self-employment may explain part of the decline in the share of nonroutine cognitive-task–intensive occupations. The employment share of routine-task–intensive occupations increased or remained stable in all countries on which there are consistent data, except Moldova and Turkey. The employment share of nonroutine manual-task–intensive occupations rose in all countries except Armenia and Moldova. The expansion of elementary occupations in a context of economic growth suggests there was considerable growth in the demand for low-skilled services.

FIGURE 2.7

The share of employment, by occupational category, early 2000s to mid-2010s

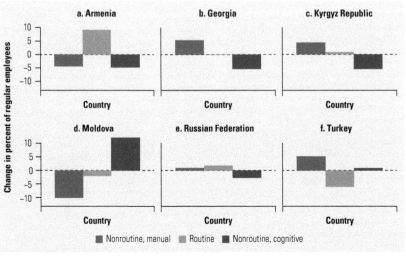

Source: World Bank calculations based on household surveys and labor force surveys.

Thus, changes in occupational structure have differed considerably across Europe and Central Asia. Some regions, particularly Western and Southern Europe, are undergoing a process of job polarization, while the economies of the former Soviet Union have seen a growth in nonroutine manual-task–intensive occupations and a fall in the share of highly skilled nonroutine cognitive-task–intensive occupations. The impact of occupational change on the distribution of earnings also likely differs across the region. The next subsection analyzes this impact in seven countries in Europe and Central Asia (Bussolo, Torre, and Winkler 2018).[16]

Job Polarization and Earnings in Selected Countries

This subsection reviews detailed information on trends in earnings in selected countries in the western and eastern parts of Europe and Central Asia. It examines earnings data on three countries in the west (Germany, Poland, and Spain) from the early 1990s to 2013. In the east, it investigates data on four countries (Georgia, Kyrgyz Republic, Russia, and Turkey) over a slightly shorter period.

Job polarization in the three countries in the west was accompanied by a decline in earnings among low-wage workers relative to the earnings of high-wage workers. Most EU countries experienced strong growth in the years between the fall of the Berlin Wall and the global financial crisis. While income inequality did not change much overall (chapter 1), labor incomes became more unequal in several countries. From the early 1990s to 2013, the Gini index of labor income rose by about 8 points in Germany and Spain and by about 5 points in Poland. This increase in inequality mainly reflected slower earnings growth among low-wage workers; the earnings of workers in the two bottom deciles of the wage distribution rose at least 10 percentage points less than the earnings of workers at the median of the distribution and more than 30 percentage points less than the earnings of workers at the top. In the United States, job polarization was accompanied by wage polarization, that is, growth in wages at the two extremes of the earnings distribution. In the EU, however, the polarization in occupations did not translate into a greater rise in the wages of low-paid workers relative to workers at the median; rather, the distribution of wages became more regressive in general (figure 2.8, panels a, c, and e).

The deterioration in earnings inequality in Europe was partly driven by job polarization. In Germany, Poland, and Spain, occupational changes played a big role in accounting for the relative wage decline among low-paid workers (see figure 2.8, panels b, d, and f). This analysis separates changes in the overall distribution of wages (figure 2.8, panels a, c, and e) into changes deriving from occupational shifts and changes deriving from other factors (figure 2.8, panels b, d, and f), for example the entry of new workers with better skills or shifts in demand that increase the wages for some skill occupations (box 2.3). In these three countries, declining relative demand for occupations intensive in routine tasks displaced many workers who could not compete for high-skill jobs. These workers were forced to compete for jobs at the bottom of the wage distribution, resulting in a relative reduction in wages and an expansion in employment in jobs intensive in nonroutine manual skills (the least well-paid workers). Simulation results show that moving from a routine-task–intensive job to a job intensive in nonroutine manual tasks—the usual transition for the relatively low skilled employed in routine intensive occupations—implied a reduction of almost 30 percentage points in

FIGURE 2.8 Changes in wages, Germany, Poland, and Spain, 1990s to 2013

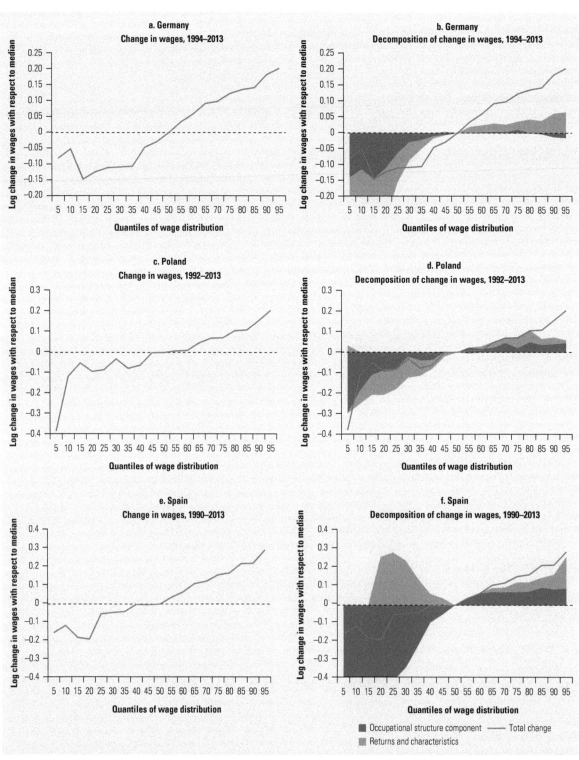

Source: Bussolo, Torre, and Winkler 2018.

BOX 2.3 Decomposing the Change in Wages: The Role of Occupational Change

Analysis of the factors explaining changes in wages requires, initially, establishing the possible drivers. In this sense, characteristics such as educational attainment, age, sector, or task-specific skills can be thought of as assets that workers accumulate and for which they receive returns on the labor market. The simultaneous accumulation of these assets and changes in the associated returns affect trends in the distribution of earnings. Moreover, the returns to these assets can be thought of as specific to each job. Returns to education, for instance, need not be the same across occupations. But occupations are not distributed randomly within the population. Individuals with a certain set of characteristics may be more likely to be found in certain occupations. This is a representation of the occupational structure and is the result of the interaction of both labor demand and the supply of skills. Bussolo, Torre, and Winkler (2018) carry out a decomposition of changes in wages in seven countries of Europe and Central Asia over 20 years within such a framework and provide estimates of the extent to which changes in the characteristics of individuals, changes in the returns to these characteristics, and changes in the occupational structure account for trends in earnings.

A standard method for decomposing changes in wages between two periods (for instance, 1993 and 2013) is the Oaxaca-Blinder method, which decomposes the change between two earnings distributions by analyzing the changes in the means of the relevant factors, such as individual characteristics, returns to characteristics, and occupational structure. Bussolo, Torre, and Winkler (2018) perform a decomposition inspired by Bourguignon and Ferreira (2005) and Inchauste et al. (2014) that generalizes the Oaxaca-Blinder methodology to changes in the whole earnings distribution, rather than only the means. This decomposition is carried out with the use of counterfactual simulations in which the earnings distribution in the final year is simulated by retaining, alternatively, the characteristics of individuals, the returns to these characteristics, and the set of

parameters defining the occupational structure of the earnings distribution in the initial year. Thus, the decomposition relies on simulating the earnings distribution in 2013 as if the occupational structure parameters—for instance, the probability of an individual with tertiary educational attainment to be in a nonroutine cognitive-task–intensive occupation—had been the same as those in 1993. The change between the actual earnings distribution and the simulated earnings distribution is explained in this case by the change in the parameters of the occupational structure. A similar exercise is carried out with the characteristics of individuals and the respective returns. A residual component is needed because the counterfactual simulation can only be carried out on observed characteristics and cannot account for changes in unobservable variables.

Figures 2.8 and 2.9 in the text show the results of the decomposition of the changes in wages. In blue is indicated the occupational structure component, that is, the part of the change in wages that can be accounted for by changes in the occupational structure. The remaining two components—the change accounted for by variations in the characteristics of individuals, such as educational attainment, and their returns—is shown, added up, in green. The orange line indicates the actual changes observed between the initial year of the analysis and the last year of the analysis. For presentational purposes the residual component, which would account for the remaining difference between the actual change and the explained components, is not depicted.

The results indicate that, in Germany, Poland, and Spain, changes in the parameters defining the occupational structure were particularly damaging for the earnings of those at the bottom of the wage distribution. For instance, the probability of household heads with only secondary educational attainment to working in nonroutine manual-task–intensive jobs—typically the lowest paid in the economy—rose by 12 percentage points in Spain, while, among household spouses with similar educational profiles, it increased by 19 percentage

(Continued)

BOX 2.3 Decomposing the Change in Wages: The Role of Occupational Change *(continued)*

points in Germany and 14 percentage points in Poland. Individuals with secondary education are found more often in low-paid occupations now than before, explaining part of the relative decline in wages at the bottom of the distribution.

The results of the decomposition for Georgia, the Kyrgyz Republic, the Russian Federation, and

Turkey show that the occupational structure component accounts for a small part of the change in wages. The relative improvement in wages at the bottom of the distribution in these countries is explained more by the changes observed in the characteristics of individuals and in the associated returns.

labor market earnings. Conversely, the transition to a job intensive in nonroutine cognitive tasks implied an increase of around 25 percentage points. Thus, many formerly middle-paid workers experienced a significant cut in earnings.

By contrast, earnings inequality fell in the former Soviet Union economies because the employment share and relative earnings of high-skilled workers declined. The employment share of occupations intensive in nonroutine cognitive skills fell (see above). This was accompanied by a drop in the earnings of high-skilled workers, who are typically the most well-paid workers, relative to the earnings of other workers. For example, in Georgia and the Kyrgyz Republic from the early 2000s to the mid-2010s, the top two deciles of the distribution of earnings experienced earnings growth about 20 to 40 percentage points lower than the median (figure 2.9). In Russia, the labor market incomes of high earners rose by about 50 percentage points less than the corresponding incomes of the median between 1994 and 2014. Most of the relative loss in earnings at the top of the wage distribution in the east can be explained by a reduction in the returns to education (Bussolo, Torre, and Winkler 2018). In contrast, low earners experienced earnings growth significantly above the median. These changes resulted in a strong decrease in the inequality of labor income in Georgia (from a Gini coefficient of 0.48 in 2002 to 0.45 in 2015), Russia (from a coefficient of 0.55 in 1994 to 0.39 in 2014) and Turkey (from a Gini coefficient of 0.42 in 2002 to 0.36 in 2013). In the Kyrgyz Republic, the Gini coefficient of the labor market remained at around 0.44.

Thus, economies of the former Soviet Union avoided the deterioration in wage inequality experienced in Western Europe. In Europe, the demand for low-skill workers could not keep up with the increase in supply caused by the influx of displaced routine workers, leading to rising inequality, while in the former Soviet Union countries, the demand for high-skill workers was not as strong as the growing supply of skilled workers, resulting in falling inequality. While the absence of job polarization in the east and falling inequality may have helped avoid the kinds of distributional tensions experienced in the west, it may also indicate a lack of economic dynamism. Policy distortions in the east may mean that highly educated workers are not paid wages commensurate with their productivity (box 2.4). Moreover, the absence of job polarization in a subregion subject to the same

FIGURE 2.9 Wage changes, Georgia, Kyrgyz Republic, Russian Federation, and Turkey, 1990s to 2010s

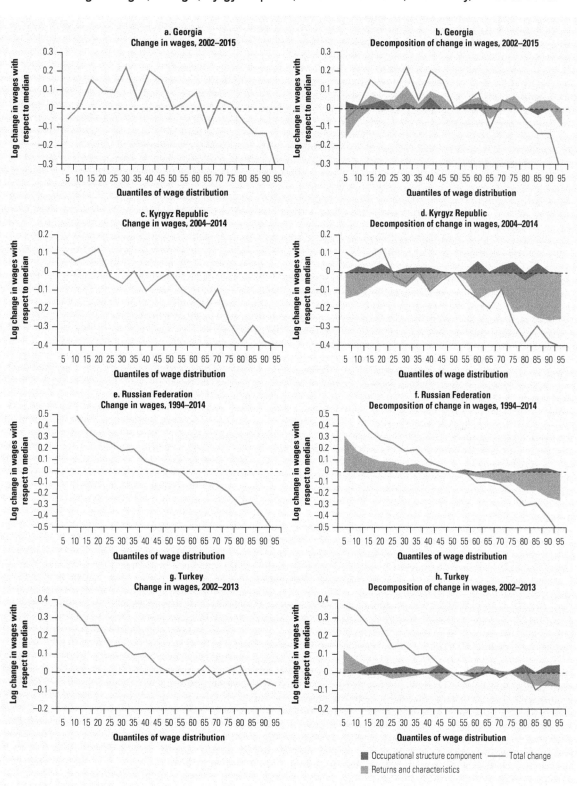

Source: Bussolo, Torre, and Winkler 2018.

BOX 2.4 **Teachers and Drivers: Low Wages in High-Skill Occupations in the Former Soviet Union Economies**

One of the characteristics of the wage structure in former Soviet Union economies is that the occupations of high-skill workers do not necessarily pay high wages. Consider, for example, teaching professionals (ISCO category 23), a job which typically requires at least a high school degree and is intensive in nonroutine cognitive tasks, versus drivers and mobile plant operators, International Standard Classification of Occupations (ISCO) category 83, jobs that usually do not require any formal schooling qualification and are intensive in nonroutine manual tasks. Figure B2.4.1 presents the distribution of these occupations within the overall wage distribution in three countries—Georgia, Germany, and the Kyrgyz Republic—in the mid-1990s to early 2000s. In Germany, the expected pattern is found. Teachers typically earn wages in the upper deciles of the wage distribution, while drivers typically earn wages in the middle deciles. The pattern in Georgia and the Kyrgyz Republic is the opposite: teaching professionals are found in the middle to the bottom of the wage distribution, and drivers are mostly found from the middle to the top of the distribution. The prevalence of low wages among teachers may have resulted in an incentive for workers in these occupations to move to jobs where, even if overqualified, such as driving jobs, they can earn higher wages. Indeed, the distributions of teaching professionals and drivers in the most recent year (not shown) have moved to the right and the left, respectively, suggesting that shifts out of nonroutine cognitive-task–intensive occupations and into other occupations may have reduced this counterintuitive wage difference.

FIGURE B2.4.1 Distribution of teaching professionals, drivers, and mobile plant operators, initial year

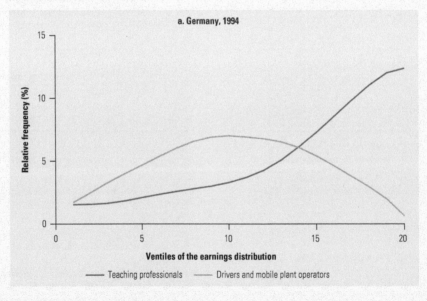

(Continued)

BOX 2.4 **Teachers and Drivers: Low Wages in High-Skill Occupations in the former Soviet Union Economies** (continued)

FIGURE B2.4.1 Distribution of teaching professionals, drivers, and mobile plant operators, initial year (continued)

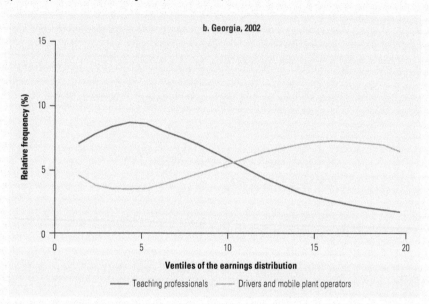

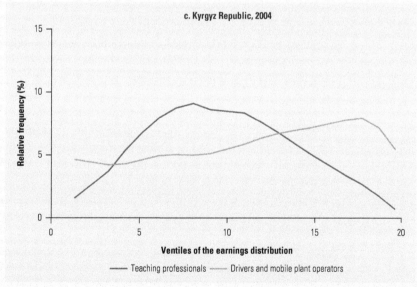

Source: Bussolo, Torre, and Winkler (2018).
Note: The figure plots the relative distribution of teaching professionals (ISCO code 23) and drivers and mobile plant operators, International Standard Classification of Occupations (ISCO) category 83 on the overall earnings distribution in the initial year of the analysis. All curves are smoothed by a locally weighted regression. All values include the self-employed. Similar patterns are observed if the self-employed are excluded.

technological and globalization forces as the west may suggest a static labor market in which innovation and technological change are weak, and the process of creative destruction—whereby some occupations shrink and others expand—is muted.

Economic insecurity increases in times of intense occupational change. Because there are returns to specialization in any employment activity, changing occupations can represent a short-term and potentially also a long-term decrease in productivity and earnings for any given individual. Even if, from the perspective of society, occupational change represents dynamism and growth, a high turnover in occupations can be a source of economic distress from an individual's point of view. Moreover, the fact that the distribution of the winners and losers of occupational change can be highly polarized adds a distributional dimension to the inherent tension emerging from the shift in jobs by individuals.

An Increasing Generational Divide, and the Young Are Losing Ground

The economic transformations in Europe and Central Asia in 1990–2010 had differing effects across generations. The changes impaired the economic prospects of youth relative to the changes experienced by older generations at the same age. Until early adulthood, the economic welfare of an individual is largely the same as that of the individual's immediate family. Among people aged 16–30, however, the surrounding society becomes a more influential factor, and the experiences of individuals during this formative period may shape the fortunes and attitudes of these individuals for a lifetime (Chauvel and Schröder 2014). As the economic environment changes, different birth cohorts will have different experiences, and the cohort to which an individual belongs becomes an important determinant of the individual's welfare.

This generational divide may be masked in analyses of vertical inequality. For instance, inequality may be increasing between generations, but inequality within each generation may be declining. Thus, measures of aggregate inequality may not change, while tensions between or within generations rise. Also, young generations tend to be smaller in number than older ones in the aging countries of Europe and Central Asia and account for an even smaller share of total income (because earnings are typically lower at the beginning of one's career). Thus, a decline in the earnings of young generations may not have a large impact on aggregate income distribution, while it may become an important source of distributional tension.

Five stylized facts point to the difficulties facing younger workers and thus raising distributional tensions between generations, as follows:

- Nonstandard employment (part-time, temporary, and agency work) is becoming more common in the region, and younger cohorts are engaged in these types of employment more intensively relative to older cohorts.

- Job tenure has decreased among young workers.
- The declining fortunes of the young are associated with their labor market earnings: college graduates have seen the growth of their wages decrease substantially.
- The position of the young relative to the middle aged and, particularly, the elderly has been deteriorating in Southern and Western Europe during the last decades, while, in Central and Northern Europe, former Soviet Union economies, and Turkey, the situation has been relatively stable.
- In those regions where the income levels of younger generations have declined compared with that of older generations, inequality among the young has also widened.

New Types of Jobs for Younger Workers

Nonstandard employment is becoming more common in the region, and, together with shorter tenures, may partly explain the narrowing wage prospects and the greater within-cohort inequality among younger generations. Traditionally, security and stability in labor markets have been achieved through formal employment involving permanent contracts of indefinite duration. This is the benchmark against which workers in postwar societies in Europe and Central Asia have typically measured themselves. In recent decades, however, new forms of employment have become more common, partly because of changes in labor policies that have diversified the type of contracts available (chapter 3). This nonstandard employment includes part-time and temporary employment.[17] The share of nonstandard employment in total employment rose steadily and substantially in Central, Southern, and Western Europe, while in Northern Europe, the share remained relatively stable, but at a high level (more than 30 percent) (figure 2.10). In Southern Europe, the share shot up from 8 percent in the early 1980s to 29 percent in the early 2010s, and in Western Europe from around 18 percent to close to 34 percent in the same period. In Central Europe, where data are available only from the late 1990s, the increase was from 10 percent in 1997 to almost 21 percent in 2013. In the Baltic States, the share of nonstandard employment hovered between 10 percent and 12 percent during the same period.

Data on the economies of the former Soviet Union and Turkey cover a more limited time span and show mixed trends. Albania, Armenia, and Georgia have experienced declines in the share of nonstandard employment in total employment, while in the Kyrgyz Republic, Moldova, and Turkey, the share has increased. In terms of composition, in many countries, such as Croatia, Hungary, Poland, Portugal, and Slovenia, the overall expansion in nonstandard employment was driven by the growing share of (full-time) temporary employment (figure 2.11). In several other countries, such as Austria, Ireland, and the Netherlands, the rise in permanent part-time employment was the bigger contributor. Yet, in others, such as Denmark, Sweden, and the United Kingdom, no significant change in the share of nonstandard employment was observed, but the composition of this employment changed, including a shift from permanent part-time to temporary

FIGURE 2.10
Nonstandard employment (NSE) has expanded in most of Europe and Central Asia
Nonstandard employment as percent of total employment

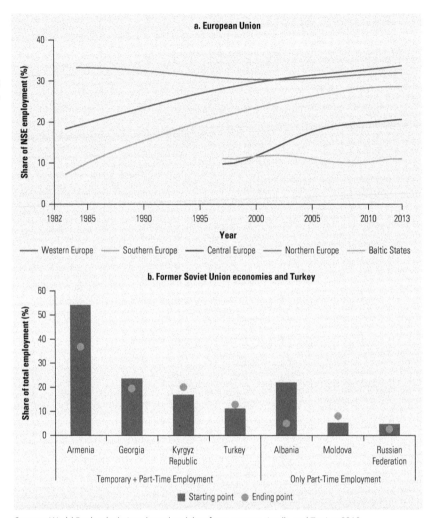

Sources: World Bank calculations based on labor force surveys; Apella and Zunino 2018.
Note: Panel a: each line depicts the smoothed (locally weighted regression) average of the prevalence of nonstandard employment (temporary and part-time employment) by region. Panel b: starting point and ending point, respectively: Albania, 2002, 2013; Armenia, 1998, 2015; Georgia, 2002, 2015; Kyrgyz Republic, 2004, 2014; Moldova, 1998, 2013; Russian Federation, 1994, 2014; Turkey, 2004, 2013.

employment in Sweden and a reverse shift in Denmark and, to a lesser degree, the United Kingdom. The education and task profile of workers in nonstandard employment also changed (box 2.5).

Younger workers are more engaged in nonstandard employment. Various groups may exhibit variations in their willingness to engage in temporary or part-time employment, and employers may vary in their willingness to hire certain groups of workers under such conditions. In the subregions with the largest rise in the share of nonstandard employment, Southern and Western Europe, a greater share of younger age-groups tend to take on nonstandard employment, and the expansion in the share of nonstandard employment was greater among the young (figure 2.12). In Southern Europe, the share of nonstandard employment among the 20–24 age-group rose from 15 percent in the early 1980s to well above 60 percent in 2013. In Western Europe, the share of nonstandard employment in the same age-group increased from around 15 percent to more than 40 percent in the same period,

FIGURE 2.11 The composition of nonstandard employment differs in countries and regions

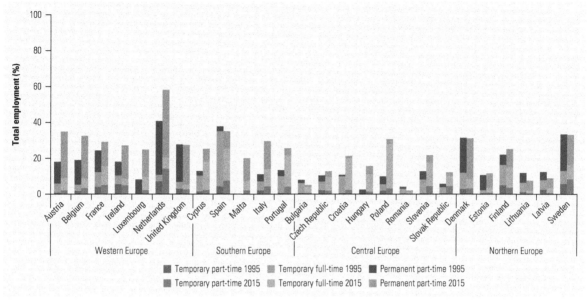

Source: World Bank calculations based on labor force surveys.

BOX 2.5   The Changing Education and Task Profile of Nonstandard Employment

Workers in nonstandard employment are more well educated today than in the 1990s (figure B2.5.1). However, this is not unique to nonstandard employment and reflects the more widespread access to education in all countries in the west. The spread of education access in Southern Europe appears to have been more pronounced relative to nonstandard employment. Coupled with the difference in the education profile of workers in nonstandard employment versus workers in standard employment, this shift widened the divide, sustaining, even deepening, the vulnerability of workers involved in nonstandard employment.

The jobs of workers in nonstandard employment increasingly involve tasks that require more complex skills, mimicking the broader trend in employment. In most of the European Union, the trend is toward occupations more intensive in nonroutine cognitive tasks, while in the former Soviet Union economies, the pattern of occupational change has been more

heterogeneous. Overall, the task content of nonstandard jobs seems to follow a similar pattern, though with notable exceptions. In Europe, standard employment has become more intensive in all nonroutine cognitive tasks, such as analyzing information or thinking creatively, while in nonstandard employment, this has been observed only among jobs requiring interpersonal relationships, such as supervising subordinates or interacting with customers; in many countries, it has not been observed among nonstandard jobs involving analytical tasks (figure B2.5.2). The broader decline in manual tasks in standard employment has also been observed in nonstandard employment.[a] These parallel trends between the task content in nonroutine cognitive and manual tasks are also found in the economies of the former Soviet Union, although the changes are smaller in magnitude relative to those elsewhere in Europe (Apella and Zunino 2018). There is a clear divergence with respect to routine cognitive tasks—those involving a need for precision in a

(Continued)

BOX 2.5 **The Changing Education and Task Profile of Nonstandard Employment** *(continued)*

structured work environment—in Europe. While there has been a consistent decline in these tasks among standard employees, there have been increases in nonstandard employment, particularly in some countries in Central and Eastern Europe. The expansion identified by Keister and Lewandowski (2016) in routine cognitive-task intensity in overall employment in many of these countries is explained mostly by the spread of nonstandard employment. Thus, tasks that appear to be disappearing in Southern Europe are becoming more highly concentrated in more flexible forms of employment, particularly in certain countries.

FIGURE B2.5.1 Changes in the education profile of workers, by employment type

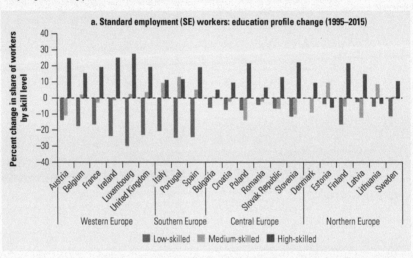

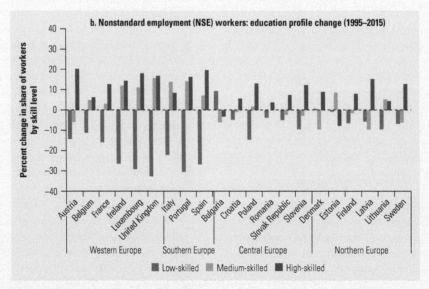

Source: Calculations based on data of EU-LFS (European Union Labour Force Survey) (database), Eurostat, European Commission, Luxembourg, http://ec.europa.eu/eurostat/statistics-explained/index .php/EU_labour_force_survey_%E2%80%93_data_and_publication.

(Continued)

BOX 2.5 **The Changing Education and Task Profile of Nonstandard Employment** (continued)

FIGURE B2.5.2 Changes in task content, by employment type
Similar trends in nonroutine cognitive analytical and manual tasks; diverging trends in routine cognitive and nonroutine cognitive interpersonal tasks

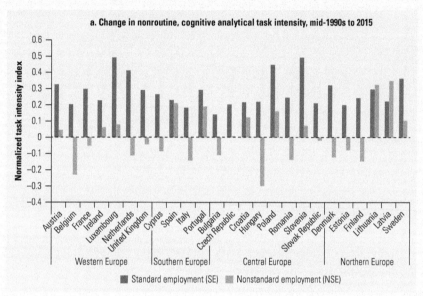

a. Change in nonroutine, cognitive analytical task intensity, mid-1990s to 2015

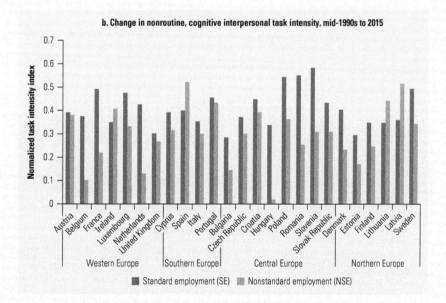

b. Change in nonroutine, cognitive interpersonal task intensity, mid-1990s to 2015

(Continued)

BOX 2.5   **The Changing Education and Task Profile of Nonstandard Employment** (continued)

FIGURE B2.5.2 Changes in task content, by employment type (continued)

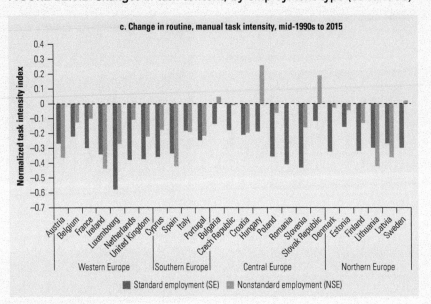

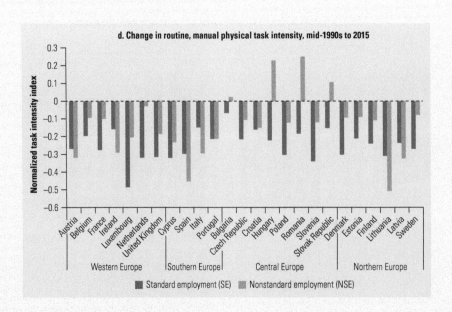

(Continued)

The Changing Education and Task Profile of Nonstandard Employment *(continued)*

FIGURE B2.5.2 **Changes in task content, by employment type** *(continued)*

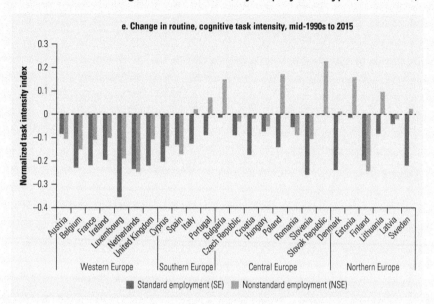

Source: Calculations based on data of EU-LFS (European Union Labour Force Survey) (database), Eurostat, European Commission, Luxembourg, http://ec.europa.eu/eurostat/statistics-explained/index .php/EU_labour_force_survey_%E2%80%93_data_and_publication.
a. A notable outlier is Hungary, where intensity in manual tasks, both routine and nonroutine, has risen considerably in nonstandard employment. This derives from a surge in the share of nonstandard employment among agricultural laborers and garbage collectors, which represented 27 percent of nonstandard employment in Hungary in 2015, while the same occupations constituted only 1 percent in 1997.

while the share of the remaining age-groups expanded from close to 20 percent to around 30 percent. A similar pattern is observed in Central and Northern Europe (figure 2.13). In the latter, while the overall share of nonstandard employment did not change, the share of nonstandard employment rose by around 20 percentage points among the 20–24 age-group. In Central Europe, younger workers always show a greater share of nonstandard employment relative to older individuals, while the rise in the share of nonstandard employment was greatest among the young. The significant increases in nonstandard employment among the young were largely driven by a rise in temporary employment in Croatia, Hungary, Italy, Poland, Portugal, and Slovenia and, to a lesser degree, in France and Sweden. Part-time employment also grew substantially as a share of youth employment (from 15 percent to 25 percent), including involuntary part-time employment.[18]

FIGURE 2.12 Rising nonstandard employment (NSE), Southern and Western Europe

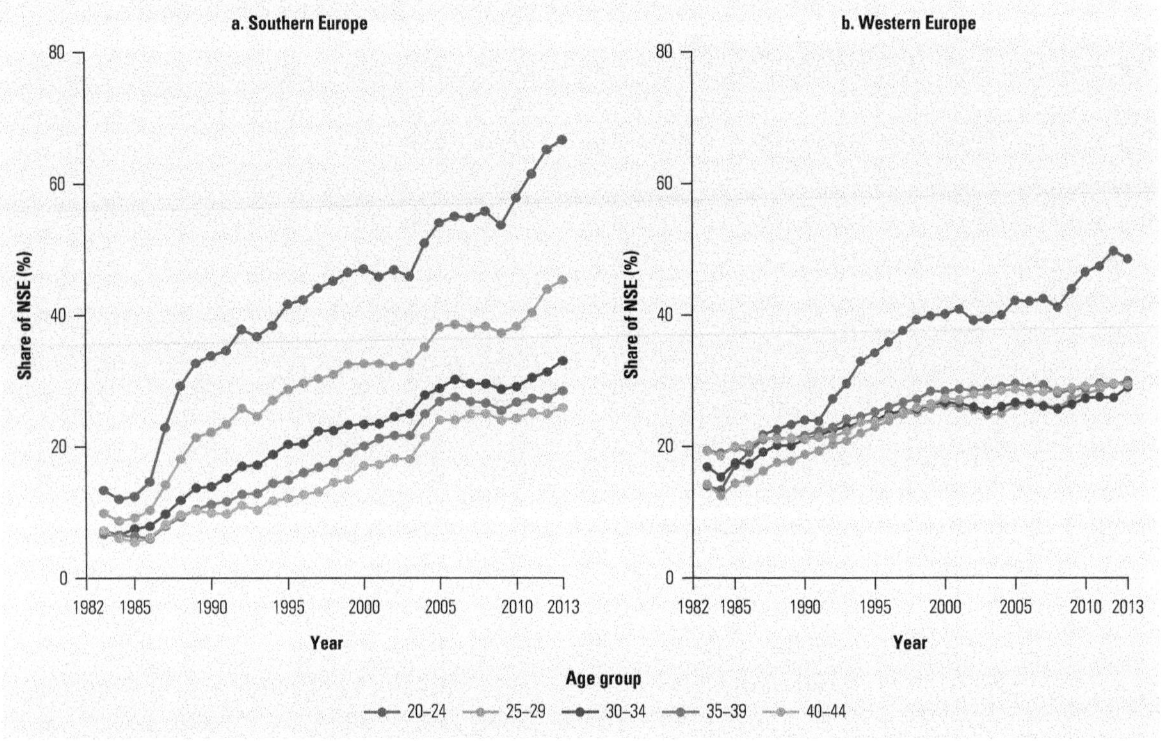

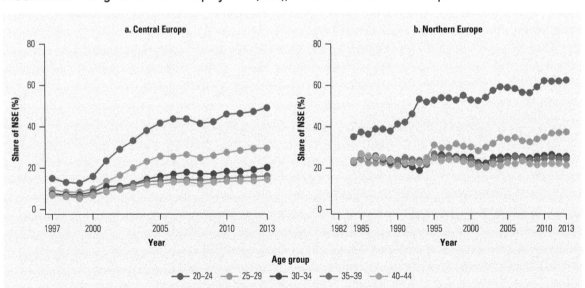

Source: World Bank calculations based on data of labor force surveys.
Note: Each line depicts the smoothed (locally weighted regression) average of the prevalence of nonstandard employment (temporary and part-time employment) by age-group.

FIGURE 2.13 Rising nonstandard employment (NSE), Central and Northern Europe

Source: World Bank calculations based on data of labor force surveys.
Note: Each line depicts the smoothed (locally weighted regression) average of the prevalence of nonstandard employment (temporary and part-time employment) by age-group.

Shorter Job Tenure among Younger Workers

One consequence of the greater prevalence of temporary contracts—one form of nonstandard employment—may be an increase in employee turnover and, thus, a reduction in average job tenure. Some studies argue that employment regulations that impose high costs for firing workers lower the incentives to either hire or fire workers so that job tenure becomes longer (Hopenhayn and Rogerson 1993; Lazear 1990). Employment protection legislation is strongly linked to cross-country differences in tenure levels (Eurofound 2015). Auer and Cazes (2000) find that differences in job tenure in Europe, Japan, and the United States derive from differences in labor market institutions and the labor market behavior of workers. Analyzing employer–employee data in Germany, Boockmann and Steffes (2010) find that labor market institutions (mainly work councils) play a pronounced role in reducing mobility and thus prolonging tenure. Because the shift from permanent to temporary contracts reflects an easing of labor market protections for workers and involves reduced costs in shedding workers, it might be expected that this shift was accompanied by a reduction in job tenure.

At first glance, however, job tenure seems to have expanded in Europe (figure 2.14). In most subregions in 1992–2013, the average job tenure was stable at close to 10.0 years. In the Baltic States, it was close to 7.5 years. The average job tenure rose by almost one year in Southern Europe, the region with the highest average job tenure, more than 12 years in 2013. However, job tenure tends to rise with the unemployment rate; so the rise in Southern Europe, the region affected the most by the 2008–09 financial crisis, is not surprising. Moreover, countries in that region have a high share of long tenured workers, who are generally more difficult to fire during recessions (Abraham and Medoff 1984; Jovanovic 1979).

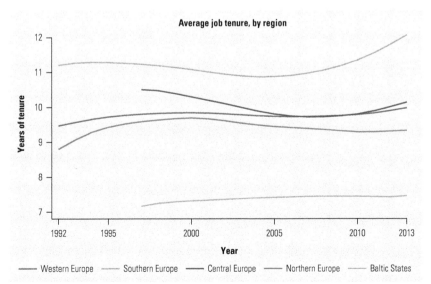

Average job tenure, by region

— Western Europe   — Southern Europe   — Central Europe   — Northern Europe   — Baltic States

FIGURE 2.14
Average job tenure has been mostly stable in Europe and Central Asia

Source: Based on data of labor force surveys.
Note: Each line depicts the smoothed (locally weighted regression) average of the prevalence of nonstandard employment (temporary and part-time employment) by region.

The picture of overall stability in tenure across Europe may hide diverse trends among older and younger workers. The impact of recent transformations—rapid technological change and the easing of labor market protections—may have different effects on job tenure across age-groups. Older workers tend to have longer job tenure relative to younger workers because older workers are often endowed with more specific human capital, and employers are thus less likely to fire them. However, older workers tend to have completed fewer years of education, and the more well-educated (younger) workers are likely to represent the lower costs or greater benefits associated with specific skills. Likewise, technological change may increase the need for retraining and thus drive greater demand for younger skilled workers, who are also further from retirement and thus more suitable for retraining (Rodriguez and Zavodny 2003). In countries with strict labor market regulations, allowing more temporary contracts may induce greater competition between those for whom short-term contracts are usually tailored, young people and the pool of the unemployed (Boeri 1999). Greater competition should raise turnover and reduce average tenure among these groups.

Job tenure has decreased among younger workers in Europe. Among the 25–29 age-group, the average job tenure has declined in all regions (figure 2.15). In Southern Europe, for instance, job tenure fell from 4.2 years in 1993 to 3.6 years in 2013, while, in Western Europe, it narrowed from 4.4 years to 3.5 years, decreases of 15 percent and 20 percent, respectively. The reduction was smaller among older age-groups: around 10 percent (1.5 years) for the 45–49 age-group in the same regions and between 7 percent and no change among the 60–64 age-group. The decline in job tenure among younger generations is evident even after one controls for cyclical and composition effects (Bussolo, Capelle, and Winkler 2018).

FIGURE 2.15 Tenure is decreasing among the young, but less among the middle and older age-groups

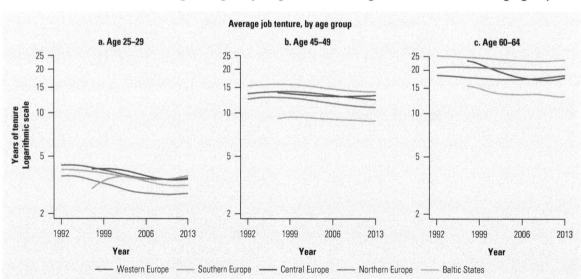

Average job tenure, by age group

Source: Based on data of labor force surveys.
Note: Each line depicts the smoothed (locally weighted regression) average of job tenure by age-group. The vertical axis is expressed in logarithmic terms.

The stability of overall average job tenure results from a change in the composition of the labor force. While job tenure has fallen among younger individuals, older individuals with, on average, long job tenures have considerably boosted their labor force participation rate. In this sense, the trends in average tenure seem to be more in line with the predictions of Boeri (1999) in terms of changes in employment regulation rather than those of Rodriguez and Zavodny (2003) with respect to technological change. The evidence that younger generations are facing shorter job tenures is in line with the findings of Eurofound (2015), which show that the trend is associated with the weakening of employment protection provided by law and by trade unions. Given the weak individual bargaining power of young workers, the trend toward the interpersonal employment relationship may affect them disproportionately. O'Higgins (2010) argues that the increased flexibility of employment protection in transition economies in Europe and Central Asia has particularly affected the job stability of young people, among whom average tenure has fallen to the levels in Western European countries (figure 2.15).

The Young Are Faring Worse than Older Generations

In modern societies, children are expected to achieve, over the course of their lifetimes, a better living standard than their parents (Chetty et al. 2016). This is typically what happens in a growing economy because the average productivity of the young workers entering the labor force exceeds that of older workers when they entered the labor force. Thus, even though the greater experience of older workers means that their productivity and earnings will exceed that of younger workers at any given time, as the young workers age they will catch up and eventually surpass the older generation. However, a slowdown in growth may interrupt this process and reduce the difference in earnings between younger and older generations.

The recent slowdown in growth—not entirely caused by the global financial crisis—affected the income prospects of younger generations disproportionately. In Northern and Western Europe, the income growth rate among older household heads—tied to previous trends in income given the contributive nature of most pension systems—has been constant throughout the last two decades, while the income growth rate among younger household heads has declined. The income of middle-aged household heads—the 45–54 age-group—in these two regions showed a pattern similar to that of older household heads, suggesting that the slowdown in growth particularly affected the young (figure 2.16). In Southern Europe, moreover, the income of younger household heads has declined, while that of older household heads continued to grow. Thus, the youngest generations—today's 25–34 age-group—have experienced much slower income growth relative to older household heads across the EU15.[19]

Contrasting with the western, more developed countries of the region, in Central Europe, the Baltic States, Russia, and Turkey households incomes for all age groups have increased in the past decade (figure 2.17). Only in Turkey does the income of older heads of household show a slower growth rate, providing an explanation for the steady decline in the ratio of the average incomes of the older group to the younger group. The incomes of the 25–34 and 45–54 age-groups is

FIGURE 2.16 Household income, by age of household head, Western, Northern, and Southern Europe

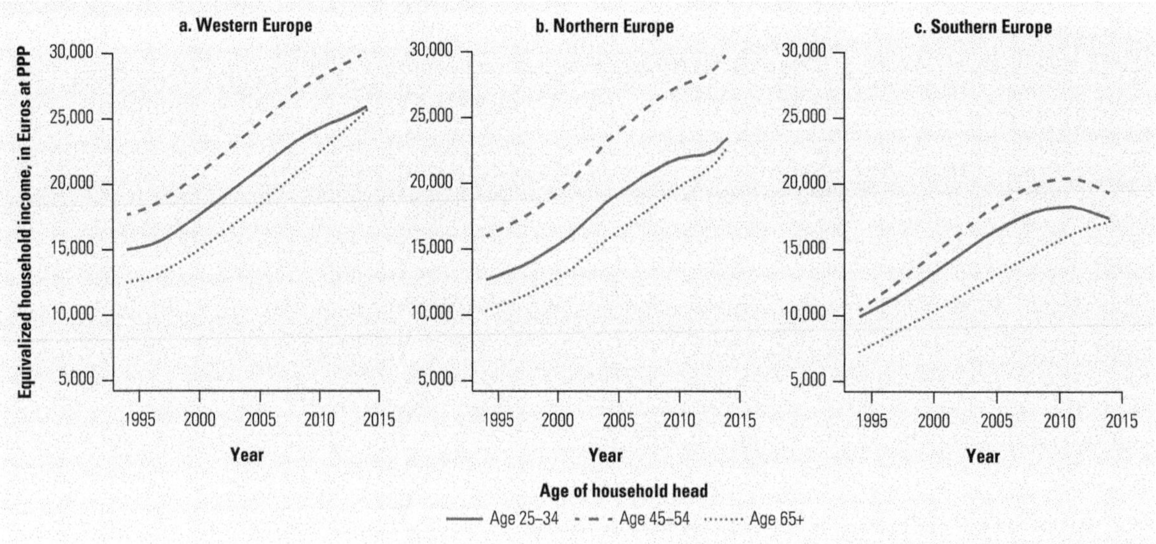

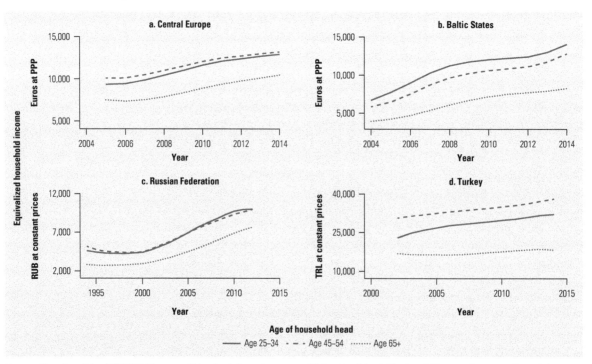

Sources: Based on data of ECHP (European Community Household Panel) (database), Eurostat, European Commission, Luxembourg, http://ec.europa .eu/eurostat/web/microdata/european-community-household-panel; EU-SILC (European Union Statistics on Income and Living Conditions) (database), Eurostat, European Commission, Luxembourg, http://ec.europa.eu/eurostat/web/microdata/european-union-statistics-on-income-and-living-conditions. *Note:* PPP = purchasing power parity.

FIGURE 2.17 Household income, by age of household head, Central Europe, Baltic States, Russian Federation, and Turkey

Sources: Based on data of EU-SILC (European Union Statistics on Income and Living Conditions) (database), Eurostat, European Commission, Luxembourg, http://ec.europa.eu/eurostat/web/microdata/european-union-statistics-on-income-and-living-conditions; household income, consumption, and expenditure surveys; RLMS–HSE (Russia Longitudinal Monitoring Survey–Higher School of Economics) (database), Higher School of Economics, National Research University, Moscow, http://www.hse.ru/en/rlms/. *Note:* PPP = purchasing power parity.

similar in all transition countries, while, in Turkey and the rest of Europe, the middle age-group enjoys significantly higher incomes. This suggests that the wage returns to experience is relatively low in transition economies.

The earnings prospects of young generations in Southern and Western Europe appear to be deteriorating. The flat profile of the earnings of workers with only a high school diploma suggests these individuals are receiving low returns to experience (figures 2.18 and 2.19, panel a).[20] Moreover, average earnings did not improve among successive cohorts. The impact of the 2008–09 financial crisis may

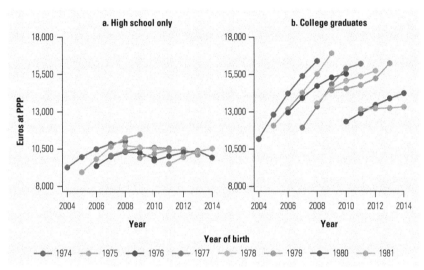

FIGURE 2.18
Average annual earnings, 30–34 age-group, Southern Europe, 2004–14

Source: Based on data of EU-SILC (European Union Statistics on Income and Living Conditions) (database), Eurostat, European Commission, Luxembourg, http://ec.europa.eu/eurostat/web /microdata/european-union-statistics-on-income-and-living-conditions.
Note: Each line depicts the smoothed (locally weighted regression) average labor market earnings from age 30 to age 34 of each birth cohort. PPP = purchasing power parity.

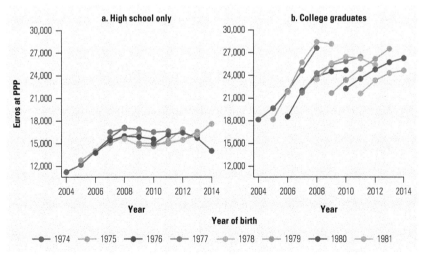

FIGURE 2.19
Average annual earnings, 30–34 age-group, Western Europe, 2004–14

Source: Based on data of EU-SILC (European Union Statistics on Income and Living Conditions) (database), Eurostat, European Commission, Luxembourg, http://ec.europa.eu/eurostat/web /microdata/european-union-statistics-on-income-and-living-conditions.
Note: Each line depicts the smoothed (locally weighted regression) average labor market earnings from age 30 to age 34 of each birth cohort. PPP = purchasing power parity.

be partly responsible for this lack of growth. However, the wage profile is similar even among cohorts that were 30–34 years old before the crisis, suggesting that low earnings prospects are a structural characteristic of the labor market among individuals with only a high school diploma. The wages of college graduates from older generations did rise substantially (the slope of the wage profile in figures 2.18 and 2.19 is steep), but the youngest cohorts that entered their prime earnings years during or after the financial crisis, experienced a considerably lower increase in wages. In Southern Europe, the youngest generations have a practically flat wage profile, similar to that of workers with only a high school diploma. The flattening of the wage profile among young college graduates may reflect either a decline in returns to experience or greater job turnover. More frequent shifts in and out of jobs or even between jobs reduce the average wage, especially among younger generations. Indeed, there is some evidence to support the second hypothesis: there has been a decline in the average job tenure of younger generations relative to older generations in Europe (see above).

Trends in wages across generations have been more varied in Central and Northern Europe (figures 2.20 and 2.21). The average income of workers with only a high school diploma has increased across successive cohorts. Among college graduates, the flattening of the wage profile is evident in Central Europe, albeit with a smaller magnitude than in Southern and Western Europe. In Northern Europe, cohorts entering the prime earnings period during the crisis (cohorts born in 1978 and 1979, for instance) faced only limited earnings growth thereafter, but this pattern is reversed among later generations, who enjoyed income increases similar to those of generations born in the early 1970s.

FIGURE 2.20
Average annual earnings, 30–34 age-group, Central Europe, 2004–14

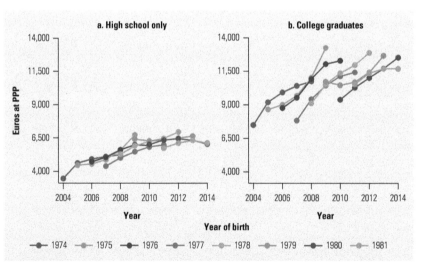

Source: Based on data of EU-SILC (European Union Statistics on Income and Living Conditions) (database), Eurostat, European Commission, Luxembourg, http://ec.europa.eu/eurostat/web /microdata/european-union-statistics-on-income-and-living-conditions.
Note: Each line depicts the smoothed (locally weighted regression) average labor market earnings from age 30 to age 34 of each birth cohort. PPP = purchasing power parity.

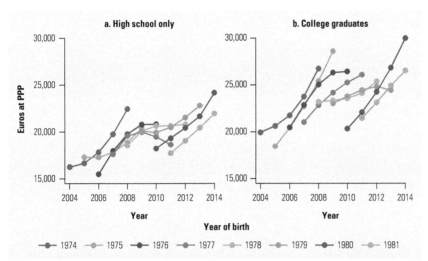

FIGURE 2.21
Average annual earnings, 30–34 age-group, Northern Europe, 2004–14

Source: Based on data of EU-SILC (European Union Statistics on Income and Living Conditions) (database), Eurostat, European Commission, Luxembourg, http://ec.europa.eu/eurostat/web /microdata/european-union-statistics-on-income-and-living-conditions.
Note: Each line depicts the smoothed (locally weighted regression) average labor market earnings from age 30 to age 34 of each birth cohort. PPP = purchasing power parity.

Increased Inequality Among the Young

Weak income growth among younger generations in Southern and Western Europe has been accompanied by widening inequality. While income inequality across a given generation tends to rise over time, younger generations in Southern and Western Europe are facing higher income inequality at every point of the life cycle relative to older generations.[21] For example, Bussolo, Jappelli, Nisticò, and Torre (2018) find that income inequality among Italians born in the 1930s was similar to that of a relatively equal country, such as Japan (Gini coefficient of approximately 0.31) (figure 2.22).[22] By contrast, income inequality among Italians born in the 1980s was similar to a highly unequal country such as Chile (Gini coefficient of approximately 0.48). The equivalent intergenerational rise in the Gini coefficient was much smaller in Germany (4 points) and in France (1 point). The intergenerational rise in inequality is even higher if the analysis is restricted to labor income rather than total income.[23] So, successive generations are experiencing an increase in inequality that exceeds the amount expected as generations age.

Persistent Spatial Disparities across the Region

As technological change, agglomeration economies, trade, and other market forces transform the economic and labor market landscape across countries, some individuals may be systematically excluded from economic opportunities. If place of birth or residence limits the access of people to quality education or good jobs, it will also limit their productive capacity and their opportunities to

FIGURE 2.22
Income inequality is much higher among cohorts born in the 1980s

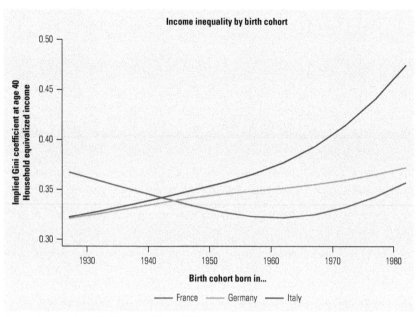

Source: Bussolo, Jappelli, Nisticò, and Torre 2018.

join the middle class, and may thus fuel discontent and perceptions of unfairness. Evidence on Europe and Central Asia points to place of birth as an important factor in the inequality of opportunity in gaining access to tertiary education, a job, and higher income (EBRD 2016). Moreover, despite the relatively high international emigration rates in many countries in Eastern Europe and Central Asia, internal mobility rates are low, reflecting limited opportunities to move to obtain better jobs (Arias et al. 2014). Recognizing that economic growth may be an unbalanced process (World Bank 2009), spatial disparities, particularly if persistent and not mitigated by targeted policies to promote convergence in living standards, can contribute to rising distributional tensions and populism. People in some places may feel left behind and sense their restricted ability to influence policy making and the allocation of resources in society (World Bank 2017a). This section explores trends in such spatial disparities in Europe and Central Asia.

Spatial Disparities Are Common in the Region

Differences in income persist between regions in many countries of Europe and Central Asia. National indicators of welfare may mask even vast differences across regions within countries. The use of the coefficient of variation as a measure of disparities in consumption or disposable income between regions reveals that spatial inequalities in welfare are common within countries. The greatest inequalities occur in the Slovak Republic, Tajikistan, and Russia and the lowest in Denmark (figure 2.23). In the European Union, the highest disparities are in Southern Europe, including Greece, Italy, and Spain, where levels are higher than the OECD average of 0.14 (OECD 2016). The varying geographical aggregations at which disparities

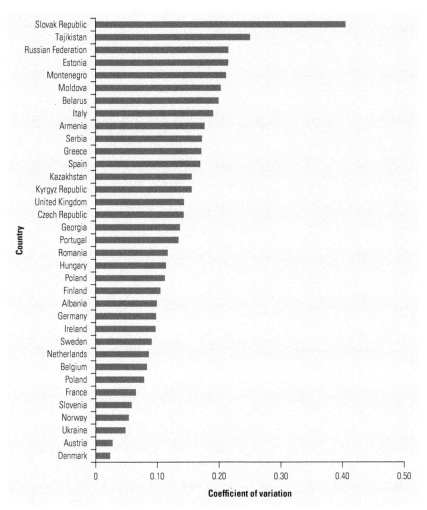

FIGURE 2.23
Spatial disparities in welfare are not uncommon in the region
Coefficient of variation of disposable income or consumption, by region, circa 2013

Sources: OECD 2016; World Bank calculations rely on harmonized data on other, non-OECD countries.

are measured across several countries may pose a challenge in comparing inequalities across regions. Nonetheless, the disparities are also evident between urban and rural areas. A comparison between urban and rural areas using a welfare index constructed based on information on durables and the socioeconomic characteristics of households in the 2016 round of the Life in Transition Survey (LiTS) shows that living standards are higher in urban areas than in rural areas in all countries of Europe and Central Asia covered by the data except Greece (figure 2.24).[24] The greatest urban–rural disparities by this measure occur in Bulgaria, Georgia, Romania, and Tajikistan.

The share of inequality explained by inequality between within-country regions has risen in some countries. One summary measure of this regional inequality indicates the inequality between geographical areas in average per capita consumption as a share of the maximum possible inequality between these areas, taking into account the size and number of regions.[25]

FIGURE 2.24
Gaps between urban and rural areas are largest in Georgia and Tajikistan and are negative only in Greece
Urban–rural gap in welfare index, 2015

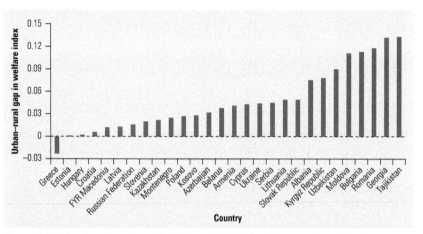

Source: Calculations based on data of the 2016 round, LiTS (Life in Transition Survey) (database), European Bank for Reconstruction and Development, London, http://www.ebrd.com/what-we-do /economic-research-and-data/data/lits.html.
Notes: The welfare index ranges from 0 to 1 and is constructed using a principal component analysis and 12 variables of household durables, including phone (landline or cell), computer, washing machine, car, bike, motorbike, as well as proxies for household socioeconomic status, including Internet access, adequate heating, a week's holiday each year, a meal of meat, chicken, or fish every second day, ability to meet unexpected expenses through own resources equivalent to the national poverty threshold, and access to a bank account. All variables are transformed to 0 if the household cannot afford the asset and 1 if the household is in possession of the asset or does not have it for other reasons, for example, Internet is not available at the location of the household.

The importance of inequality between within-country regions and between urban and rural areas has increased in several countries, although data are not available for all countries of Europe and Central Asia (figures 2.25 and 2.26). Increases are noticeable in Armenia, Moldova, and Serbia. Between-region inequality has narrowed in the Kyrgyz Republic, in addition to inequality between urban and rural areas in Kazakhstan and Poland, for instance.

Spatial disparities in welfare have increased in many countries in the region. Despite increases in average household consumption over the past decade, inequalities across geographical areas persist and have increased in several countries. The gap in consumption between urban and rural areas has widened in 10 of the 14 countries depicted in figure 2.27 (panel a), mostly in the eastern part of the region, and the gap between the richest and poorest regions has increased in 12 of the countries (figure 2.27, panel b).

Regional disparities have also widened in the EU. Regional disparities in disposable income within countries increased over the last two decades in some countries in Southern Europe as well as in other European countries such as Belgium, the Czech Republic, the Netherlands, the Slovak Republic, and the United Kingdom (figures 2.28 and 2.29). Regional disparities declined in others, such as Finland and Germany. Focusing on regional output measured by per capita GDP within country regions, the coefficient of variation shows an average rising trend in regional disparities within EU countries in 2000–15. Thus, some regions are lagging, despite a reduction in within-country inequality that led to a convergence in the EU. Pooling all within-country regions in the EU also indicates there was an increase in dispersion during this period.

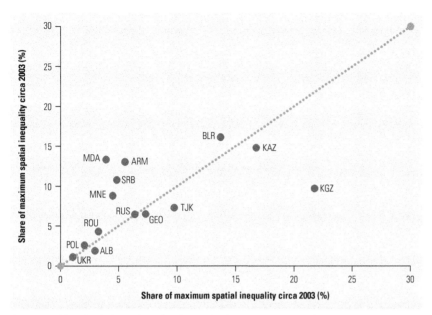

FIGURE 2.25
Between-region inequality has widened in some countries

Source: World Bank calculations based on harmonized mean consumption data on 14 countries in Europe and Central Asia.
Note: Maximum spatial inequality corresponds to a scenario where, given the size and the ranking of the regions in terms of mean income, households with the lowest incomes are allocated to the poorest regions, while households with the highest incomes are allocated to the richest regions, and households in the middle are allocated in similar fashion to the remaining regions. The values illustrated in the figure express between-region inequality, that is, the average difference in mean incomes, as a ratio of maximum spatial inequality. See Elbers, Lanjouw, and Lanjouw (2003) for a detailed explanation of the methodology. Dotted line represents no change in values between 2003 and 2013.

In line with spatial differences in living standards, the concentration of poverty also has a spatial dimension. Subnational poverty rates vary significantly within countries. In Tajikistan, for instance, the poverty rate—the share of people with incomes below US$5.50 a day in constant 2011 prices in U.S. dollars purchasing power parity (PPP)—in the poorest region is 72 percent, more than twice the rate of the region with the lowest rate (31 percent). In Romania, the poverty rate in the least well-off region is two and a half times higher than the rate in the wealthiest region. Similarly, the at-risk-of-poverty measure at the Nomenclature of Territorial Units for Statistics–3 level shows that the poorest region in France has a rate three times higher than the rate in the region with the lowest poverty rate; this ratio is around seven in the United Kingdom.[26]

The spatial concentration of poverty is rising. As living standards have improved, poverty rates have declined across countries in the last decade or so. However, particularly important for potential concerns over emerging distributional tensions is the accompanying rise in geographical dispersion. In seven countries in the eastern part of the region where the poverty rates—the share of people living on less than US$5.50 a day at 2011 constant PPP prices—are more than 10 percent, the difference in poverty rates across regions (measured by the coefficient of variation) has increased (figure 2.30). In Armenia, for example, the difference in poverty rates between the less well-off and the more well-off regions rose from 25 percentage points to 38 percentage points in 2003–2013.

FIGURE 2.26
Inequality between urban and rural areas has increased in some countries

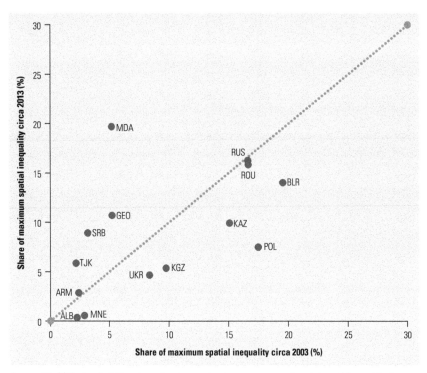

Source: World Bank calculations based on harmonized mean consumption data on 14 countries in Europe and Central Asia.

Note: Maximum spatial inequality corresponds to a scenario where, given the size and the ranking of the regions in terms of mean income, households with the lowest incomes are allocated to the poorest regions, while households with the highest incomes are allocated to the richest regions, and households in the middle are allocated in similar fashion to the remaining regions. The values illustrated in the figure express between-region inequality, that is, the average difference in mean incomes, as a ratio of maximum spatial inequality. See Elbers, Lanjouw, and Lanjouw (2003) for a detailed explanation of the methodology. Dotted line represents no change in values between 2003 and 2013.

FIGURE 2.27
Gaps in mean consumption, circa 2003–13

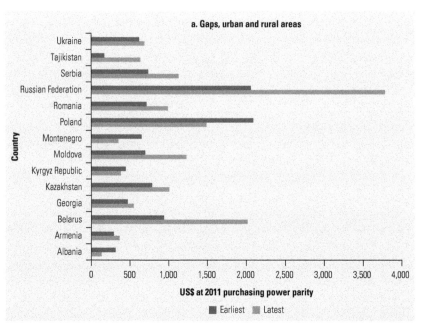

(Continued)

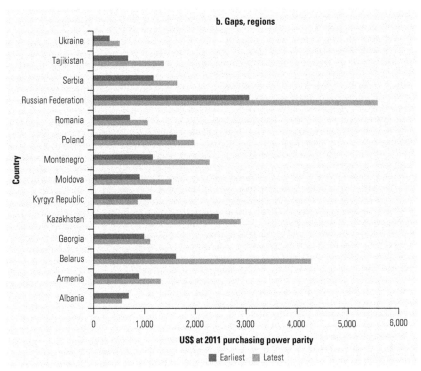

FIGURE 2.27
Gaps in mean consumption, circa 2003–13 *(continued)*

Source: World Bank calculations based on harmonized mean consumption data on 14 countries in Europe and Central Asia.

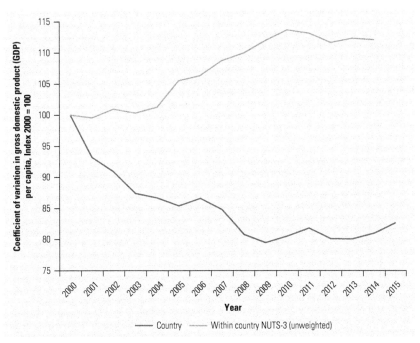

FIGURE 2.28
Between-region spatial inequalities within countries have increased in the European Union

Source: Farole, Goga, and Ionescu-Heroiu 2018.
Note: Country refers to the coefficient of variation across European Union countries, signaling convergence in gross domestic product (GDP). The within-country coefficient of variation measure is at the Nomenclature of Territorial Units for Statistics–3 level (NUTS-3). GDP per capita is measured in purchasing power standard (PPS).

FIGURE 2.29
Regional disparities in
disposable income rose,
were unchanged, or
declined
*Coefficient of variation in
regional disposable income,
1995 and 2014*

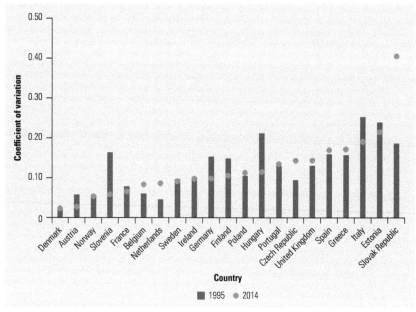

Source: OECD 2016.

FIGURE 2.30
The spatial dispersion of
poverty rates has increased
*Coefficient of variation of
poverty rates at US$5.50 a
day (2011 purchasing power
parity), circa 2003–13*

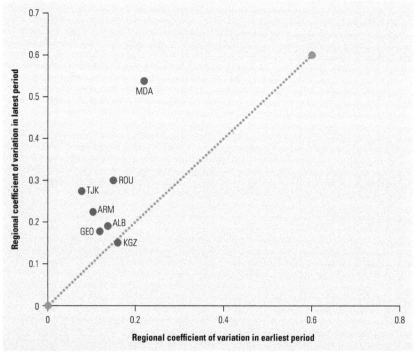

Source: World Bank calculations using harmonized mean consumption data of 7 countries in Europe
and Central Asia.
Note: Dotted line indicates no change in value between earliest and latest period.

Access to Opportunities Is More Limited among Residents of Certain Areas

Differences in individual endowments are a major reason for disparities in welfare between regions and between rural and urban residents. Income may be lower because of the characteristics of individuals in an area; for example, they may not be as well educated—education, the age of the head of household, and household demographic composition and size are considered here—or because the returns to these characteristics are lower given location-specific factors. In 14 countries in Europe and Central Asia on which harmonized data are available, characteristics play a key role in driving income disparities between geographical areas, such as between leading versus lagging regions, the richest versus the poorest regions, and, especially, urban versus rural areas (figure 2.31). In most of the countries under consideration, the educational attainment of the household head accounts for a large share of the characteristics component, pointing to the influence of education on gaps in living standards. The role of education is not surprising, given the close correlation of educational attainment with welfare in the region.

There are also spatial gaps in schooling quality. Europe and Central Asia stands out as one of the regions with the highest educational attainment and learning outcomes. Yet, gaps in access remain, particularly among certain groups and areas, and schooling does not always translate into learning. For example, across

FIGURE 2.31 **Differences in characteristics and in returns to characteristics help explain welfare gaps across geographical areas, circa 2013**
Decomposition of spatial disparities in mean consumption per capita in characteristics vs. returns (share of the gap explained by each component)

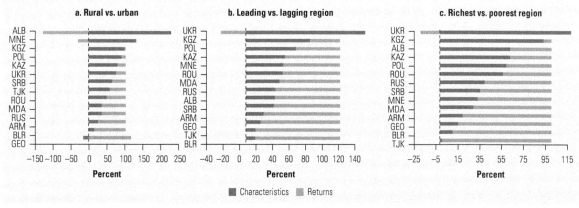

Source: Calculations using harmonized mean consumption data on 14 countries in Europe and Central Asia.
Note: Laggers are defined based on average harmonized mean consumption below the national average. Regressors include demographics (age and gender of the household head), educational attainment of household heads, and household composition (size, demographic composition). The panels indicate the dominant explanation for welfare disparities between geographical areas: characteristics, returns to characteristics, or both. In the Kyrgyz Republic, for example, 93 percent of the welfare difference between the richest and the poorest regions is explained by differences in the characteristics of households and individuals in these areas. In Georgia, 84 percent of the differences derive from difference in the returns to characteristics. Country codes: ALB = Albania; ARM = Armenia; BLR = Belarus; GEO = Georgia; KAZ = Kazakhstan; KGZ = Kyrgyz Republic; MDA = Moldova; MNE = Montenegro; POL = Poland; ROU = Romania; RUS = Russian Federation; SRB = Serbia; TJK = Tajikistan; UKR = Ukraine.

all countries in Europe and Central Asia that implemented the 2015 round of the test of the Programme for International Student Assessment (PISA), a share of students were found not to have developed the foundational cognitive skills they need to succeed in the labor market.[27] The share of functionally illiterate students (15-year-old students who scored below level 2 on the PISA reading section) was 77 percent in Kosovo and 71 percent in FYR Macedonia, but also quite high in EU countries such as Bulgaria (42 percent), Romania (39 percent), and the Slovak Republic (32 percent). Disadvantages in schooling quality are evident along the spatial dimension, creating a divide based on geographical location. Thus, children in a same grade in a same country are losing out on accessing quality education depending on where they live. The largest gaps in 2015 PISA scores in countries on which data are available occurred in Bulgaria and Moldova (around a two-year schooling gap between urban and rural areas), followed by the Slovak Republic and Romania (figure 2.32). In Romania, 83 percent of low-performing schools are in rural areas (World Bank 2018a).

Other factors may also lead to lower productivity and lower returns in certain geographical areas. Across countries, differences in returns are relevant in explaining disparities in mean consumption between rural and urban areas and between regions (see figure 2.31). These differences in returns may be capturing spatial gaps in public service delivery, service infrastructure, communication networks, access to markets, local governance coverage, social capital, or the business environment. Access to basic services has expanded in many countries. Yet, a spatial divide exists, including differences in quality. In Russia, some regions are systematically affected by the limited presence of the state (box 2.6). In Moldova, 95 percent of the urban population is connected to piped water, but this is so among only 54 percent of the rural population, of which only 39 percent have the service within the dwelling (World Bank 2016b). Albania presents a similar situation. There, the share of households with access to a steady water supply ranges from 47 percent in Durrës County to 88 percent in Shkodër County (World Bank 2015). Access to services does not refer only to basic infrastructure, which is more relevant in the developing countries in the region, but also access to technology. The Czech Republic, France, Portugal, and Spain show regional gaps of around 20 percentage points in the share of households with broadband connections.[28]

Quality may also vary. In Moldova, firms face lower-quality services depending on where they are located (figure 2.33). Other region-related factors may likewise keep some areas from providing residents with access to opportunities. Evidence from the eastern and the western parts of the region—Kazakhstan and Italy—shows that firms face a business environment that differs depending on location.[29]

Even if gaps in access to education and other services were to be addressed, the difference in returns across regions cannot be bridged if barriers to internal mobility limit the ability of residents in some areas to benefit from agglomeration and urbanization. This is an example of horizontal inequality whereby there are significant impediments in switching between groups. Evidence on the region points to low internal mobility compared with populations in other countries, despite evidence of agglomeration economies and gaps in unemployment rates between regions (Arias et al. 2014; Restrepo Cadavid

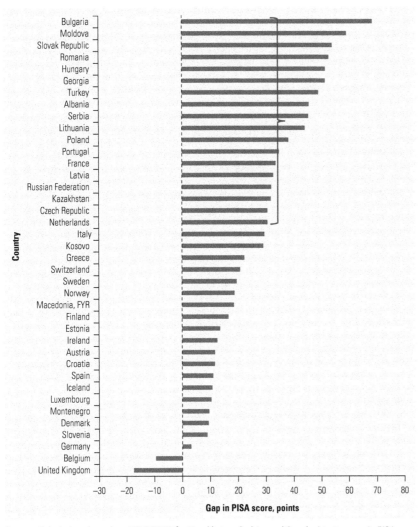

FIGURE 2.32

Gaps in PISA reading scores: often equivalent to a year of schooling, urban and rural areas

Source: Calculations based on 2015 (2012 for Kazakhstan, Serbia, and Sweden) test scores in PISA (Programme for International Student Assessment) (database), Organisation for Economic Co-operation and Development, Paris, http://www.oecd.org/pisa/pisaproducts/.
Note: Urban schools are located in a city or large city (more than 100,000 people). Rural schools are located in a town, a small town, or village, hamlet, rural area (fewer than 100,000 people). A gap in PISA scores of 30 points, covered by the red bracket, is estimated as the equivalent of one year of schooling. See Woessmann (2016).

BOX 2.6   A Closer Look at Spatial Disparities in the Russian Federation

An understanding of the obstacles in the Russian Federation's quest for development begins with the country's expansive geography and the difficulties in governing such a vast territory. Russia is the world's largest country, and its geographical endowments encompass harsh climatic conditions and a dominance of natural resources in peripheral regions that have shaped Russia's development policies. During the Soviet era, labor and capital were forcibly moved toward the east to exploit Siberia's vast natural resources, develop military capabilities, and support a more even distribution of population and economic activity. The resulting economic structure was physically more dispersed throughout the territory, yet inefficient and distorted. Efforts to reverse this policy legacy have often been undermined by the

(Continued)

BOX 2.6   A Closer Look at Spatial Disparities in the Russian Federation
(continued)

inherited economic, social, physical, and relational networks that hindered progress toward more efficient and equitable regional development.

Today, Russia has the highest level of inequality among large, emerging economies such as Brazil, China, and India. Russian regions experienced some convergence in income in the last decade as poorer regions grew more quickly (controlling for other factors). Moreover, there appear to be positive spillovers from one region to another, that is, factors that raise incomes and reduce poverty in one region raise incomes and reduce poverty in neighboring regions. However, immense disparities in living standards persist. Households in Sakhalin Oblast (which has the highest gross regional product per capita) experience living standards similar to those in Singapore, while households in Ingushetia (which has the lowest gross regional product per capita) experience living standards closer to those in Honduras. Poverty rates range from less than 10 percent in resource-rich Tatarstan and large metropolitan areas of Moscow and St. Petersburg to almost 40 percent in the poorest regions in the North Caucuses, Siberia, and the Far East. In the richest

and most populous regions, including Moscow, St. Petersburg, and natural resource–rich regions, inequality is high, meaning the numbers of the poor are large, though the areas do not exhibit the highest poverty rates.

The transformation from unbalanced growth to inclusive development requires a shift in policies, including a focus on richer regions where poverty and inequality are concentrated. Russia's prevailing policy approach since the transition has been more equalizing than other countries. Poor regions depend heavily on federal transfers. These drivers of convergence have become less sustainable, which became evident when Russia underwent the recent oil price crisis and sanction regime. The policies also appear to have hindered the ability of poor regions to boost their comparative advantage. Regions are still characterized by significant disparities in access to services, and some regions are affected systematically by the low profile of the state. This invariably translates into disparities in outcomes. Addressing disparities in access to services and thereby leveling the playing field remains at the heart of policies seeking to improve both efficiency and equity.

Source: World Bank 2017b.

et al. 2017). Less than 30 percent of the population reported they would be willing to move to another part of the country for a job; younger, single, more well-educated men were more likely to move. Barriers to internal mobility, including those related to weaknesses in housing and land markets, can leave some trapped in lagging areas (chapter 3).

Closing spatial disparities by ensuring that people build the human capital they need and that they can access opportunities will lead to more inclusive growth. There are important reasons to pay attention to spatial inequalities, especially their potential to foster location-related discontent. One reason is equity, which implies that location of residence should be neutral with respect to income, educational attainment, ownership of assets, and access to economic opportunity. Another reason is voice and accountability: spatial disparities may affect the agency and bargaining power of people living in different places and their ability to influence policy making and the allocation of resources in society (World Bank 2017d). If individuals in some areas are systematically excluded from

FIGURE 2.33 Moldova: indicators of service quality, by region, 2013

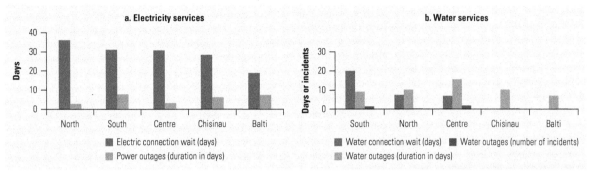

Source: World Bank 2016b.

economic gains and from emerging and changing opportunities given their lower skills, limited labor mobility, or other reasons, spatial inequalities may widen, and some groups will be left further behind.

Rising Inequality of Opportunity, Particularly in the East

If the access of people to opportunities is determined by circumstances beyond their control, this may lead to distributional tensions and to a growing sense of unfairness. Widening inequality of opportunity can also impair aggregate growth. It has been suggested that the existence of strong and persistent inequalities in the initial opportunities open to individuals can generate inequality traps that represent severe constraints to the future growth of an economy by preventing entire groups from full participation in economic and social life (Bourguignon, Ferreira, and Menéndez 2007; World Bank 2006).[30]

Inequality of Opportunity Is Declining, but Is Still Evident in the West

Inequality of opportunity—the impact of circumstances at birth on income and other welfare outcomes—is an important reason behind the existence of income inequality in Europe. The contribution of inequality of opportunity to income accounts for between 25 percent and 60 percent of total income inequality (measured according to the Gini index) in most European countries (Checchi, Peragine, and Serlenga 2016).[31] Moreover, inequality of opportunity and income inequality were strongly related across Europe in both 2005 and 2011 (figure 2.34). The Nordic countries had low levels of income and opportunity inequality; the Mediterranean and Continental European countries exhibited intermediate levels in these inequality dimensions; and the Eastern European countries showed a relatively high level of income inequality, but were more mixed with respect to inequality of opportunity.

There were no significant changes in the estimated level of inequality of opportunity in income in 2005–11 (comparing the two panels of figure 2.34). Measuring inequality of opportunity over longer periods is difficult, given the lack of data.

FIGURE 2.34
Income inequality, Europe, 2005 and 2011

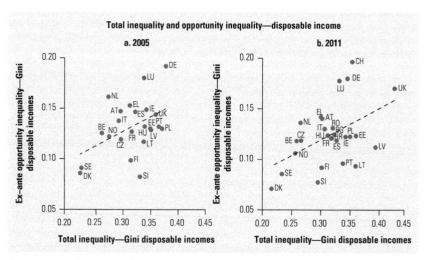

Source: Checchi, Peragine, and Serlenga 2016.

However, for the four largest economies in the EU, namely, France, Germany, Italy, and the United Kingdom, the data are sufficient for this measurement.[32] Depending on how inequality is calculated, inequality of opportunity accounts for about a third (based on the mean log deviation calculation) to a half (based on the Gini coefficient) of total income inequality in the four countries (figure 2.35, panel a, for the Gini). Inequality of opportunity in income in these countries was either stable or weakly decreasing (in Germany and the United Kingdom) in 1993–2014, suggesting that inequality of opportunity reflects embedded features of national socioeconomic systems that are little affected by temporary changes in economic activity. Inequality of opportunity with respect to education declined steadily, especially in Italy, over the period (figure 2.35, panel b).

Inequality of opportunity tends to decline with age (figure 2.36).[33] The observed inequality of opportunity exhibits an inverted U-shaped pattern over the life cycle; in France and Italy, it has a clearer decreasing pattern. After a certain age, which varies across countries, the effect of the circumstances at birth seem to weaken. This differs from the pattern of income or consumption inequality, which generally rises with age. The cohort analysis shows a more mixed picture: in Germany and the United Kingdom, inequality of opportunity declines across generations, that is, the younger generation experience less inequality of opportunity, while the data on France and Italy are characterized by an inverted U.

Improved access to education in Europe is not always associated with declines in inequality of opportunity across generations. Figure 2.37 shows, for Germany and Italy, the contribution to inequality of opportunity of (1) the intergenerational persistence in education (whether an individual's educational attainment is strongly related to the educational attainment of the parents), (2) the returns to education in the labor market, and (3) networking activity associated with parental background.[34] In Italy, the first two variables decline, which, other things being equal, should produce a decline in inequality of opportunity, but the third variable rises; so inequality of opportunity is roughly the same at the end of the period as at the beginning. In Germany, the contribution of the returns to education falls, while the

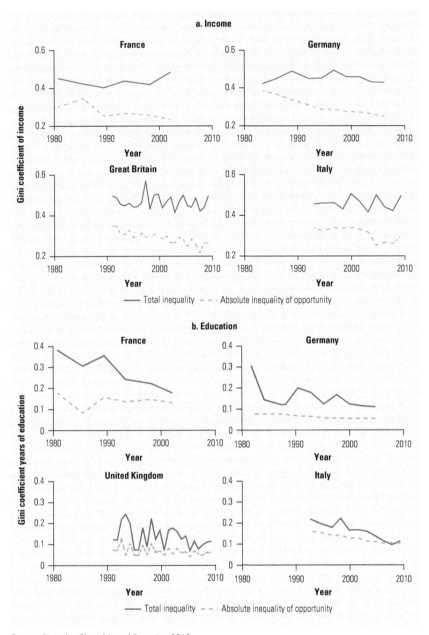

FIGURE 2.35
Trends in inequality of opportunity: France, Germany, Italy, United Kingdom

Source: Bussolo, Checchi, and Peragine 2018.
Note: The education outcome is measured by years of education.

contribution of parental networking is roughly unchanged by the end of the period; so inequality of opportunity declines.

Thus, increased equality of opportunity in education, mainly because of the expansion of tertiary education in most countries in recent decades, has not always resulted in greater equality of opportunity in income. Three of the many possible explanations are likely important. First, parental networking may be playing a role in helping young workers find desirable jobs. Second, the decline in the returns to education may be loosening the link between educational

FIGURE 2.36 Decomposition of inequality of opportunity in age and cohort effects, France, Germany, Italy, United Kingdom

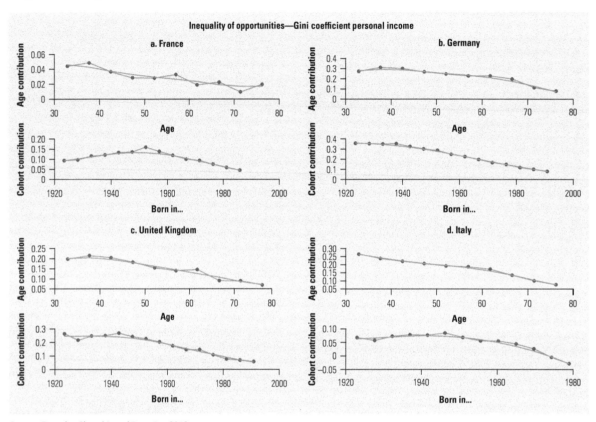

Source: Bussolo, Checchi, and Peragine 2018.
Note: Estimated contributions of birth cohorts and age-groups in explaining the dynamics of inequality of opportunity, according to Deaton's decomposition; see Deaton (1997). Blue line and markers indicate the actual values, and green line indicates the smoothed values.

FIGURE 2.37
Decomposition of inequality of opportunity

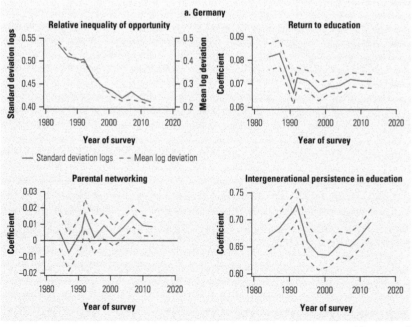

(Continued)

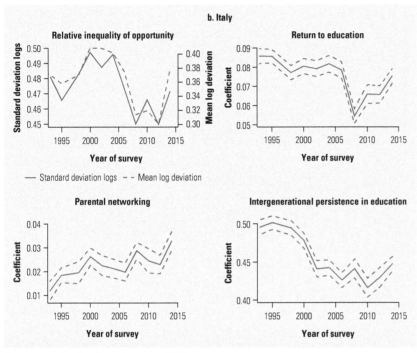

FIGURE 2.37

Decomposition of inequality of opportunity *(continued)*

Source: Bussolo, Checchi, and Peragine 2018.
Note: The first quadrant plots the relative inequality of opportunity, while the other three quadrants report the estimated structural parameters (with one standard error confidence interval) that contribute to the measured inequality of opportunity.

attainment and incomes. Third, while access to education measured in years of education or the degrees obtained has become more equal, the quality of education may still vary greatly. There are still spatial gaps in quality. Deficiencies are also evident among children of disadvantaged socioeconomic backgrounds, as revealed by the results of the PISA test in 2015. In the Slovak Republic, for example, the gap between socioeconomic groups is the equivalent of five years of schooling; the gaps in Austria, the Czech Republic, and France are also large (Ridao-Cano and Bodewig 2018).

Increasingly Unequal Access to Opportunities in the East

Inequality of opportunity is greater in the east. In three-quarters of the transition countries studied by Brock, Peragine, and Tonini (2016), a third or more of total income inequality is associated with individual circumstances or inequality in opportunity (figure 2.38).[35] In general, inequality of opportunity is greater in the formerly planned economies than in the western countries in the LiTS 2016 sample.[36] On average, the inequality of opportunity in acquiring labor income averages 0.11 in the 15 countries that are part of the EU, compared with 0.12 in the remaining 18 countries, despite the relatively high estimates for Bulgaria, Estonia, Greece, Hungary, and Latvia, where inequality of opportunity is above the regional average. However, inequality of opportunity is much lower in the transition economies than in other emerging economies (for example, Brazil and India) or in the United States.[37]

FIGURE 2.38
Income inequality and inequality of opportunity in obtaining income

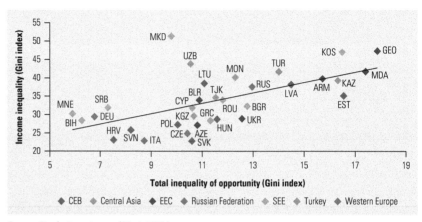

Source: Brock, Peragine, and Tonini 2016.
Note: CEB = Central Europe and the Baltic States; EEC = Eastern Europe and the Caucasus; SEE = South-Eastern Europe.

Inequality of opportunity varies substantially across the transition countries and often between neighboring countries. It is high in several transition countries that are now EU members and that also have more well-developed institutions. Differences in inequality of opportunity within the eastern subregions of Europe and Central Asia are largest in southeastern Europe, where Bosnia and Herzegovina, Montenegro, and Serbia display some of the lowest estimates, comparable with that of Germany. By contrast, inequality of opportunity in Bulgaria, Kosovo, and Romania is estimated to be above the median of the transition region. Inequality of opportunity is generally high in Eastern Europe, the Caucasus, and Central Asia.

Transition countries with high inequality of opportunity also tend to exhibit high income inequality (see figure 2.38). The relationship is stronger among countries with higher inequality and weaker in countries with lower inequality. Some countries show high inequality of opportunity, but moderate or low income inequality. However, low inequality of opportunity and high income inequality together, as in FYR Macedonia, are rare.

Access to education is an important determinant of inequality of opportunity in the east, and it has become more unequal. In the transition region, workers with a tertiary degree earn, on average, 31 percent more in income than those workers with only a secondary degree (Brock, Peragine, and Tonini 2016). Returns to education of this magnitude are comparable with returns in some Western European countries, such as the Netherlands and Spain, but are lower than the corresponding returns in Eastern Europe in the early years of transition (Badescu, D'Hombres, and Villalba 2011; Bartolj et al. 2012). Individual birth circumstances are more important determinants of access to tertiary education among the generation that came of age in the early 2000s than among the generation that started education before the transition (Brock, Peragine, and Tonini 2016). This result is confirmed by the data of the three waves of the LiTS and by making a finer partition of the population into five separate cohorts to describe 40-year trends in equality of opportunity in education.[38] Figure 2.39 reports, for each of five cohorts, the inequality of opportunity in tertiary education, as measured by the dissimilarity index.[39] The panels show that, although some differences within subregions exist, access to

FIGURE 2.39 Inequality of opportunity in tertiary education

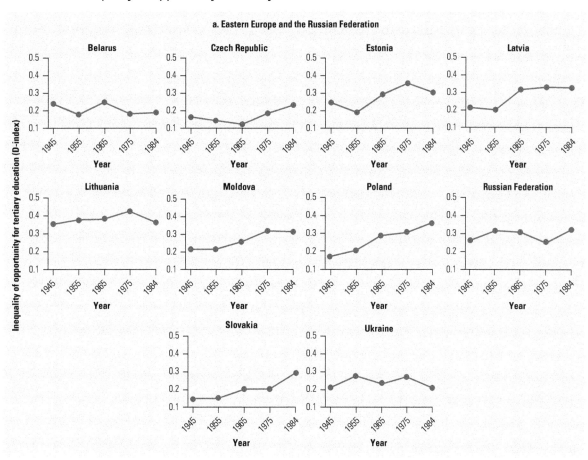

a. Eastern Europe and the Russian Federation

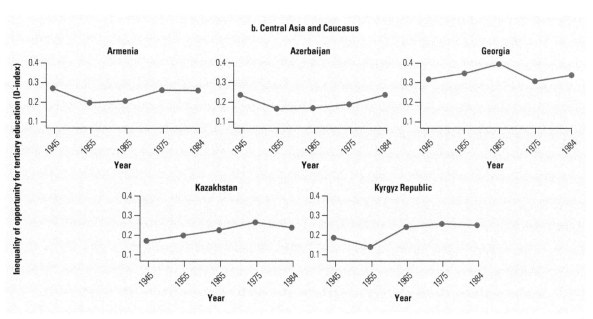

b. Central Asia and Caucasus

(Continued)

FIGURE 2.39 Inequality of opportunity in tertiary education (continued)

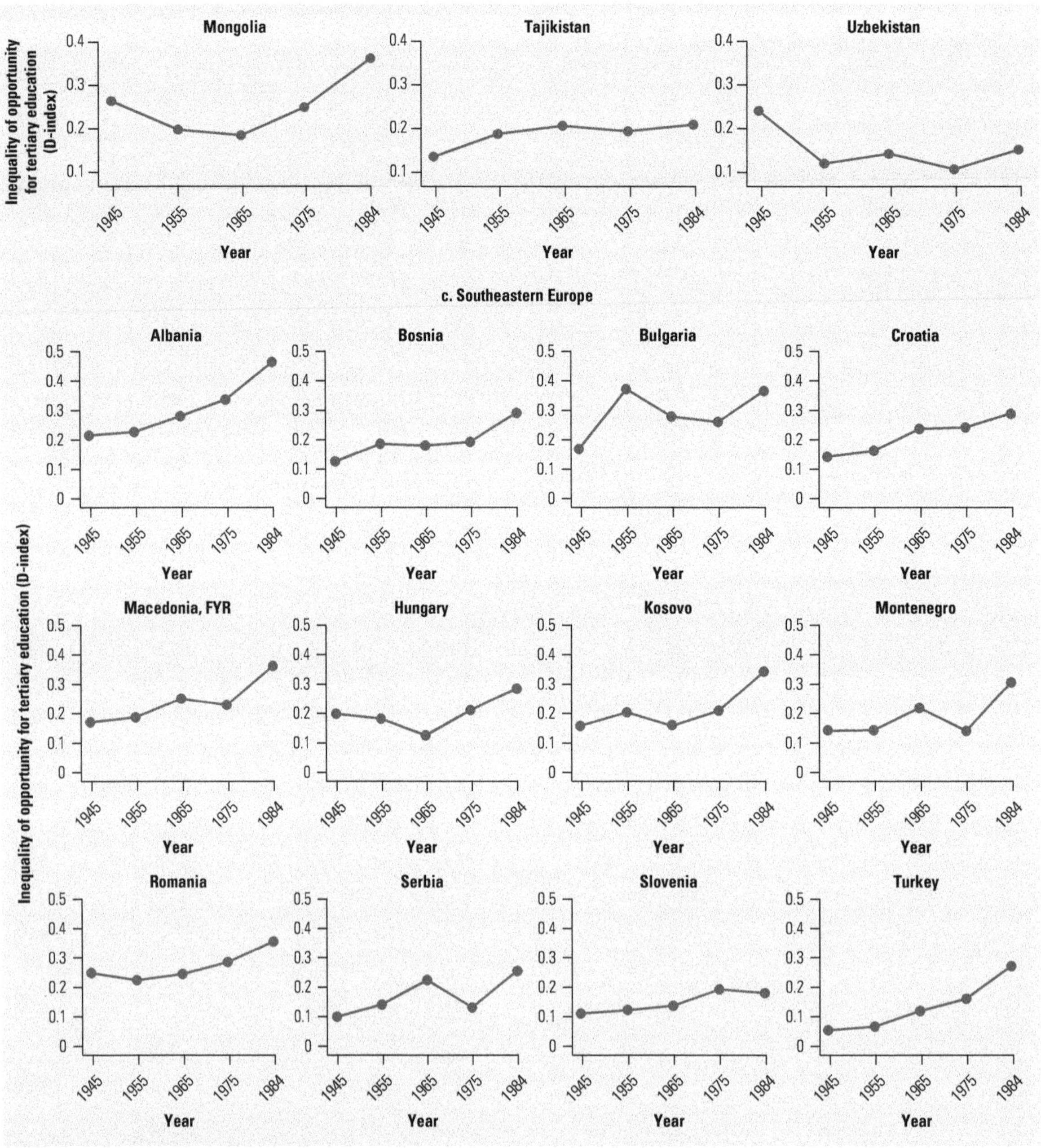

c. Southeastern Europe

Source: Calculations based on data of the 2016 round, LiTS (Life in Transition Survey) (database), European Bank for Reconstruction and Development, London, http://www.ebrd.com/what-we-do/economic-research-and-data/data/lits.html.
Note: The panels show a dissimilarity index of inequality of opportunity, based on a probit regression of the variable indicating the completion of some tertiary education on individual circumstances.

tertiary education in most countries in Eastern Europe has become more unfair over time, that is, more dependent on the individual's circumstances. This is particularly true of Eastern Europe. Birthplace and gender contribute less to the measured inequality affecting the oldest cohort than to that affecting the younger cohorts.

The increase in inequality of opportunity in education is confirmed in figure 2.40, which shows the trend in intergenerational mobility in education, calculated across cohorts, for countries in Europe and Central Asia (box 2.7).

Examination of mobility trends among cohorts grouped by income reveals that the lower-middle- and high-income countries in the region exhibit greater mobility, on average, relative to upper-middle-income countries. However, all three

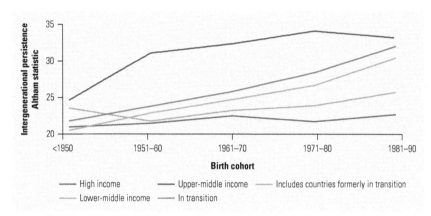

FIGURE 2.40

Intergenerational persistence in education, Europe and Central Asia

Source: Tiwari et al. 2018.
Note: The figure shows the Altham (1970) measure of mobility applied to a pooled sample of the 2006, 2010, and 2016 rounds of the LiTS. See LiTS (Life in Transition Survey) (database), European Bank for Reconstruction and Development, London, http://www.ebrd.com/what-we-do/economic-research-and -data/data/lits.html.

BOX 2.7 Calculating Measures of Intergenerational Mobility

Intergenerational mobility—the extent to which individuals may expect to do better in life, usually in terms of income or profession, than their initial circumstances might suggest—is one of the fundamental cornerstones of development. In an absolute sense, intergenerational mobility is understood in terms of the attainment of a higher status or higher standing (education, income, employment, living standards) relative to one's parents. It involves freeing oneself from the tethers of the social position of one's parents to reach a higher position on the socioeconomic ladder through one's effort.

The ideal dataset for the analysis of intergenerational mobility would consist of a vector of the income or earnings of the children, paired with the corresponding vector of the income of the parents. (The literature has typically used the father's income.) This would allow an estimation of the association between the two vectors. A stronger association between the two would imply lower

mobility, and, conversely, a weaker association would imply greater mobility.

There are several challenges in calculating intergenerational income and earnings elasticities. First, there are only a few countries in the world in which one may construct matched parent-child pairs in income or earnings. Even if this is possible, it cannot be done for a sufficiently long period to capture unbiased estimates of persistence satisfactorily. Second, even if matched data on parental income or earnings are available, they are often available only for a particular point in time. This forces one to make inferences about the relationship based on a snapshot of income rather than long-term income. Third, in many developing and transition countries where formal labor markets are not well developed and there is still a heavy reliance on often informal self-employment, data on income and earnings are likely to exhibit significant measurement errors.

(Continued)

BOX 2.7 Calculating Measures of Intergenerational Mobility *(continued)*

For these reasons, educational attainment is often used to analyze intergenerational mobility. There are several advantages to this. First, educational attainment is a good proxy for overall economic status. There are positive and nontrivial returns to education in almost all labor markets. Even in the post-transition countries in the sample here, where there is some degree of notional universality of education at least to secondary education, there is significant heterogeneity in attainment, and there are positive returns to higher educational attainment. Second, education is often also the most important conduit for the transmission or reproduction of societal privilege or advantage, and it is therefore a useful way to examine social mobility. Third, there is much less noise in

the measurement of educational attainment than in calculating other direct measures of income in the settings under study.

Tiwari et al. (2018) measure intergenerational mobility of education using the Altham statistic. Originally proposed by Altham (1970), the statistic essentially summarizes the degree of association between the rows and columns of any given matrix, relative to the degree of association between the rows and columns of another matrix. Specifically applying this statistic to the transition matrices of educational attainment among parents and children relative to a hypothetical matrix that would denote perfect mobility yields a measure of the degree of persistence between parental and child educational attainment.

Source: Based on Tiwari et al. 2018.

country groups have witnessed a decline in mobility. Among the lower-middle-income countries, the decline is steady among all cohorts born after the 1950s, though the decline appears to be slightly sharper among the youngest cohort. The mobility of the youngest cohort in the upper-middle-income countries has increased slightly. However, this group is still less well off than the generation of their parents and grandparents who would have been born before the 1950s or in the 1960s. In countries still undergoing a transition from the planned to the market economy and in countries that have now completed the transition and joined the EU, there appears to be a steady downward slide among all cohorts and a somewhat sharper deterioration among the two youngest cohorts.

Greater inequality of opportunity in access to education among young cohorts may be traced to the impact of the transition on university systems. First, tertiary education, which used to be universally free, is often now associated with nontrivial costs. Even where education is still nominally free, scholarships to cover the cost of living, generous before the transition, have been effectively phased out, resulting in much higher opportunity costs for an education. Second, the once strong and closely controlled link between tertiary education and jobs has effectively disappeared, while the transition has placed a premium on new skills. Third, parents with tertiary educational attainment have gained from the transition to the extent that, before the transition, manufacturing jobs, which did not typically require a university degree, were relatively high status. As a result of these forces, parental education has become more important in explaining access to tertiary education, signaling a deterioration in the equality of opportunity.

The persistence or widening of inequality of opportunity in the east may have implications for the social contract. The transition has been accompanied by the expectation that the inequality linked to individual effort and talents would increase. In a sense, beyond the popular support for a free market economy and political liberalization, a fair return on individual effort was a main motivation behind supporters of the transition. However, the persistence of inequality because of exogenous factors, such as social background and ethnicity, is a violation of the principle of fair returns and may weaken popular support for the market economy and the implicit social contract.

Distributional Tensions and the Path to a Middle-Class Society

Emerging distributional tensions are making the middle class more fragile and less attainable for some groups. The distributional tensions generated by labor market polarization, generational differences, spatial disparities, and inequality of opportunity are reducing the productive capacity and ability of some groups to benefit from economic opportunity. Relative to older generations, younger generations are facing a deterioration in economic security—a defining element of middle-class status—because of shorter average job tenure and greater reliance on temporary and part-time jobs. Many middle-class workers who depend on jobs that are intensive in routine tasks have become unemployed or are experiencing lower earnings because of technological change.

The middle class is composed of "those who work from 8 am to 5 pm and receive a monthly salary," said a Turkish man (Dávalos et al. 2016, 33).

"People who belong to the middle class should not be under constant stress that they might lose their jobs," said a Serb (Dávalos et al. 2016, 13).

The rise in inequality of opportunity is also reducing the labor market prospects of individuals of lower social or family backgrounds. In the east, the access of such individuals to higher education is becoming more limited because parental background is an increasingly important determinant of access. People living in remote regions may experience difficulties in access to key services, particularly quality education, that reduce their job prospects.

Has the Middle Class Declined in the Region?

The middle class accounts for a large share of the population in Europe and Central Asia. There are several ways of measuring the size of the middle class (box 2.8). Based on data on 20 countries in the Luxembourg Income Study (LIS) database and a definition of the middle class in relative terms as all persons with incomes between 75 percent and 125 percent of the median income, the middle class accounted for an average 38 percent of the population in Europe and Central Asia in around 2013.[40] (For information on country groups and more data, see annex 2A, tables 2A.2 and 2A.3.) The lower and upper ends of the distribution accounted for 29 percent and 33 percent, respectively. The middle class generally comprises the largest group in Western Europe, though the three groups are roughly equal in size in Southern Europe. In Continental and Nordic Europe, the middle class is substantially bigger. In about half the Eastern European countries, the upper end of the distribution represents the largest group. The distribution of population in

BOX 2.8 Defining the Middle Class

The composition of the middle class has been the focus of academic research, mainly in sociology, at least since Max Weber's (1922) work on status groups and classes. There are multiple approaches to defining the middle class (see Atkinson and Brandolini 2013; Banerjee and Duflo 2008; Foster and Wolfson 2010; Vaughan-Whitehead 2016). Two main approaches can be identified: the objective and the subjective approaches.[a]

The objective approach
In this approach, the research defines ex ante certain thresholds to demarcate the middle from the lower and upper classes. This approach is objective in the sense that certain thresholds are applied, though the choice of the thresholds is subjective. The thresholds can be selected in the income space or in the population space.

Income space. A first set of objective approaches defines the middle in the income space according to selected income thresholds. These thresholds can be defined in a relative or absolute way. Relative objective indicators tend to define the middle according to income bounds around the median. For instance, the International Labour Organization defines the middle class as the population between 60 percent and 200 percent of the median (Vaughan-Whitehead 2016). The Pew Research Center (2015) applies the range of 67 percent to 200 percent of the median. Other authors use a more dense definition of the middle class, for example, 75 percent to 125 percent of the median, as a threshold (Birdsall, Graham, and Pettinato 2000; Gornick and Jäntti 2013; Thurow 1987).

A problem involved in the application of relative thresholds is that the income bounds vary across countries depending on the level of the median. To relate the middle class to a specific purchasing power, other researchers have applied absolute thresholds. In this case also, different thresholds have been used, for instance, people living above the median poverty line in developing countries or above another cutoff, such as US$10-a-day purchasing power parity (PPP) (Banerjee and Duflo

2008; Birdsall 2010; Loayza, Rigolini, and Llorente 2012; Ravallion 2010). Another absolute approach involves deriving an appropriate income level from a measure of vulnerability to relate middle-class status and a feeling of economic security.

Population space. The middle class can also be defined according to a selected part of the income distribution within the population space. Unlike the income space approach, the relative size of the population is fixed in this approach. The approach thus conceptualizes the middle position in the distribution in terms of the enjoyment of a particular social status.

The subjective approach
The middle class can also be defined based on the subjective perception of what it means to belong to the middle class. Ravallion (2012) discusses the use of subjective welfare indicators as a way of determining a socially subjective poverty line. Ferreira et al. (2013) take this a step further by inferring absolute thresholds for the middle class based on the probability individuals will answer middle class to a question about their own social status. The main limitations of the subjective approach derive from the fact that individual answers vary considerably depending on the way the question is framed and that inferences based on the answers may be highly biased because of latent heterogeneity.

Advantages and disadvantages of selected definitions
All definitions of the middle class involve compromises and are characterized by advantages and disadvantages (for an elaborate discussion, see Foster and Wolfson 2010). In the objective approach, the researcher defines cutoff points that are arbitrary to a certain extent. This is not true of the subjective approach, which relies on the perceptions among individuals that they belong to the middle class; however, these perceptions may not be confirmed by relative or absolute income measures and may be culturally determined. This is a particular disadvantage in cross-country research

(Continued)

BOX 2.8 Defining the Middle Class *(continued)*

and is the reason the objective approach is favored in this chapter.

In the objective approach, the income position of the middle class in the population space does not depend on differences in average or median incomes across countries. Thus, income growth does not affect the size of the population. Moreover, inequality is also ignored because the size of the middle class is fixed, regardless of the relative income position. The income space approach is therefore applied in this chapter.

However, the income space approach is also associated with disadvantages. While income may be defined relative to the median income, the size of the population may vary depending on trends in inclusive growth. Moreover, in cross-country research, the middle class may be characterized by different incomes across countries. This problem does not arise if the

middle class is defined on the basis of an absolute income threshold. Yet, in the latter approach, the relative position of an individual in a society is ignored. For instance, applying a fairly low absolute income threshold to a rich country could result in placement of the entire population in the upper class.

In acknowledgment of the advantages and disadvantages of each definition of the middle class, both a relative and an absolute objective income space approach are adopted in this chapter. For the relative definition, the thresholds at 75 percent to 125 percent of the equivalized disposable household median income are used. In the absolute definition, the middle class represents the share of households with disposable incomes between US$11- and US$28-a-day PPP. Vulnerability is taken into account by linking the middle class to a certain level of economic security.

a. Another approach is to follow the median over time (for example, Aaberge and Atkinson 2013; Nolan, Roser, and Thewissen 2016; Thewissen et al. 2015). This approach can be useful for tracking trends in living standards, but it does not allow an exploration of the composition of the middle class in terms of income or demographics. It is therefore not discussed in more detail here.

the Czech Republic, the Slovak Republic, and Slovenia resembles that in Nordic European countries, that is, smaller poorer groups and a large middle class, whereas the two extremes of the distribution are larger in Russia and Serbia and, especially, Estonia and Georgia.

Defined by the relative measure, the size of the middle class in Europe and Central Asia did not change significantly from the mid-1990s to the early 2010s. The middle class shrank in half the countries and expanded in the other half of the countries (figure 2.41). In many countries in which the population share of the middle class declined, the reduction was not substantial. In Germany, for example, the share fell from 43 percent in 1994 to 39 percent in 2014. In Slovenia, the country with the steepest decline, the share dropped from 48 percent in 1997 to 40 percent in 2012.

It is also useful to determine a fixed level of income that defines the middle class and assess the changes in the composition of the middle class in absolute terms. Because median incomes differ greatly across countries, the relative middle-class definition used above groups people at quite different levels of welfare. For example, 75 percent of the median income in Georgia in 2013 was US$1,594 PPP, whereas the corresponding income in Finland in the same year was US$11,951 PPP. Defining the middle class in absolute terms thus enables comparisons among individuals at the same levels of welfare across countries. An absolute definition can be used to include in the middle class people who are

FIGURE 2.41 Trends in the relative size of the middle class, Europe and Central Asia

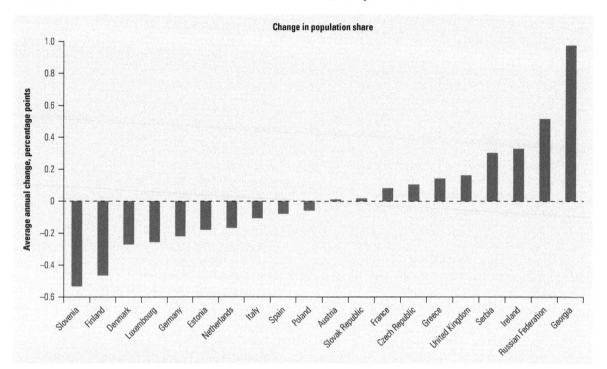

Source: Calculations based on data of LIS Database (Luxembourg Income Study Database), LIS Cross-National Data Center in Luxembourg, Luxembourg, http://www.lisdatacenter.org/our-data/lis-database/.
Note: See annex 2A, table 2A.2 for more detail. The middle class is defined as the share of the population with incomes between 75 percent and 125 percent of the median income. The middle-class population shares were measured around 1995 and 2014.

able to avoid falling into poverty in the face of unexpected shocks, which is an attribute that people likely view as essential to a middle-class lifestyle. In this analysis, the lower threshold defining the middle class is the income associated with a 5 percent probability of poverty—defined as falling below an income of US$5.50 a day in constant 2011 PPP prices—over a four-year period, calculated on the basis of the observed characteristics of households, including assets (see box 2.8 for details).[41] Based on this analysis, individuals with incomes between US$11- and US$28-a-day PPP are included in the middle class. Another vulnerable group consists of people with incomes between US$5.50- and US$11.00-a-day PPP. This group is not poor, but, because it experiences a high probability of falling into poverty (given its distance to the poverty line), it is not considered part of the middle class.

Around 2015, the middle class determined by this absolute definition included 45 percent of the population in developing Europe and Central Asia.[42] However, the vulnerable and the poor, together, represented more than 50 percent of the population (figure 2.42).[43] Apparent from this latter statistic alone, Europe and Central Asia may be a middle-income region, but it is not a middle-class society. Of course, the shares of the poor and vulnerable vary a great deal across countries. In 2015, the poor accounted for 37 percent, and the vulnerable 45 percent of the population of the lower-middle-income

FIGURE 2.42 Income classes, subregions of Europe and Central Asia, excluding the EU15

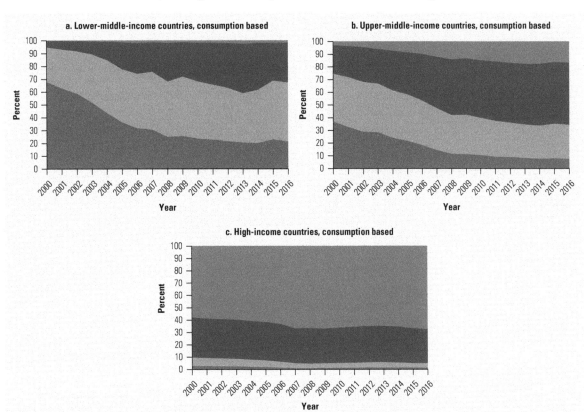

Source: Calculations based on World Bank data.
Note: EU15 = Austria, Belgium, Denmark, Finland, France, Germany, Greece, Ireland, Italy, Luxembourg, Netherlands, Portugal, Spain, Sweden, and United Kingdom; Lower-middle-income countries = Armenia, Georgia, Kosovo, Kyrgyz Republic, Moldova, and Tajikistan; Upper-middle-income countries = Albania, Belarus, Bosnia and Herzegovina, Bulgaria, Croatia, Kazakhstan, FYR Macedonia, Montenegro, Romania, Russian Federation, Serbia, and Turkey; High-income countries = Estonia, Hungary, Lithuania, Poland, Slovak Republic, and Slovenia; PPP = purchasing power parity.

countries of Europe and Central Asia. Nonetheless, this analysis is not irrelevant for the region's richer countries. The vulnerable account for 28 percent of the population in upper-middle-income countries and almost 30 percent in high-income countries. (The more advanced EU15 countries are not included; see the note to figure 2.42.)

Poverty has declined, but the expansion of the middle class has decelerated. While the population share of the poor fell sharply from 2000 to 2015 in the two middle-income-country groups, the expansion of the middle class was more pronounced in the first half of the 2000s than more recently (see figure 2.42). Indeed, in some countries, the middle-class expansion even reversed. For example, in the Kyrgyz Republic, the population share of the middle class dropped from a peak of 6 percent in 2009 to 4 percent in 2014. The share of the middle class in Albania fell from 25 percent in 2008 to 18 percent in 2012, and, in Serbia, from 43 percent in 2008 to 38 percent in 2013.

The population share of the middle class changed little over the last decade in the high-income countries, while the share of the vulnerable rose from about 25 percent to almost 30 percent.

A Focus on Size Neglects the Reality of the Changing Middle Class

While the size of the middle class has not changed significantly, its composition has shifted, indicating that some groups have now more difficulty reaching middle-class status or maintaining it. Among these groups, people in their working-age years, especially those of more recent cohorts, have more trouble.

The probability that an individual of working age belongs to the middle or upper class has declined relative to 25 years ago. In other words, in 2013, an individual of working age is more likely found at the poorer end of the income distribution.[44] Thus, the share of the working-age population expanded among lower-income groups in 17 of the 20 countries, while it tended (on average) to shrink for the middle and upper income groups, as shown in annex 2A, table 2A.3. A more detailed analysis focusing on the 26–40 and the 41–55 age-groups shows that the share of the working-age population in poorer groups rose in France, Italy, and Poland from the fall of the Berlin Wall to 2013, while the share of the working-age population among richer groups increased by less or fell (figure 2.43). The steep income gradient that once placed most of the working-age population in the top deciles has become flatter because individuals of working age have dispersed along the income distribution.

The decline in the share of the working-age population in the middle class reflects the limited increases in earnings among lower-income entrants in the labor force in recent years. The rise in earnings among younger workers is well below the rise older generations had enjoyed after they had entered the labor force (see figures 2.16 and 2.17). Individuals who had expected to join the middle class as they gained experience found themselves stuck among the poor or vulnerable. This phenomenon has not led to a substantial reduction in the population share of the middle class because more retirees are now part of the middle class given their larger incomes (from pensions) relative to the incomes of younger working-age individuals. Thus, rough stability in the size of the middle class masks the presence of considerable disappointment among working-age individuals.

The expansion in the share of single-adult households has raised vulnerability. In about a generation, the share of people living in single-adult households—households each with only one adult, irrespective of the number of children—has risen significantly in most countries and at all incomes. The increase has been close to or above 10 percentage points in the Czech Republic, France, Germany, Italy, Luxembourg, the Netherlands, Russia, Spain, and the United Kingdom (figure 2.44). This meant that the share of single-adult households, in some cases, more than doubled from the early 1990s to 2013 (see annex 2A, table 2A.3). This derives from a greater tendency to marry later in life, as well as the aging of the population; there are likely to be more single-adult households among older age-groups. Residence in a single-adult household is generally a good predictor of greater risk of poverty (Cappellari and Jenkins 2004). Moreover, the share of

FIGURE 2.43 Age-groups along the income distribution

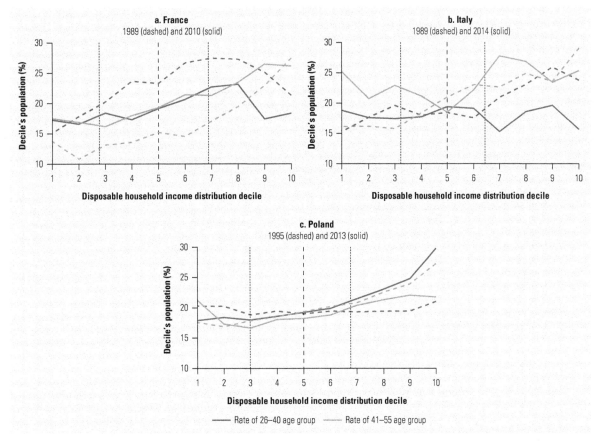

Source: Calculations based on data of LIS Database (Luxembourg Income Study Database), LIS Cross-National Data Center in Luxembourg, Luxembourg, http://www.lisdatacenter.org/our-data/lis-database/.
Note: The long dashed vertical line indicates the median disposable household income. The short dashed vertical lines indicate, respectively, 75 percent and 125 percent of the median.

single-adult households rose the most among lower-income groups (figure 2.45). Thus, the increase in the share of single-adult households indicates a general expansion in the risk of poverty.

Individual earnings inequality interacts with household income inequality. Household formation and individual labor market participation feed into each other. The earnings of one member of the household may influence the decisions of other members on participating in the labor market, and some members may choose to leave the household because of the labor market outcomes among other members. In this way, shocks to the earnings distribution among individuals may eventually be transmitted to household income distribution and vice versa. Salverda and Checchi (2015) review the literature on personal and household income distribution. A key finding they emphasize is that, in Europe since the 1990s, individual labor market participation has expanded, but household labor market participation, understood as the share of households with at least one member participating in the labor market, has not. This implies that most of the increase in individual employment has gone to households already engaged in employment, and much less has gone to reducing the number of people living in jobless households. In this sense, the

FIGURE 2.44 Cumulative change in the share of people living in single-adult households, by country

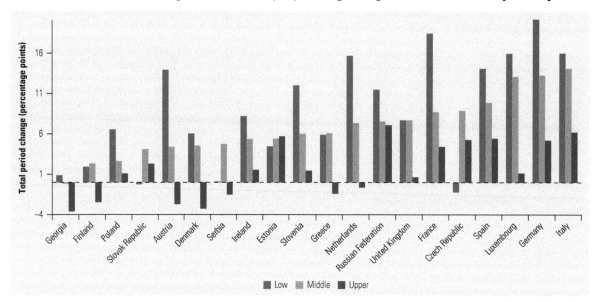

Source: Calculations based on data of LIS Database (Luxembourg Income Study Database), LIS Cross-National Data Center in Luxembourg, Luxembourg, http://www.lisdatacenter.org/our-data/lis-database/.
Note: The share of single adults is calculated as the number of individuals ages 18–65 who are the only adult in the household (regardless of whether the individual is working or whether he or she has children) as a percentage of the total working-age population.

single-breadwinner household model seems to be under pressure because there appears to be no significant transformation of jobless households into single-earner households, but, rather, there appears to be a greater transformation of single-earner households into multiple-earner households.

Employment no longer guarantees a decent position in the income distribution. The share of single-earner households among households with two adults has declined across all income groups, replaced in part by dual earner households as women have joined the labor market in large numbers (figure 2.46). These results echo those of Salverda (2018), who documents the growth in multiple-earner households at the top of the distribution across Europe. The need to have more than one earner in the household to provide for a decent flow of income and the better employment prospects of women because of improved educational attainment and changes in social preferences have made the single-male-breadwinner household, the stereotype of the postwar European middle class, a *rara avis* in many countries in the region.

Once a Hallmark of the Middle Class, Economic Security Is Now More Elusive

To quantify the rise in vulnerability to poverty in the EU, the analysis of the size of the middle class is extended in three ways. First, vulnerability is estimated separately for two periods: before the global financial crisis (2005–08) and after the crisis (2011–14) (figure 2.47). Second, all the countries on which the quality of panel data is sufficient—almost all high-income EU countries—have been added

FIGURE 2.45 Change in the share of people living in single-adult households, by income, France, Italy, Poland

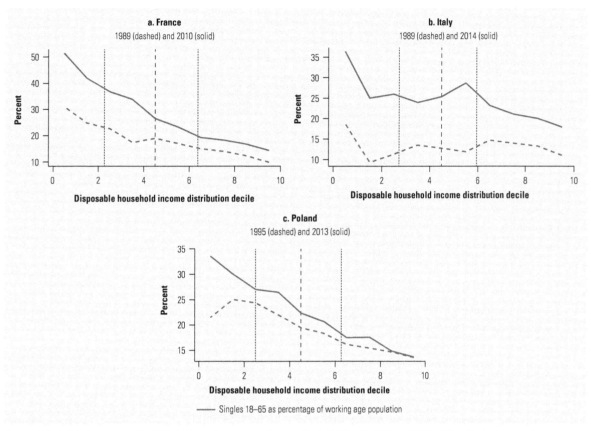

Source: Calculations based on data of LIS Database (Luxembourg Income Study Database), LIS Cross-National Data Center in Luxembourg, Luxembourg, http://www.lisdatacenter.org/our-data/lis-database/.
Note: The long dashed vertical line indicates the median disposable household income. The short dashed vertical lines indicate, respectively, 75 percent and 125 percent of the median.

FIGURE 2.46 The decline in single-breadwinner households across the region

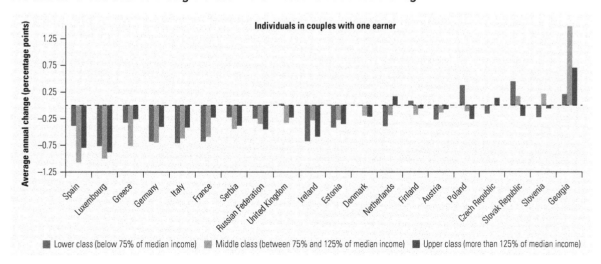

to the calculation of the thresholds for membership in the middle class.[45] Third, a poverty line of US$21.70-a-day PPP is adopted (instead of the US$5.50 line used above). This corresponds to a newly defined international poverty line for high-income countries, which is roughly equal to the EU's regional poverty line (the at-risk-of-poverty measure).[46] Given this higher poverty line, the middle-class threshold also increases to US$37-a-day PPP, based on the approach used above. This poverty line replaces the threshold of US$11-a-day PPP, which is based on panel data on Bulgaria, Croatia, and Romania (box 2.9). These countries are among the poorest in the EU (though not the poorest in Europe and Central Asia); so, the earlier approach provides a definition of the middle class in absolute terms that can be applied to a large group of countries in Europe and Central Asia. Here, the

FIGURE 2.47
The middle class in the European Union has become more vulnerable

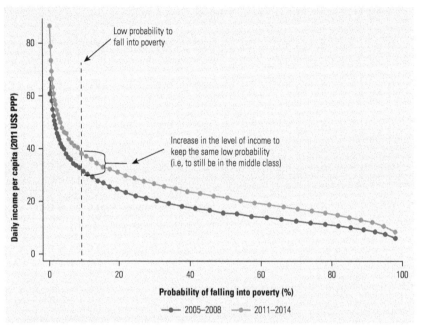

Source: Based on data of EU-SILC (European Union Statistics on Income and Living Conditions) (database), Eurostat, European Commission, Luxembourg, http://ec.europa.eu/eurostat/web /microdata/european-union-statistics-on-income-and-living-conditions.
Note: The two curves in the figure have been obtained using pooled data for Austria, Belgium, Bulgaria, Cyprus, Denmark, Estonia, France, Greece, Hungary, Iceland, Latvia, Lithuania, Netherlands, Norway, Poland, Slovak Republic, Slovenia, and Spain during the two periods indicated.

BOX 2.9   **Defining the Absolute Middle-Class Threshold, a Vulnerability Approach**

Absolute thresholds of the middle class based on vulnerability to poverty are defined using panel data. Specifically, the probability of falling into poverty or remaining poor (at US$5.50-a-day PPP), over an established period is estimated using the EU-SILC's four-year panels for a sample of

countries.[a] The income level associated with a spectrum of probabilities is then identified. This approach allows falling into poverty to be modeled with various household and individual characteristics that capture lifetime income and stocks (assets) rather than only income flows, and the

(Continued)

BOX 2.9 **Defining the Absolute Middle-Class Threshold, a Vulnerability Approach** *(continued)*

same variables are used to predict levels of income. Thus, vulnerability is not only a function of income, but also of income-generating assets.

In defining the absolute middle-class thresholds used throughout the chapter (and changes in the composition of the middle class over time), panel data are pooled across an eight-year period that captures the 2008–09 global financial crisis, the postcrisis, and the recovery periods for the three poorest countries in the European Union (Bulgaria, Croatia, and Romania) to identify the predicted income level associated with different quantiles of the poverty probability distribution. The lower threshold is defined as the predicted income associated with a 5 percent or greater probability of falling into poverty, which is what is observed in poverty transition matrices for the set of three countries.

For example, the probability of falling into poverty (conditional on being nonpoor) between 2009 and 2012 stood at 9 percent in Romania, but this dropped to 4 percent and 5 percent in 2010–13

and 2011–14, respectively, highlighting the impact of the crisis. The same methodology can be used to determine how vulnerability to poverty has changed since before the crisis, especially by evaluating the income level associated with the middle class at different points in time.

Figure B2.9.1 plots, for Romania, the relationship between the predicted income per capita in 2011 U.S. dollars purchasing power parity (PPP) and the probability of falling into poverty. The data are split into 50 quantiles, and the mean predicted income and mean probability are plotted for each of the 50 cells. The figure shows that, for a given probability of falling into poverty (set at 5 percent, which is the average probability of transitioning from poor to nonpoor across the three countries and the entire period), an income level above which an individual could be considered middle class can be identified: the average for the three countries is US$11 a day if all panels are pooled, though it is slightly lower in Romania.

FIGURE B2.9.1 The vulnerability-income function: identifying the middle-class threshold

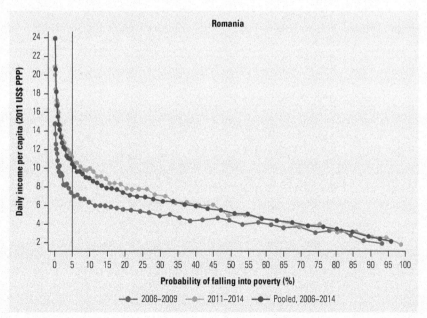

a. See EU-SILC (European Union Statistics on Income and Living Conditions) (database), Eurostat, European Commission, Luxembourg, http://ec.europa.eu/eurostat/web/microdata/european-union-statistics-on-income-and-living-conditions.

focus is on vulnerability in high-income countries; so, a poverty line and definition of the middle class that are more appropriate for high-income countries is used.

For a given income, the probability of falling into poverty has increased in the region or, conversely, more income is needed to maintain the same probability of falling into poverty. Thus, in figure 2.47, the vulnerability curve in the more recent period has shifted above and to the right of the curve in the earlier period. The income associated with an 8 percent probability of falling into poverty rose from US$34 a day in 2005–08 to US$40 a day in 2011–14 (table 2.2).[47] A 20 percent increase in the initial income is needed to counteract the greater vulnerability. This insurance premium varies across countries. In Bulgaria and Latvia, it is more than double the initial income. The rise in vulnerability is consistent with perceptions that people are increasingly less likely to feel they belong to the middle class, even though their income or consumption suggests they do.[48]

Rising distributional tensions are also evident in the fact that many people with qualifications that made them part of the middle class before the crisis are now at risk of falling into poverty (figure 2.48). The educational and occupational profile of the group of individuals who are vulnerable to falling into poverty (that is, those individuals who are at or near the lower threshold of the high-income middle class) changed substantially between the precrisis and postcrisis periods. For example, the share of

TABLE 2.2 Income Associated with an 8 Percent Probability of Falling into Poverty

Country	Predicted income, US$ PPP		Probability of falling into poverty, percent	
	2005–08	2011–14	2005–08	2011–14
Eastern Europe				
Bulgaria	14	32	9	9
Estonia	21	36	8	8
Poland	31	32	7	8
Hungary	30	32	8	9
Slovak Republic	20	31	10	7
Slovenia	33	39	8	8
Southern Europe				
Greece	40	43	8	9
Cyprus	54	46	8	8
Spain	32	47	8	8
Continental Europe				
Austria	41	51	8	8
France	32	37	8	8
Belgium	37	36	8	8
Netherlands	38	42	8	8
Nordic Europe				
Denmark	42	44	8	9
Iceland	37	50	3	8
Lithuania	25	29	7	9
Latvia	22	44	8	7
Norway	48	56	7	9
European Union	34	40	8	8

Source: Based on data of EU-SILC (European Union Statistics on Income and Living Conditions) (database), Eurostat, European Commission, Luxembourg, http://ec.europa.eu/eurostat/web /microdata/european-union-statistics-on-income-and-living-conditions.
Note: The quantile selected is based on the probability closest to 8 percent (by country panel).

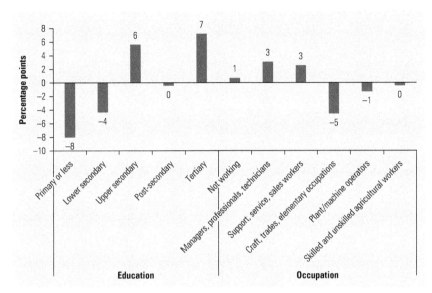

FIGURE 2.48

The profile of those vulnerable to poverty now looks like the middle class of yesterday

Percentage point change in the share of the vulnerable population between the precrisis and postcrisis periods

Source: Calculations based on data of EU-SILC (European Union Statistics on Income and Living Conditions) (database), Eurostat, European Commission, Luxembourg, http://ec.europa.eu/eurostat /web/microdata/european-union-statistics-on-income-and-living-conditions.

the vulnerable population with upper-secondary education or higher rose (6 and 7 percentage points for upper-secondary and tertiary, respectively), while the share of the vulnerable population with lower secondary or less declined by an even greater magnitude (8 and 4 percentage points with primary or less and lower-secondary, respectively). The share of professionals and support, service, or sales workers increased by 3 percentage points between the precrisis and postcrisis periods, while the share of individuals with elementary occupations fell by 5 percentage points. Thus, people who are vulnerable to poverty have the skills that once made them part of the middle class, but now those skills are not sufficient to achieve middle-class status.

Is the state equipped to reduce the emerging distributional tensions that have increased economic insecurity and access to economic opportunities among some groups, making the middle class more elusive? Many social protection policy instruments are designed to support or explicitly target specific groups of individuals or households. If the composition of these groups or the challenges they face are changing, policies may become less effective in responding to and addressing inequalities. Chapter 3 explores whether the design of policies is up to the task in a context of growing distributional tensions.

Annex 2A. Statistical Tables

TABLE 2A.1 Summary Statistics on Occupational Categories

	Occupations intensive in routine tasks	Occupations intensive in nonroutine, cognitive tasks	Occupations intensive in nonroutine, manual tasks
Routine-task intensity index O*NET task content indexes (average)	1.930	0.188	0.079
Routine, manual	9.308	6.336	8.191
Routine, cognitive	9.929	8.973	8.495
Nonroutine, cognitive, personal	8.538	10.635	8.734
Nonroutine, cognitive, analytical	8.651	11.105	8.120
Nonroutine, manual, physical	10.867	7.952	11.309
Nonroutine, manual, personal	2.905	3.513	3.037
Examples (ISCO 88, submajor groups)	Office clerks (41), metal, machinery and related trades workers (72), stationary-plan and related operators (81)	Corporate managers (12), physical, mathematical and engineering science professionals (21), life science and health associate professionals (32)	Personal and protective services workers (51), sales and services elementary occupations (91), drivers and mobile-plant operators (83)

Sources: Based on Occupation Classifications Crosswalks: From O*NET-SOC to ISCO (database), Institute for Structural Research, Warsaw, April 6, 2016, http://ibs.org.pl/en/resources/occupation-classifications-crosswalks-from-onet-soc-to-isco/; O*NET OnLine (database), Employment and Training Administration, U.S. Department of Labor, Washington, DC, https://www.onetonline.org/.

TABLE 2A.2 Size of Income Class, by Country

		Population share, percent					
		Relative definition			Absolute definition		
Country	Year	Lower	Middle	Upper	Lower	Middle	Upper
		(1)	(2)	(3)	(1)	(2)	(3)
Eastern Europe and Central Asia							
Czech Republic	2013	23	47	30	5	57	38
Estonia	2013	34	29	37	13	55	33
Georgia	2013	36	26	38	82	16	2
Poland	2013	29	38	33	22	56	21
Russian Federation	2013	31	33	35	12	55	32
Serbia	2013	32	34	34	56	40	4
Slovak Republic	2013	25	44	31	11	63	26
Slovenia	2012	28	40	31	4	39	57
Southern Europe							
Greece	2013	32	34	35	21	53	26
Italy	2014	32	32	35	12	38	50
Spain	2013	33	31	36	11	35	54
Continental Europe							
Austria	2013	26	42	32	1	13	86
France	2010	27	42	31	2	21	76
Germany	2013	28	39	33	1	18	81
Luxembourg	2013	28	39	32	1	9	90
Netherlands	2013	26	44	30	1	17	81
British Isles							
Ireland	2010	30	35	34	3	27	70
United Kingdom	2013	30	34	35	3	28	69
Nordic Europe							
Denmark	2013	27	44	29	1	10	89
Finland	2013	27	43	30	1	15	84
Average		29	38	33	13	33	54

Source: LIS Database (Luxembourg Income Study Database), LIS Cross-National Data Center in Luxembourg, Luxembourg, http://www.lisdatacenter.org/our-data/lis-database/.

TABLE 2A.3 Working-Age Population and Old-Age Dependency, by Income Class and Country

Country	Years	Working-age population rate			Old-age dependency ratio		
		Lower	Middle	Upper	Lower	Middle	Upper
		Average annual change (percentage points)			Average annual change (percentage points)		
		(1)	(2)	(3)	(4)	(5)	(6)
Eastern Europe and Central Asia							
Czech Republic	1996–2013	0.3	−0.1	−0.1	−0.7	0.7	0.2
Estonia	2000–2013	−0.4	0.1	0.2	1.7	0.0	0.0
Georgia	2010–2013	−0.1	0.3	0.0	−0.2	−1.8	−0.4
Poland	1995–2013	0.3	0.2	0.1	0.1	0.3	0.0
Russian Federation	2000–2013	0.1	0.2	0.3	0.2	−0.1	0.1
Serbia	2006–2013	0.3	0.0	−0.4	−0.2	0.4	0.8
Slovak Republic	2004–2013	0.0	−0.2	0.1	−0.1	0.6	0.5
Slovenia	1997–2012	0.3	−0.2	0.1	0.0	0.8	0.0
Southern Europe							
Greece	1995–2013	0.4	−0.3	0.0	−1.0	1.3	0.4
Italy	1989–2014	0.2	−0.2	−0.4	−0.2	0.7	0.7
Spain	1995–2013	0.3	−0.1	−0.1	−0.6	0.5	0.4
Continental Europe							
Austria	1994–2013	0.2	−0.1	0.0	−0.2	0.4	0.3
France	1989–2010	0.2	0.0	−0.1	−0.5	0.4	0.2
Germany	1994–2013	0.1	−0.2	−0.2	0.4	0.9	0.3
Luxembourg	1991–2013	0.4	0.0	−0.3	−0.7	0.4	0.4
Netherlands	1999–2013	0.7	−0.1	−0.3	−1.0	1.0	0.1
British Isles							
Ireland	1994–2010	0.6	0.2	0.2	−0.9	0.2	0.2
United Kingdom	1991–2013	0.4	−0.1	−0.1	−0.9	0.6	0.2
Nordic Europe							
Denmark	1995–2013	0.1	−0.3	−0.4	−0.2	0.7	0.2
Finland	1995–2013	−0.3	−0.2	0.0	0.5	0.7	0.2
Average		0.2	−0.1	−0.1	−0.2	0.4	0.2

Notes

1. The available data do not cover the full period for all countries in the region.
2. See Milanović (1998) for a more detailed analysis of the changes in inequality during the transition in Central and Eastern Europe. Not only did income inequality increase strongly, but also income dispersion widened across countries. In 1987–88, the lowest Gini index of income inequality was 19 (the Czech Republic), and the highest 26 (Poland). In 1993–95, the lowest was 20 (the Slovak Republic), and the highest was 34 (Bulgaria).
3. See EU-SILC (European Union Statistics on Income and Living Conditions) (database), Eurostat, European Commission, Luxembourg, http://ec.europa.eu/eurostat/web /microdata/european-union-statistics-on-income-and-living-conditions.
4. This is because the sampling strategies used in household surveys are not suited to capture outliers. In some surveys, rare observations are deleted to ensure respondent anonymity, and richer individuals are more likely not to respond to some items in the survey (Ceriani, Fiorio, and Gigliarano 2013).

5. Trends in inequality between the rich and the poor have been the focus of much academic attention in recent years. The *World Inequality Report 2018* (Alvaredo et al. 2018) is an example of the sort of detailed analysis that is being carried out on vertical inequality and on the concentration of income and wealth at the top.

6. See WID (World Inequality Database), Paris School of Economics, Paris, https://wid.world/.

7. In more than half the countries of Europe and Central Asia, a majority of individuals surveyed in 2015–16 believed that inequality had widened over the previous four years, while most countries actually experienced a decline in inequality over the period according to household survey measures of inequality (EBRD 2016).

8. For a recent survey that attempts to measure the relative importance of these three factors, see OECD (2017); World Bank (2016a).

9. The decomposition analysis aims at addressing what if questions. In this case, it is used to answer the question, what would the distribution of earnings look like if the only change was in occupational structure?

10. Autor (2014) and the World Bank (2016a) use broad occupational categories (1-digit level, major groups, of the International Standard Classification of Occupations [ISCO]). This report uses the 2-digit classification (submajor groups of ISCO) to capture more effectively the differences between occupations (see box 2.2). Data limitations preclude the use of the finer 3- and 4-digit classifications for the entire region.

11. The task content approach and the occupational groups approach usually show similar results given that, ultimately, they rely on the same information: the distribution of occupations in the economy. However, some differences may emerge. Occupations with a high routine-task intensity usually have a high nonroutine, manual-task intensity, but occupations intensive in nonroutine, manual tasks do not necessarily exhibit high routine-task intensity. Occupations with a high routine-task intensity index have a nonroutine, manual physical index of 10.867 (the average for all occupations is 10.29) (annex 2A). Occupations with a high nonroutine, manual physical index have a routine-task intensity index of 0.079, even lower than that of occupations intensive in nonroutine, cognitive tasks. This particular correlation of tasks may result, in a context of deroutinization, in a decrease in nonroutine, manual-task intensity in overall employment (as the task content approach would show), together with growth in the share of occupations intensive in nonroutine, manual tasks (as the occupational groups approach would show).

12. See Bussolo, Torre, and Winkler (2018) for an illustration of task intensity along the wage distribution and how jobs intensive in nonroutine, manual tasks are among the lowest paid in Western Europe.

13. This excludes self-employment. The inclusion of self-employment does not alter the general trends.

14. Ridao-Cano and Bodewig (2018) use an alternative grouping of occupations, relying not only on task intensity, but also on the skill profile of the workers employed in the occupations. They find that employment among low-skill occupations has decreased throughout the EU, implying an absence of job polarization. This is because routine manual-task–intensive occupations are grouped together with nonroutine manual-task–intensive occupations in the low-skill occupational category. In the EU, the share of routine manual-task–intensive occupations has declined more than the share of nonroutine manual-task–intensive occupations has increased, and the overall change in employment among the low-skill group is therefore negative. The classification used in this report relies exclusively on the task intensity of occupations to provide a common approach for the whole region and abstract from differences in occupation-specific skill demand because there are notable differences across countries (for instance, see box 2.4, teachers and drivers). In the classification used here, routine manual-task–intensive occupations are included in the middle group given the high routine-task intensity of these occupations.

15. This decrease in the share reflects a greater increase in employment in the other two occupation categories rather than an actual decrease because the absolute number of jobs in all categories rose throughout the period.

16. The countries analyzed have been selected based on the availability of wage and occupation data in 1990–2013 among which there is a gap of at least 10 years between the earliest and the latest data.

17. The International Labour Organization's definition of nonstandard employment includes agency work, which is not shown in the figures in this report.

18. Close to a third of all part-time work is involuntary across the EU. The share is as high as 60 percent in crisis-affected economies in Southern Europe (Fries-Tersch, Tugran, and Bradley 2017).

19. The EU15 is Austria, Belgium, Denmark, Finland, France, Germany, Greece, Ireland, Italy, Luxembourg, the Netherlands, Portugal, Spain, Sweden, and the United Kingdom.

20. This analysis is based on techniques developed by Beaudry, Green, and Sand (2014) to measure shifts in the wage profile of college graduates in the United States. The analysis focuses on the labor market earnings of individuals with high school diplomas only (International Standard Classification of Education 4) or with at least some tertiary education (International Standard Classification of Education 5 or higher), based on EU-SILC data for Southern and Western Europe. See EU-SILC (European Union Statistics on Income and Living Conditions) (database), Eurostat, European Commission, Luxembourg, http://ec.europa.eu/eurostat/web/microdata/european-union-statistics -on-income-and-living-conditions.

21. This is because shocks to income tend to cumulate, that is, workers who suffer a decline in income in one period—for example, losing a job, being out of work for an extended period, or having to accept a lower-paying job—are no more likely than others to enjoy a rise in income in the next period. Likewise, workers who enjoy an increase in income— for example, a rise in the demand for one's skills—are no more likely to suffer a decline in the next period. Thus, the distribution of income becomes more spread out over time, leading to a rise in inequality (see Deaton and Paxson 1994).

22. The authors perform an age-cohort-time decomposition of income inequality in three European countries (France, Germany, and Italy) on which consistent long-term data are available.

23. In Italy, the implied Gini coefficient of labor income at age 40 among the cohort born in the 1930s is 0.22, while among the cohort born in the 1980s, it is 0.33. In France, which experienced a small widening in inequality in overall income, the difference between the implied Gini coefficient of labor market income at age 40 among the cohort born in the 1930s was 0.23, while among the cohort born in the 1980s, it was 0.49. In the case of Germany, the corresponding difference is 9 points in the Gini coefficient among men, but it is close to zero among women.

24. A welfare index was computed for this study using the 2016 round of LiTS, including assets and other proxies of socioeconomic status. For the survey, see LiTS (Life in Transition Survey) (database), European Bank for Reconstruction and Development, London, http://www.ebrd.com/what-we-do/economic-research-and-data/data/lits .html.

25. This inequality decomposition relies on the methodology demonstrated in Elbers, Lanjouw, and Lanjouw (2003).

26. Data of EU poverty maps (for instance, see Simler 2016); EU-SILC (European Union Statistics on Income and Living Conditions) (database), Eurostat, European Commission, Luxembourg, http://ec.europa.eu/eurostat/web/microdata/european-union -statistics-on-income-and-living-conditions.

27. See PISA (Programme for International Student Assessment) (database), Organisation for Economic Co-operation and Development, Paris, http://www.oecd.org/pisa /pisaproducts/.

28. Data for 2014 from OECD (2016).

29. For Italy and other EU countries, see Ridao-Cano and Bodewig (2018). For Kazakhstan, see World Bank (2017c).

30. For an empirical analysis of the relationship between inequality of opportunity and growth in a sample of U.S. states, see Marrero and Rodríguez (2013), who decompose

total inequality into inequality of opportunity and inequality of effort, showing that the GDP per capita growth rate is negatively correlated with the former and positively correlated with the latter. A similar line of research has been followed by Ferreira et al. (2014) through a cross-country analysis involving a sample of 84 countries.

31. Checchi, Peragine, and Serlenga (2016) use the EU-SILC database to examine family background, gender, age, and country of origin as circumstances outside one's control. For the database, see EU-SILC (European Union Statistics on Income and Living Conditions) (database), Eurostat, European Commission, Luxembourg, http://ec.europa.eu/eurostat /web/microdata/european-union-statistics-on-income-and-living-conditions.

32. The analysis is based on a dataset compiled by the Luxembourg Income Study and on the following primary national surveys. France: Household Budget Survey conducted by the Banque de France in 1978–2005 and consisting of six surveys covering 97,306 individuals. Germany: German Socio-economic Panel, consisting of 11 surveys in 1984–2013 covering 156,338 individuals. Italy: Survey on Household Incomes and Wealth collected by the Bank of Italy in 1993–2014 and consisting of 11 surveys covering 112,690 individuals. Switzerland: Swiss Household Panel consisting of six surveys in 1999–2014, covering 43,102 individuals. United Kingdom: the British Household Panel and, after 2009, the Understanding Society–Household Longitudinal Survey, consisting of 24 waves in 1991–2014, originally covering 434,253 individuals. The analysis examined family background, gender, age, and place of birth as circumstances beyond the control of the individual.

33. The analysis is based on Deaton's decomposition of inequality of opportunity (Deaton 1997; Bussolo, Checchi, and Peragine 2018).

34. The analysis is based on an estimation of a structural model of inequality of opportunity in which it is assumed that parental background affects the incomes of the children directly (through education) and indirectly (through networking, education quality, role models, and the like). Inequality of opportunity is measured by either the standard deviation of logs or the mean log deviation. See Bussolo, Checchi, and Peragine (2018) for details.

35. The analysis is based on three waves of the LiTS (2006, 2010, 2016) and focuses on 15 countries in three macroregions (Eastern Europe, Central Asia and the Caucasus, and Russia). The study involves about 40,000 individuals divided into five 10-year cohorts to detect 50-year trends starting with individuals born in 1945; the last cohort includes individuals who began their education after the fall of the Berlin Wall). Brock, Peragine, and Tonini (2016) consider gender, birthplace, and ethnic and family background as circumstances beyond one's control. For the LiTS, see LiTS (Life in Transition Survey) (database), European Bank for Reconstruction and Development, London, http://www .ebrd.com/what-we-do/economic-research-and-data/data/lits.html.

36. See LiTS (Life in Transition Survey) (database), European Bank for Reconstruction and Development, London, http://www.ebrd.com/what-we-do/economic-research-and -data/data/lits.html.

37. However, comparisons of inequality of opportunity across countries are hampered because the relevant studies rely on different methodologies, outcomes, and circumstances. See EqualChances.org (database), University of Bari and World Bank, Washington, DC, http:// www.equalchances.org/. The database is the first online repository of internationally comparable information on inequality of opportunity and socioeconomic mobility.

38. The analysis is based on the 2006, 2010, and 2016 waves, LiTS (Life in Transition Survey) (database), European Bank for Reconstruction and Development, London, http://www .ebrd.com/what-we-do/economic-research-and-data/data/lits.html.

39. The outcome of interest is a binary variable that takes the value of 1 if the individual has attained some tertiary education and 0 otherwise. The circumstances considered are gender, birthplace, and ethnic and family background.

40. The LIS consists of a harmonization effort across household surveys around the world. Presently, the collection of harmonized microdata includes about 50 countries and spans over five decades. See LIS Database (Luxembourg Income Study Database), LIS Cross-National Data Center in Luxembourg, Luxembourg, http://www.lisdatacenter .org/our-data/lis-database/.

41. The estimates are based on panel data of the EU-SILC surveys. See EU-SILC (European Union Statistics on Income and Living Conditions) (database), Eurostat,

European Commission, Luxembourg, http://ec.europa.eu/eurostat/web/microdata/european-union-statistics-on-income-and-living-conditions.

42. Countries included in this calculation are Albania, Armenia, Bosnia and Herzegovina, Bulgaria, Belarus, Estonia, Georgia, Croatia, Hungary, Kazakhstan, Kosovo, the Kyrgyz Republic, Lithuania, FYR Macedonia, Moldova, Montenegro, Poland, Romania, Russia, Serbia, the Slovak Republic, Slovenia, Tajikistan, and Turkey.

43. The vulnerable group accounted for about a third, and the poor for 11 percent of the population.

44. The ratio of the working-age population to the total population rises with income. The more well off show a higher ratio than the middle class, which exhibits a higher ratio than the less well off. The ratio is represented by an upward sloping line, as in figure 2.43. This can be expected and is derived from a life-cycle approach; see, for instance, Attanasio and Székely (2000) for an example of these life-cycle approaches to household analysis. As they pass through the life cycle, individuals have less income when they are young, reach a maximum around at around ages 55–60, and their incomes tend to level off or decline in the later parts of their lives. Similarly, at the beginning of their formation, households tend to include adults who are working and providing for young dependents. Later the offspring leave the household, while the parent(s) continue to work. Finally, the parents quit working. So, for both individuals and households, the life cycle of income follows a rising line that flattens at the end, almost an inverted U pattern. This is why working-age people are overrepresented at the higher quantiles of the distribution and underrepresented at the bottom, giving rise to the upward sloping line of the working-age population.

45. The EU countries on which the quality of panel data is adequate include Austria, Belgium, Bulgaria, Cyprus, Denmark, Estonia, France, Greece, Hungary, Iceland, Latvia, Lithuania, the Netherlands, Norway, Poland, the Slovak Republic, Slovenia, and Spain. Several new member states are not included. For a handful of countries on which there are precrisis panel data, which excludes a number of new member countries, longitudinal weights were either missing for some years or could not be generated in a way consistent with the process used with the remaining countries.

46. The measures capture individuals whose income is less than 60 percent of the median of equivalized disposable income. World Bank (2018b) follows Jolliffe and Prydz's (2016) methodology to establish a poverty line for this group of countries, which is US$23.50-a-day PPP.

47. The probability level is based on observed transitions into poverty, conditional on being nonpoor, during the period.

48. The measurement of vulnerability is based on a permanent or long-term level of income, not simply on a volatile income flow in a specific year (box 2.9). The thresholds shown in table 2.2 predict incomes that an average person with certain assets, living in a certain area, and in a typical household could expect to earn in the two periods. The increased income needed to maintain the same low probability of falling into poverty can be translated into a corresponding expanded accumulation of assets or some permanent rise in the returns to those assets.

References

Aaberge, Rolf, and Anthony B. Atkinson. 2013. "The Median as Watershed." Discussion Paper 749 (August), Research Department, Statistics Norway, Oslo.

Abraham, Katharine G., and James L. Medoff. 1984. "Length of Service and Layoffs in Union and Nonunion Work Groups." *Industrial and Labor Relations Review* 38 (1): 87–97.

Acemoglu, Daron, and David H. Autor. 2011. "Skills, Tasks, and Technologies: Implications for Employment and Earnings." In *Handbook of Labor Economics*, vol. 4, part B, edited by Orley C. Ashenfelter and David Card, 1043–1171. San Diego: North-Holland.

Altham, Patricia M. E. 1970. "The Measurement of Association of Rows and Columns for an r × s Contingency Table." *Journal of the Royal Statistical Society.* Series B (Methodological), 32 (1): 63–73.

Alvaredo, Facundo, Lucas Chancel, Thomas Piketty, Emmanuel Saez, and Gabriel Zucman. 2018. *World Inequality Report 2018.* Paris: World Inequality Lab, Paris School of Economics.

Atkinson, Anthony B., and Andrea Brandolini. 2013. "On the Identification of the 'Middle Class'." In *Income Inequality: Economic Disparities and the Middle Class in Affluent Countries,* edited by Janet C. Gornick and Markus Jäntti, 77–100. Stanford, CA: Stanford University Press.

Apella, Ignacio Raul, and Gonzalo Zunino. 2018. "Nonstandard Forms of Employment in Developing Countries: A Study for a Set of Selected Countries in Latin America and the Caribbean and Europe and Central Asia." Working paper, World Bank, Washington, DC.

Arampatzi, Efstratia, Martijn Burger, Elena Ivanova Ianchovichina, Tina Röhricht, and Ruut Veenhoven. 2015. "Unhappy Development: Dissatisfaction with Life on the Eve of the Arab Spring." Policy Research Working Paper 7488, World Bank, Washington, DC.

Arias, Omar S., Carolina Sánchez-Páramo, María Eugenia Dávalos, Indhira Santos, Erwin R. Tiongson, Carola Gruen, Natasha de Andrade Falcão, Gady Saiovici, and César A. Cancho. 2014. *Back to Work: Growing with Jobs in Europe and Central Asia.* Washington, DC: World Bank.

Attanasio, Orazio P., and Miguel Székely. 2000. "Household Saving in Developing Countries, Inequality, Demographics, and All That: How Different are Latin America and South East Asia?" IDB Working Paper 427 (July), Inter-American Development Bank, Washington, DC.

Auer, Peter, and Sandrine Cazes. 2000. "The Resilience of the Long-Term Employment Relationship: Evidence from the Industrialized Countries." *International Labour Review* 139 (4): 379–408.

Autor, David H. 2014. "Skills, Education, and the Rise of Earnings Inequality among the 'Other 99 Percent'." *Science* 344 (6186): 843–51.

Autor, David H., and David Dorn. 2013. "The Growth of Low-Skill Service Jobs and the Polarization of the US Labor Market." *American Economic Review* 103 (5): 1553–97.

Autor, David H., David Dorn, Lawrence F. Katz, Christina Patterson, and John Van Reenen. 2017. "Concentrating on the Fall of the Labor Share." *American Economic Review: Papers and Proceedings* 107 (5): 180–85.

Autor, David H., Lawrence F. Katz, and Melissa S. Kearney. 2006. "The Polarization of the U.S. Labor Market." NBER Working Paper 11986 (January), National Bureau of Economic Research, Cambridge, MA.

———. 2008. "Trends in U.S. Wage Inequality: Revising the Revisionists." *Review of Economics and Statistics* 90 (2): 300–23.

Autor, David H., Frank Levy, and Richard J. Murnane. 2003. "The Skill Content of Recent Technological Change: An Empirical Exploration." *Quarterly Journal of Economics* 118 (4): 1279–1333.

Badescu, Mircea, Béatrice D'Hombres, and Ernesto Villalba. 2011. "Returns to Education in European Countries: Evidence from the European Community Statistics on Income and Living Conditions (EU-SILC)." JRC Scientific and Technical Research Report EUR 24850 EN, Institute for the Protection and Security of the Citizen, Joint Research Center, European Commission, Ispra, Italy.

Banerjee, Abhijit Vinayak, and Esther Duflo. 2008. "What Is Middle Class about the Middle Classes around the World?" *Journal of Economic Perspectives* 22 (2): 3–28.

Bartolj, Tjaša, Aleš Ahčan, Aljoša Feldin, and Sašo Polanec. 2012. "Evolution of Private Returns to Tertiary Education during Transition: Evidence from Slovenia." *Post-Communist Economies* 25 (3): 407–24.

Beaudry, Paul, David A. Green, and Benjamin M. Sand. 2014. "The Declining Fortunes of the Young since 2000." *American Economic Review* 104 (5): 381–86.

Birdsall, Nancy. 2010. "The (Indispensable) Middle Class in Developing Countries; or, The Rich and the Rest, Not the Poor and the Rest." Working Paper 207 (March), Center for Global Development, Washington, DC.

Birdsall, Nancy, Carol Graham, and Stefano Pettinato. 2000. "Stuck in the Tunnel: Is Globalization Muddling the Middle Class?" CSED Working Paper 14 (August), Center on Social and Economic Dynamics, Brookings Institution, Washington, DC.

Boeri, Tito. 1999. "Enforcement of Employment Security Regulations, On-the-Job Search, and Unemployment Duration." *European Economic Review* 43 (1): 65–89.

Boockmann, Bernhard, and Susanne Steffes. 2010. "Workers, Firms, or Institutions: What Determines Job Duration for Male Employees in Germany?" *Industrial and Labor Relations Review* 64 (1): 109–27.

Bourguignon, François, and Francisco H. G. Ferreira. 2005. "Decomposing Changes in the Distribution of Household Incomes: Methodological Aspects." In *The Microeconomics of Income Distribution Dynamics in East Asia and Latin America*, edited by François Bourguignon, Francisco H. G. Ferreira, and Nora Lustig, 17–46. Washington, DC: World Bank.

Bourguignon, François, Francisco H. G. Ferreira, and Marta Menéndez. 2007. "Inequality of Opportunity in Brazil." *Review of Income and Wealth* 53 (4): 585–618.

Brock, Michelle, Vito Peragine, and Sara Tonini. 2016. "Education, Income, and Policy Preferences: Inequality of Opportunity in Transition Economies." Paper presented at the World Bank conference, "Equity and Development: Ten Years On," Washington, DC, October 20–21.

Bussolo, Maurizio, Damien Capelle, and Hernan Winkler. 2018. "Job Tenure: Labor Market Policies, Globalization, and the Growing Intergenerational Divide." Paper presented at the Institute of Labor Economics, the World Bank, and the Network on Jobs and Development's "2018 Jobs and Development Conference," Bogotá, Colombia, May 11–12.

Bussolo, Maurizio, Daniele Checchi, and Vito Peragine. 2018. "The Long-Term Evolution of Inequality of Opportunity." LIS Working Paper 730 (January), Luxembourg Income Study, Cross-National Data Center, Luxembourg.

Bussolo, Maurizio, Tulio Jappelli, Roberto Nisticò, and Iván Torre. 2018. "Inequality across Generations in Europe." Background paper, World Bank, Washington, DC.

Bussolo, Maurizio, Iván Torre, and Hernan Winkler. 2018. "Does Job Polarization Explain the Rise in Earnings Inequality? Evidence from Europe." Background paper, World Bank, Washington, DC.

Cappellari, Lorenzo, and Stephen P. Jenkins. 2004. "Modelling Low Income Transitions." *Journal of Applied Econometrics* 19 (5): 593–610.

Ceriani, Lidia, Carlo Vittorio Fiorio, and Chiara Gigliarano. 2013. "The Importance of Choosing the Data Set for Tax-Benefit Analysis." *International Journal of Microsimulation* 6 (1): 86–121.

Chauvel, Louis, and Martin Schröder. 2014. "Generational Inequalities and Welfare Regimes." *Social Forces* 92 (4): 1259–83.

Checchi, Daniele, Vito Peragine, and Laura Serlenga. 2016. "Inequality of Opportunity in Europe: Is There a Role for Institutions?" *Research in Labor Economics* 43: 1–44.

Chetty, Raj, David Grusky, Maximilian Hell, Nathaniel Hendren, Robert Manduca, and Jimmy Narang. 2016. "The Fading American Dream: Trends in Absolute Income Mobility since 1940." NBER Working Paper 22910 (December), National Bureau of Economic Research, Cambridge, MA.

Dávalos, María Eugenia, Giorgia DeMarchi, Indhira V. Santos, Barbara Kits, and Isil Oral. 2016. "Voices of Europe and Central Asia: New Insights on Shared Prosperity and Jobs." World Bank, Washington, DC.

Deaton, Angus S. 1997. *The Analysis of Household Surveys: A Microeconometric Approach to Development Policy*. Washington, DC: World Bank; Baltimore: Johns Hopkins University Press.

Deaton, Angus S., and Christina Paxson. 1994. "Intertemporal Choice and Inequality." *Journal of Political Economy* 102 (3): 437–67.

Dicarlo, Emanuele, Salvatore Lo Bello, Sebastian Monroy-Taborda, Ana Maria Oviedo, Maria Laura Sanchez-Puerta, and Indhira Santos. 2016. "The Skill Content of Occupations across Low and Middle Income Countries: Evidence from Harmonized Data." IZA Discussion Paper 10224 (September), Institute of Labor Economics, Bonn, Germany.

EBRD (European Bank for Reconstruction and Development). 2016. *Transition Report 2016–17; Transition for All: Equal Opportunities in an Unequal World*. London: EBRD.

Eden, Maya, and Paul Gaggl. 2015. "On the Welfare Implications of Automation." Policy Research Working Paper 7487, World Bank, Washington, DC.

Elbers, Chris, Jean O. Lanjouw, and Peter F. Lanjouw. 2003. "Micro-Level Estimation of Poverty and Inequality." *Econometrica* 71 (1): 355–64.

Eurofound (European Foundation for the Improvement of Living and Working Conditions). 2015. *New Forms of Employment*. Research Report. Luxembourg: Publications Office of the European Union.

Farole, Thomas, Soraya Goga, and Marcel Ionescu-Heroiu. 2018. *Rethinking Lagging Regions: Using Cohesion Policy to Deliver on the Potential of Europe's Regions*. World Bank Report on the European Union. Washington, DC: World Bank.

Ferreira, Francisco H. G., Christoph Lakner, María Ana Lugo, and Berk Özler. 2014. "Inequality of Opportunity and Economic Growth: A Cross-Country Analysis." Policy Research Working Paper 6915, World Bank, Washington, DC.

Ferreira, Francisco. H. G., Julián Messina, Jamele Rigolini, Luis F. López-Calva, María Ana Lugo, and Renos Vakis. 2013. *Economic Mobility and the Rise of the Latin American Middle Class*. Washington, DC: World Bank.

Foster, James E., and Michael C. Wolfson. 2010. "Polarization and the Decline of the Middle Class: Canada and the U.S." *Journal of Economic Inequality* 8 (2): 247–73.

Fries-Tersch, Elena, Tugce Tugran, and Harriet Bradley. 2017. *2016 Annual Report on Intra-EU Labour Mobility*. May. Brussels: European Commission.

Goos, Maarten, and Alan Manning. 2007. "Lousy and Lovely Jobs: The Rising Polarization of Work in Britain." *Review of Economics and Statistics* 89 (1): 118–33.

Goos, Maarten, Alan Manning, and Anna Salomons. 2014. "Explaining Job Polarization: Routine-Biased Technological Change and Offshoring." *American Economic Review* 104 (8): 2509–26.

Gornick, Janet C., and Markus Jäntti. 2013. *Income Inequality: Economic Disparities and the Middle Class in Affluent Countries*. Stanford, CA: Stanford University Press.

Hardy, Wojciech, Roma Keister, and Piotr Lewandowski. 2016. "Technology or Upskilling? Trends in Task Composition of Jobs in Central and Eastern Europe," IBS Working Paper Series 1/2016, Institute for Structural Research, Warsaw.

Hlasny, Vladimir, and Paolo Verme. 2018. "Top Incomes and Inequality Measurement: A Comparative Analysis of Correction Methods Using the EU SILC Data." *Econometrics* 6 (2): 1–21.

Hopenhayn, Hugo, and Richard Rogerson. 1993. "Job Turnover and Policy Evaluation: A General Equilibrium Analysis." *Journal of Political Economy* 101 (5): 915–38.

Inchauste, Gabriela, João Pedro Azevedo, B. Essama-Nssah, Sergio Olivieri, Trang Van Nguyen, Jaime Saavedra-Chanduví, and Hernan Winkler. 2014. *Understanding Changes in Poverty.* Directions in Development: Poverty Series. Washington, DC: World Bank.

Jolliffe, Dean Mitchell, and Espen Beer Prydz. 2016. "Estimating International Poverty Lines from Comparable National Thresholds." Policy Research Working Paper 7606, World Bank, Washington, DC.

Jovanovic, Boyan. 1979. "Job Matching and the Theory of Turnover." *Journal of Political Economy* 87 (5, part 1): 972–90.

Karabarbounis, Loukas, and Brent Neiman. 2014. "The Global Decline of the Labor Share." *Quarterly Journal of Economics* 129 (1): 61–103.

Keister, Roma, and Piotr Lewandowski. 2016. "A Routine Transition? Causes and Consequences of the Changing Content of Jobs in Central and Eastern Europe." IBS Policy Paper 05/2016 (June), Institute for Structural Research, Warsaw.

Lazear, Edward P. 1990. "Job Security Provisions and Employment." *Quarterly Journal of Economics* 105 (3): 699–726.

Loayza, Norman V., Jamele Rigolini, and Gonzalo Llorente. 2012. "Do Middle Classes Bring Institutional Reforms?" Policy Research Working Paper 6015, World Bank, Washington, DC.

Marrero, Gustavo A., and Juan G. Rodríguez. 2013. "Inequality of Opportunity and Growth." *Journal of Development Economics* 104: 107–22.

Milanović, Branko. 1998. *Income, Inequality, and Poverty during the Transition from Planned to Market Economy.* World Bank Regional and Sectoral Studies. Washington, DC: World Bank.

Nolan, Brian Thomas, Max Roser, and Stefan Thewissen. 2016. "GDP Per Capita Versus Median Household Income: What Gives Rise to Divergence over Time?" LIS Working Paper 672 (May), Luxembourg Income Study, LIS Cross-National Data Center, Luxembourg.

OECD (Organisation for Economic Co-operation and Development). 2014. "Focus on Top Incomes and Taxation in OECD Countries: Was the Crisis a Game Changer?" May, Directorate for Employment, Labour, and Social Affairs, OECD, Paris.

———. 2016. *OECD Regions at a Glance 2016.* June 16. Paris: OECD.

———. 2017. *OECD Employment Outlook 2017.* June. Paris: OECD.

O'Higgins, Niall. 2010. "The Impact of the Economic and Financial Crisis on Youth Employment: Measures for Labour Market Recovery in the European Union, Canada, and the United States." Employment Working Paper 70, International Labour Office, Geneva.

Pew Research Center. 2015. "The American Middle Class Is Losing Ground: No Longer the Majority and Falling Behind Financially." December 9, Pew Research Center, Washington, DC.

Piketty, Thomas. 2014. *Capital in the Twenty-First Century.* Cambridge, MA: Belknap Press.

Ravallion, Martin. 2010. "Poverty Lines across the World." Policy Research Working Paper 5284, World Bank, Washington, DC.

———. 2012. "Poor, or Just Feeling Poor? On Using Subjective Data in Measuring Poverty." Policy Research Working Paper 5968, World Bank, Washington, DC.

Restrepo Cadavid, Paula, Grace Cineas, Luis Eduardo Quintero, and Sofia Zhukova. 2017. "Cities in Europe and Central Asia: A Story of Urban Growth and Decline." Report AUS12288 (June 8), World Bank, Washington, DC.

Ridao-Cano, Cristobal, and Christian Bodewig. 2018. *Growing United: Upgrading Europe's Convergence Machine*. Washington, DC: World Bank.

Rodriguez, Daniel, and Madeline Zavodny. 2003. "Changes in the Age and Education Profile of Displaced Workers." *Industrial and Labor Relations Review* 56 (3): 498–510.

Salverda, Wiemer. 2018. "Household Income Inequalities and Labour Market Position in the European Union." *CESifo Forum* 19 (2): 35–43.

Salverda, Wiemer, and Daniele Checchi. 2015. "Labour-Market Institutions and the Dispersion of Wage Earnings." In *Handbook of Income Distribution*, vol. 2B, edited by Anthony B. Atkinson and François Bourguignon, 1535–1728. Oxford, UK: North-Holland.

Simler, Kenneth. 2016. "Pinpointing Poverty in Europe: New Evidence for Policy Making." Poverty and Equity Global Practice. World Bank, Washington, DC.

Stewart, Frances. 2002. "Horizontal Inequalities: A Neglected Dimension of Development." QEH Working Paper 81 (February), Queen Elisabeth House, University of Oxford, Oxford, UK.

Stewart, Frances, and Arnim Langer. 2007. "Horizontal Inequalities: Explaining Persistence and Change." CRISE Working Paper 39 (August), Centre for Research on Inequality, Human Security, and Ethnicity, Queen Elizabeth House, University of Oxford, Oxford, UK.

Stiglitz, Joseph E. 2012. *The Price of Inequality: How Today's Divided Society Endangers Our Future*. New York: W. W. Norton & Company.

Thewissen, Stefan, Lane Kenworthy, Brian Nolan, Max Roser, and Timothy Smeeding. 2015. "Rising Income Inequality and Living Standards in OECD Countries: How Does the Middle Fare?" LIS Working Paper 656 (December), Luxembourg Income Study, LIS Cross-National Data Center, Luxembourg.

Thurow, Lester C. 1987. "A Surge in Inequality." *Scientific American* 256 (5): 30–37.

Tiwari, Sailesh, Cesar Cancho, Moritz Meyer, and Alan Fuchs. 2018. "South Caucasus in Motion: Economic and Social Mobility in Armenia, Azerbaijan, and Georgia." Policy Research Working Paper 8329, World Bank, Washington, DC.

Vaughan-Whitehead, Daniel, ed. 2016. *Europe's Disappearing Middle Class? Evidence from the World of Work*. Cheltenham, UK: Edward Elgar Publishing.

Weber, Max. 1922. *Wirtschaft und Gesellschaft*. [Economy and society]. 2 vols. Tübingen, Germany: J. C. B. Mohr (Paul Siebeck).

Woessmann, Ludger. 2016. "The Importance of School Systems: Evidence from International Differences in Student Achievement." *Journal of Economic Perspectives* 30 (3): 3–32.

World Bank. 2006. *World Development Report 2007: Development and the Next Generation*. Washington, DC: World Bank.

———. 2009. *World Development Report 2009: Reshaping Economic Geography*. Washington, DC: World Bank.

———. 2015. *Next Generation Albania*. Report 95980 (April). Systematic Country Diagnostic Series. Washington, DC: World Bank.

———. 2016a. *World Development Report 2016: Digital Dividends*. Washington, DC: World Bank.

———. 2016b. *Moldova: Paths to Sustained Prosperity*. Report 107502-MD (August). Systematic Country Diagnostic Series. Washington, DC: World Bank.

————. 2017a. "Leveling the Playing Field: Rethinking the Social Contract in Europe and Central Asia (ECA)." ECA Concept Note (March), World Bank, Washington, DC.

————. 2017b. "Russian Federation: Spatial Disparities in Living Standards; Convergence without Equity: A Closer Look at Spatial Disparities in Russia." Report ACS22573 (June), World Bank, Washington, DC.

————. 2017c. "Doing Business in Kazakhstan 2017." World Bank, Washington, DC.

————. 2017d. *World Development Report 2017: Governance and the Law*. Washington, DC: World Bank.

————. 2018a. *From Uneven Growth to Inclusive Development: Romania's Path to Shared Prosperity*. Systematic Country Diagnostic Series. Washington, DC: World Bank.

————. 2018b. "Thinking CAP: Supporting Agricultural Jobs and Incomes in the EU." EU Regular Economic Report 4, World Bank, Washington, DC.

Zhang, Xiaobo, and Ravi Kanbur. 2001. "What Difference Do Polarisation Measures Make? An Application to China." *Journal of Development Studies* 37 (3): 85–98.

Are Public Policies Equipped to Respond to Distributional Tensions?

This chapter examines whether public policies have dampened or accentuated the emerging distributional tensions identified in chapter 2. The failure to address these tensions or eliminate policies that exacerbate them may have somber implications for the sustainability of the social contract. Three broad policy areas—labor markets, taxes and transfers, and barriers to labor mobility—are considered.

Labor is the main source of income for most individuals. Changes in labor markets are a principal driver of the emerging distributional tensions. How have labor market regulations, interventions, and institutions evolved, and, especially, what has been their role in managing distributional tensions among groups of workers and birth cohorts over the last couple of decades? Europe and Central Asian countries provide more employment protection and higher job quality relative to other parts of the world. Labor market regulations and institutions, such as collective wage bargaining, trade unions, and employment protection legislation, play an important role in curbing labor market inequality in Europe and Central Asia, particularly at the lower end of the wage distribution. However, a key finding of the chapter is that partial deregulation of labor markets in the 1980s and 1990s in many countries of the European Union (EU) contributed to the growth in nonstandard employment, thereby reducing job security, especially among the young cohorts. In the eastern part of the region, the overall formality of employment has expanded from low levels in the mid-1990s. The equalization of protection offered across types of contracts has prevented a similar growth in nonstandard employment. At the same time, returns to skills have declined in

113

some countries in the east, leading to unmet aspirations and continuing vulnerability among groups of workers.

Tax and benefit systems in Europe and Central Asia are crucial in reducing the inequalities generated by markets. Vertical redistribution, that is, redistribution from richer to poorer individuals in an economy, is significant in the region. This redistribution, measured as the difference between the inequality of market income and the inequality of disposable income, averages 21 points. This means that the tax and benefit systems almost cut in half the inequality of individuals' market incomes, a much larger redistribution than in other regions. However, the impact of these systems on horizontal redistribution, that is, redistribution that reduces disparities between groups, is mixed. For example, when comparing their situation in the mid 2000s with the mid 2010s, the losers of job polarization—workers in routine-task–intensive occupations and in nonroutine manual-task–intensive occupations—received limited support from transfers, but not from changes in tax policy. Changes in policy had little impact on changes in the incidence of transfers across age-groups in most of Europe and Central Asia. However, changes in policy made tax systems more progressive across age-groups in Southern and Western Europe, but tended to penalize lower-income age-groups, particularly the young, in Central and Eastern Europe. Changes in tax and transfer policies in most of Europe and Central Asia benefited dual earner households rather than single breadwinner households.

Barriers to labor mobility may exacerbate the inequality of opportunity associated with the birthplace of individuals. Labor mobility within countries is low in Europe and Central Asia, and policies often fail to tackle the market failures that discourage labor mobility, including high housing costs and underdeveloped credit markets that raise the cost of finding affordable housing in potential target areas for migration. Cumbersome residence registration requirements may impede migrants in accessing government benefits in new locations. The inadequate provision of education services in rural areas may make obtaining the qualifications required to find good jobs in urban areas difficult.

Labor Markets Are Changing, and Policy Is Not Ensuring Equal Protection

A dynamic labor market is a central element of the promise of the social contract. For most people, labor income is the largest component of overall income; so, the functioning of the labor market and resulting labor outcomes have a large impact on welfare. Enhancing the efficiency of job matching helps workers move on to better opportunities and assists firms in finding appropriate skills, thereby raising productivity. However, a very dynamic labor market may also result in significant losses among the workers who lose their jobs and are unable to locate new opportunities.

Labor market policies are critical in curbing inequality. Labor market policies can be grouped into three major types: regulations, institutions, and interventions (table 3.1). Labor market regulations and institutions (such as collective wage bargaining, trade unions, employment protection legislation) are essential

TABLE 3.1 A Typology of Labor Market Policy Instruments

Regulations: set legal employment conditions; direct costs borne mainly by firms	Institutions: formulate, enforce, and implement regulations and interventions	Interventions: correct other market failures
Statutory wage floors	Presence of unions	Earned income tax credits
Mandated individual savings	Coverage of collective bargaining	Unemployment insurance and assistance
Restrictions on hiring and contracting	Jurisdiction of labor courts	Wage (hiring or retention) subsidies
Restrictions on dismissals	Role of social partners	Other public employment programs, such as training
Procedural requirements for dismissals		Intermediation and other job-search assistance
Financial obligations upon dismissal		

Source: Adapted from World Bank 2002.

in protecting workers and in reducing wage inequality, especially at the lower end of the wage distribution (Autor, Manning, and Smith 2010; Betcherman 2015; Checchi and García-Peñalosa 2010; Pontusson, Rueda, and Way 2002; Wallerstein 1999). They may also affect adjustments in the level of employment and in hours worked in response to a macroeconomic or structural shock. Labor market interventions can be significant in supporting the incomes of unemployed workers and helping workers find jobs. In several countries, effective active labor market policies have facilitated transitions into jobs among workers affected by the relaxation of employment protections (OECD 2015).

Policy needs to keep pace with changes in the labor market. Given the importance of a stable income in people's perceptions of well-being, transformations in the labor market, such as declining job stability and shifts in occupational structure, pose a major challenge to the social contract. These phenomena affect age cohorts differently, thereby accentuating the inequality between younger and older generations. Analysis of the structure of and trends in labor market policies across the region can provide critical information for understanding their shortcomings in the face of growing job insecurity, thereby indicating directions for policy.

Reforms Are Needed so Labor Market Institutions May Maintain Their Relevance

Key labor market institutions, such as trade unions, have been central to the operation of the labor market in the region. Union membership, that is, union density, and the coverage of collective bargaining have been critical in wage setting in most EU countries. The process for setting the minimum wage involves some form of collective consultation and agreement in many countries in Europe. For instance, in Austria, Finland, Italy, and Sweden, there is no general minimum wage. Instead, in Italy and Sweden, the minimum wage within sectors is fixed by sectoral collective agreements or tripartite wage boards. In Austria and Finland, the minimum wage is set by nationwide agreement between unions and employers. In contrast,

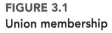

FIGURE 3.1
Union membership

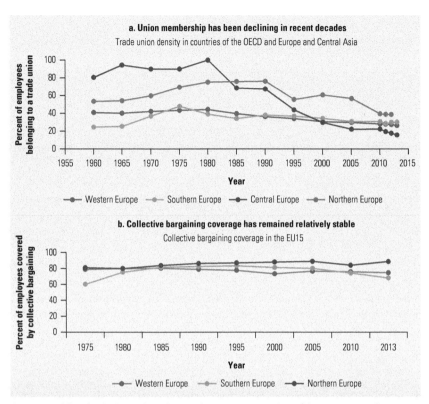

Sources: World Bank calculations based on employment statistics; data of the Organisation for Economic Co-operation and Development; ICTWSS (Database on Institutional Characteristics of Trade Unions, Wage Setting, State Intervention, and Social Pacts), Amsterdam Institute for Advanced Labour Studies, University of Amsterdam, Amsterdam, http://uva-aias.net/en/ictwss.

in Bulgaria, Hungary, and Lithuania, the minimum wage is set by the government after a nonbinding tripartite consultation process.[1] These labor market institutions have contributed greatly to reducing earnings inequality; countries with more centralized wage bargaining systems exhibit less wage inequality (European Commission 2014). The spillovers from the presence of strong labor market institutions is also a positive factor. The agreements on wages often apply not only to the groups that were bargaining, but also to other employers and employees within a region or sector. Indeed, the majority of employers apply the terms of collective contracts to their workforce irrespective of union membership.

Although union density is declining, the coverage of collective bargaining remains wide. Union density rates have fallen substantially in recent decades, particularly among eastern EU countries (figure 3.1, panel a). This could partially reflect compositional changes because union membership likely differs across cohorts, the type of contract (permanent, temporary, part time, and so on), the sector, and even gender. Only a few Nordic countries, such as Denmark and Finland, continue to show significant union density. While union density is illustrative, it offers a more complete picture only if it is combined with the coverage rates of collective bargaining. Bargaining coverage rates have remained somewhat stable in recent decades, at least in some of the larger EU countries, such as France and Italy, while declining slightly in other countries, such as Germany and Greece (figure 3.1, panel b).

Policies Supply Better Protection and Job Quality than in Other Regions . . .

Overall, Europe and Central Asia provides more employment protection compared with other parts of the world. While clear differences exist within the region, countries enjoy better employment protection, more well-regulated working hours, and higher firing costs on average, compared with the rest of the world (figure 3.2, panel a).[2] Countries in Western Europe offer better employment protection considering their history and the tradition of the welfare state in

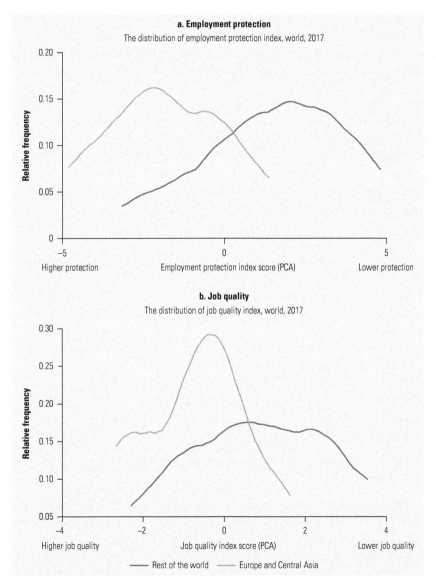

FIGURE 3.2
Employment protection and job quality, Europe and Central Asia versus the rest of the world

Source: Calculations based on data of Doing Business (database), International Finance Corporation and World Bank, Washington, DC, http://www.doingbusiness.org/data.
Note: PCA = principal component.

these countries. Following their accession to the EU, countries in Central and Eastern Europe also strengthened employment protection. Similarly, further east, Kazakhstan, the Russian Federation, and Balkan countries, such as Albania and Bosnia and Herzegovina, offer greater protection compared with countries at similar or higher levels of economic development, such as Brazil, Canada, South Africa, and the United States.

The countries in the region also offer better job quality.[3] The regulations governing the availability and quality of benefits, such as annual, sick, and family leave benefits, in the region provide an average of about 75 percent higher job quality compared with the rest of the world (see figure 3.2, panel b). For instance, Nordic countries, such as Denmark, Finland, and Sweden, are marked by generous annual and family leave policies and income protection in the case of job loss. While not quite as generous, the benefits in the Balkans, such as in Albania and Montenegro, also tend to be robust for formal sector workers and place these countries higher on the job quality index compared with several higher-income countries outside the region, including Chile, Japan, and the Republic of Korea.[4]

Job quality and the extent of protection differs within the region, however. The Western European countries continue to provide the greatest job security and job quality in the region. In 2005, the EU13 countries (in Central and Eastern Europe) had less employment protection compared with Azerbaijan, the Kyrgyz Republic, Moldova, and Ukraine.[5] Nonetheless, overall employment protection expanded in the eastern EU following EU accession (figure 3.3). For instance, the level of protection in Romania rose from 0.2 standard deviations below the regional average in 2008 to almost a full standard deviation above the regional average in 2013. Meanwhile, there was also a shift toward less protection in the eastern part of the region, most notably in Azerbaijan and the Kyrgyz Republic. Thus, in 2008, Azerbaijan allowed fixed term contracts with workers performing permanent functions. Furthermore, by 2009, Azerbaijan and the Kyrgyz Republic had eased restrictions on redundancy dismissals, for example, the elimination of third-party notification and the reassignment obligation. The latest data indicate that the eastern part of the region, for instance, Kazakhstan and Turkey, provides the least amount of job protection within the region, although protection remains substantial compared with other regions of the world. Changes in the cost of firing underscore the recent shifts within the region.

. . . but the Policies Have Fueled a Generational Divide in the West . . .

In Western Europe, partial labor market reforms to foster more flexibility in the mid-1990s resulted in a dual labor market. In Belgium, Germany, Italy, and the Netherlands, for example, the reforms focused on easing protections on temporary contracts, namely, allowing the creation of fixed term contracts for jobs that are not temporary and increases in the maximum duration and number of renewals. At the same time, they maintained the protections afforded for permanent jobs (figure 3.4). In contrast, other countries, such as Portugal and Spain, adopted

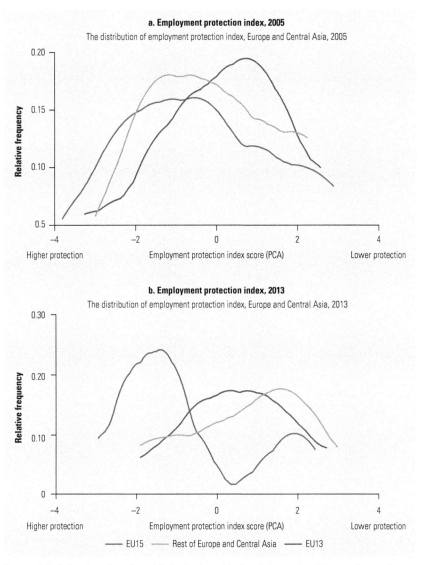

FIGURE 3.3
Employment protection differs within the region and has shifted

a. Employment protection index, 2005
The distribution of employment protection index, Europe and Central Asia, 2005

b. Employment protection index, 2013
The distribution of employment protection index, Europe and Central Asia, 2013

— EU15   — Rest of Europe and Central Asia   — EU13

Source: Calculations based on data of Doing Business (database), International Finance Corporation and World Bank, Washington, DC, http://www.doingbusiness.org/data.
Note: PCA = principal component. EU15 = Austria, Belgium, Denmark, Finland, France, Germany, Greece, Ireland, Italy, Luxembourg, Netherlands, Portugal, Spain, Sweden, and United Kingdom; EU13 = Bulgaria, Croatia, Cyprus, Czech Republic, Estonia, Hungary, Latvia, Lithuania, Malta, Poland, Romania, Slovak Republic, and Slovenia.

a broader approach toward flexibility by reducing protections for all workers, following the earlier, drastic liberalization of fixed term contracts. These changes initially had a small, positive impact on employment, especially among youth, during periods of economic growth (Aguirregabiria and Alonso-Borrego 2014; Boeri and Garibaldi 2007). However, these reforms created or exacerbated the duality in the labor market and lowered permanent employment rates through a gradual substitution of permanent with temporary workers and a reduction in conversion rates from fixed term to permanent (Bentolila and Dolado 1994; Blanchard and Landier 2002). As a result, temporary employment rates rose in many Western

FIGURE 3.4
Protections governing contracts, Central Asia and OECD Europe, 1990–2009

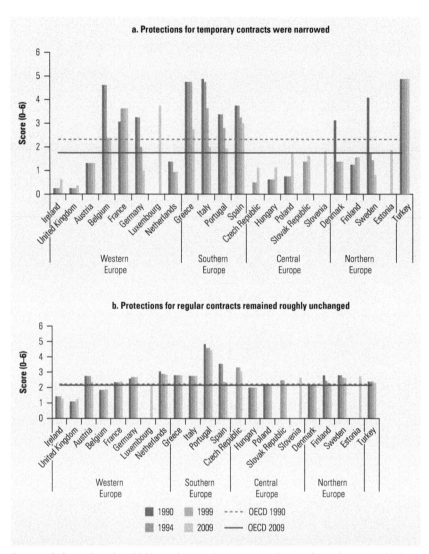

Source: calculations based on OECD Employment Protection Legislation Index and Muravyev 2010.
Note: OECD = Organisation for Economic Co-operation and Development.

European countries, including to more than 15 percent of total employment in France, the Netherlands, Poland, Portugal, and Spain. Despite the positive effect on employment, the reforms appear to have generated few income gains at the bottom of the income distribution (Causa, Hermansen, and Ruiz 2016).

Younger workers experienced a greater rise in temporary contracts relative to older workers, exacerbating the intergenerational divide. The majority of workers who already had permanent jobs and who were therefore, in some sense, insiders, continued to enjoy strong protections, dampening the impact of technological change on job losses. Meanwhile, workers newly entering the labor market, particularly youth, but also women returning after a break and people who had recently lost their jobs, the outsiders, were mostly employed on temporary contracts that were accompanied by much less protection. Indeed, in 2015, more than half the younger workers (ages 15–24) in, for instance, France, Germany, Italy, and the Netherlands had temporary contracts, and the share reached 70 percent or more in Poland, Slovenia, and Spain. In addition to experiencing less job security, workers with temporary contracts in the EU earned 14 percent less than workers with open-ended contracts (European Commission 2010). The duration of temporary employment among younger workers is rising, while the transition from temporary to permanent employment, whereby temporary employment acts as a stepping-stone, is limited to fewer than one worker in five in most countries (Fries-Tersch, Tugran, and Bradley 2017).

Policies in the western part of the region that reduced job protections also contributed to shorter job tenure among regular employees, thereby raising job insecurity for all. Tenure has decreased by an average of 1.5 years among younger cohorts over the past two decades.[6] Evidence of the importance of various factors in the rise of nonstandard employment and shorter tenure can be seen in the Europe and Central Asia region and in the United States. In the United States, despite the lack of recent policy reforms to boost labor market flexibility, all the net employment growth in the past decade (2005–15) occurred in nonstandard employment, such as temporary help agency workers, on-call workers, contract workers, and freelancers (Katz and Krueger 2016). In the western part of Europe and Central Asia, a rise in the ratio of exports plus imports over gross domestic product (GDP) by 10 percentage points was associated with a narrowing in tenure by 0.35 years, about four months. A decline in employment protection by 1— equivalent to the difference between the more well-protected 75th percentile to the 25th percentile in a sample of 29 countries—cut into tenure by a half year. A fall in GDP growth by 1 percentage point is predicted to reduce tenure by a bit less than a month. The rise of information and communication technology in the production process does not appear to have any significant effect (Bussolo, Capelle, and Winkler 2018). These results suggest that the large changes in the macroeconomic and labor market environment in Europe in the last 40 years and the policies that have accompanied them may have pushed the generations further apart in job tenure and job security.

Labor market policies in the western part of the region have fallen short in mitigating the greater vulnerability among workers. Workers in nonstandard employment contracts are more likely than workers in permanent jobs to suffer career interruptions, shorter employment spells, and lower lifetime earnings and to have less access to income protection and income-smoothing mechanisms, such as unemployment insurance. Eligibility for unemployment insurance benefits requires 9 months of contributions over the previous 12 months in Latvia and 26 weeks of contributions over the previous 36 weeks in the Netherlands; such requirements are often difficult for workers with nonstandard contracts to meet. The shorter employment spells and frequent job changes also impair the acquisition of human capital, especially firm-specific skills, given that firms have less incentive to invest in the training of nonstandard workers, partly because of the limited time of the workers on the job. Thus, the rise in nonstandard contracts may explain some of the decline in the returns to experience documented in chapter 2.

The main driver of structural transformation in the labor market may differ drastically across countries, depending on the occupational structure, skill profiles, amount of technology adaption, labor market institutions, and regulations. Box 3.1 illustrates the role that regulations and institutions have in the structural transformation of labor markets by comparing the experience of France and the United States.

Some countries have recently attempted to reduce duality in the labor market. Concerns over equity and efficiency, especially following the global financial crisis, have led to efforts to reduce labor market segmentation in Western Europe—insider: well-protected, open-ended contracts; outsider: less well-protected, temporary contracts—and to constrain the growth in temporary employment in Estonia, Italy, the Netherlands, Slovenia, and Spain. These efforts have focused on reducing the protection afforded to those in open-ended contracts or increasing the protection for temporary workers. Italy undertook a major reform to control segmentation (box 3.2). An employment relations act was passed in Slovenia in 2013 to narrow labor market segmentation, promote flexibility, and strengthen the legal protection of workers. The law aimed at limiting the difference in protection between workers on permanent versus temporary contracts by raising the protection for temporary workers (for example, requiring greater employer contributions

---

BOX 3.1 **Labor Market Institutions Pick the Winners, France versus the United States**

In France and the United States, task-biased technological change has led to changes in labor demand, while rising educational attainment has altered labor supply, generating job polarization. These forces have resulted in similar changes in the employment shares in the two countries, but different changes in levels of employment.

In the United States, overall employment increased, and the main winners were highly skilled workers involved in nonroutine cognitive or interpersonal tasks and, at the lower end, workers active in nonroutine manual tasks. By contrast, employment fell and wages declined among individuals working on routine tasks, and low levels of protection and generosity afforded by labor market institutions did not sufficiently compensate for the losses.

In France, overall employment opportunities fell. Despite this and similar to the United States, high-skilled individuals working on nonroutine tasks and workers involved in manual tasks enjoyed welfare gains. Among individuals working on routine tasks, the more highly skilled also obtained welfare gains. Stringent employment protection ensured they did not lose their jobs, and the minimum wage ensured that compensation rose. Individuals with fewer skills who could potentially work in routine occupations lost out. Insiders were protected, but unemployment increased among outsiders.

Recent reforms undertaken in France to reduce labor market protections will allow new entrants into the labor market and those with lower skills to benefit from economic growth. Meanwhile, better labor market protection, more generous compensation in the case of job loss, and better retraining opportunities could help individuals working on routine tasks in the United States.

Source: Based on Albertini et al. 2017.

BOX 3.2 Italy: Toward One Type of Employment Contract

Labor force participation has been low and unemployment high in Italy in recent decades. The government undertook a series of reforms in the 1990s and 2000s to increase labor market flexibility and raise employment and labor productivity. The reforms deregulated the use of temporary contracts, while maintaining strict firing rules on the existing stock of permanent workers. This was a political compromise to meet the demands of both employers and worker unions. However, the liberalization process resulted in labor market duality; the labor market was deeply segmented between well-protected insiders and precarious outsiders.

The introduction of temporary and atypical contracts was key in the rise of labor market duality. In 1997, the Treu reforms loosened regulations on the conversion of fixed term contracts to open-ended contracts. These measures increased flexibility at the margin by introducing temporary contracts and incentivizing part-time work. In 2001, legislation was passed to allow temporary and fixed term contracts as long as their rationale was explicitly stated in writing. In 2003, the Biagi reforms introduced new forms of atypical work arrangements and further deregulated fixed term contracts.

Most of the reforms in employment protection during this time were introduced at the margin, that is, they were applicable to new hires only. Workers hired under fixed term contracts also experienced inferior working conditions and less labor security. The losers were the usual outsiders: women, youth, and the long-term unemployed. During the global financial crisis, the largest share of employment creation was in temporary and nonstandard contracts.

The Jobs Act, the most far-reaching reform to date to tackle labor market duality, was introduced in 2014. While the Fornero law, enacted in 2012, revised the rigid dismissal scheme for open-ended contracts and abolished certain atypical contracts, it was considered a missed opportunity for several reasons, including the complex wording and weak enforcement. Meanwhile, the Jobs Act represented the most wide-ranging labor market reform since the introduction of the labor code in the 1970s. It aimed to strike a better balance between employment protection and minimal rights for all workers and covered a comprehensive set of issues: labor contracts, labor taxation and incentives, unemployment insurance, active labor market polices, public employment services, and labor inspections.

The cornerstone of the Jobs Act was the introduction of a new open-ended employment contract for all. The new open-ended contract offers greater protection and recognizes more rights (vacation, sick leave, unemployment insurance, and so on) for new hires or temporary workers converted to open-ended contracts. There was an effort to encourage employers to hire on open-ended contracts by reducing the cost of doing so. For instance, employers were given tax incentives to hire new workers on or convert current workers to the new open-ended contracts. While the existing permanent contracts were grandfathered, almost all other atypical forms of contracts were abolished. Regulation capped temporary workers at 20 percent of employees in each firm, with strict penalties for exceeding this limit. Additionally, other forms of precarious freelance contracts were either abolished or reduced in scope. Apart from guaranteeing a minimum set of rights, the new contract provided severance pay proportional to tenure if a worker was dismissed for economic reasons and established maximum monetary indemnification of workers for any form of unjust dismissal. Preliminary evidence shows that the Jobs Act contributed to employment growth in 2015–16.

Source: Based on Gatti et al. 2017.

to unemployment insurance), while decreasing protections for permanent workers (for instance, easing dismissal procedures, decreasing severance pay). Similarly, the Netherlands introduced a cap on severance payments or damages for unfair dismissal and boosting the protection for temporary workers.

While it is too early to assess the impact of these reforms, they usually did not eliminate duality in the labor market. The impact of most reforms was limited, given the strong labor market institutions and the power of various interest groups. In some cases, the reforms were introduced, but implementation lagged. In almost all countries, the reforms reduced, but did not eliminate the difference in levels of protection between different contracts. The exception was Italy's far-reaching reform program (see box 3.2). Whether the various impacts persist, especially during a future recession, remains to be seen. The duality in labor markets in the western part of Europe and Central Asia, if unaddressed, is likely to continue to exacerbate the generational divide by increasing the insecurity facing younger workers.

Labor market interventions that support workers in seeking or retaining jobs are not adequate in the face of changing skill demands. Labor market interventions include active measures (active labor market programs and labor market services, such as intermediation) and passive measures (unemployment insurance or unemployment assistance benefits). The active measures may be critical in reducing frictions in the labor market stemming from high search costs by providing support to workers in improving employability, avoiding deterioration in skills, shortening unemployment spells, and remaining attached to the labor market. Unemployment benefits—insurance or assistance—provide income smoothing through unemployment spells, which can facilitate better job matching.

The level and composition of spending on labor market interventions vary widely across the region, indicating the significant differences in the levels and types of support available. As of 2015, overall spending on labor market interventions in the EU ranged from 0.2 percent of GDP in Romania to 3.3 percent of GDP in Denmark, with an average of 1.5 percent across the 28 countries of the European Union (figure 3.5). Passive measures account for the majority of spending (at an average of 0.9 percent of GDP); the lowest levels are in Central Europe and the Baltic States, reflecting the de facto emphasis on income protection and income-smoothing measures and high coverage across the western part of the region.[7] The passive measures are also considered automatic stabilizers, that is, expanding during economic downturns to help smooth consumption and mitigate adverse impacts and contracting during recovery. The large spike in the associated spending in most countries in 2010 reflects this role, especially in Central and Southern Europe and in Ireland, which were hit hardest by the 2008–09 global financial crisis. Spending on passive measures has contracted since then (from an average of 1.1 percent of GDP in 2010 to 0.9 percent of GDP), partly because of the economic recovery, but also a lapse in benefits for the long-term unemployed, leaving a significant share of the long-term unemployed in need of support.

The low spending on active measures translates into low coverage. Many who need support are not covered by existing programs. Some countries, such as Greece, Hungary (which implemented a large public works program as a main active measure), Poland, and Spain boosted spending on active measures,

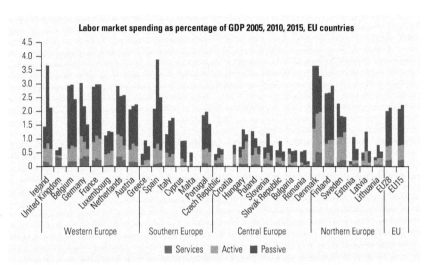

FIGURE 3.5
Spending on labor market interventions varies across the region

Source: Calculations using data of Eurostat Statistics (database), Eurostat, European Commission, Luxembourg, http://ec.europa.eu/eurostat/web/main/home.
Note: EU15 = Austria, Belgium, Denmark, Finland, France, Germany, Greece, Ireland, Italy, Luxembourg, Netherlands, Portugal, Spain, Sweden, and United Kingdom; EU28 (the current country composition of the EU) = Austria, Belgium, Bulgaria, Croatia, Cyprus, Czech Republic, Denmark, Estonia, Finland, France, Germany, Greece, Hungary, Ireland, Italy, Latvia, Lithuania, Luxembourg, Malta, Netherlands, Poland, Portugal, Romania, Slovak Republic, Slovenia, Spain, Sweden, and United Kingdom. EU = European Union; GDP = gross domestic product.

especially after the onset of the 2008–09 global financial crisis, and the Nordic countries have maintained high levels of spending. Nonetheless, spending on active measures in the EU averages only about 0.35 percent of GDP. For instance, in Greece, despite a rise in spending on a range of active labor market programs, the coverage and types of programs available remain inadequate. As of 2014, active measures serve only a small portion (about 10 percent) of registered job-seekers (Millán, Ovadiya, and Isik-Dikmelik 2017).

Moreover, even if a mix of programs exists, they are not always targeted on needs, limiting their effectiveness (World Bank 2017). Spending on active labor market programs in 12 EU countries was skewed toward relatively well-educated or skilled youth who were unemployed for a short period, rather than the low-educated, long-term unemployed with little work experience. For instance, in Croatia, low educational attainment was identified as a major barrier to employment, especially among youth and the long-term unemployed. However, active labor market programs primarily benefited individuals with more skills and greater labor market attachment, such as people who had been unemployed for less than six months, which reduced the impact of the programs (Ovadiya and Vandeninden 2017). In Bulgaria, the majority of employment promotion measures are targeted at the registered unemployed, and the number and availability of programs addressing complex needs, such as mobility and access to work experience, appear to be limited (Karacsony, Vandeninden, and Ovadiya 2017).

The inadequacy of existing programs in confronting current needs, coupled with the reduced job security faced by particular groups, indicates that labor market interventions should be rethought. While the building blocks of robust labor market interventions appear to exist in many countries in the region, the programs suffer from problems in financing, design, and, particularly, in matching needs, which limits effectiveness. The transformations in the labor market and the resulting decline in job security require a comprehensive review of labor market interventions. For instance, the changes in the task content of jobs described in chapter 2 reflect the changes in the skills demanded in the labor market, thereby highlighting the need to reskill. However, the rise in temporary contracts has reduced the incentives among firms to invest in training and the opportunities for workers to build firm-specific skills on the job. The role of unemployment benefits might be refocused relative to the broader safety net, and active measures might be redesigned, including strengthening the links between training programs and the education system to provide retraining and lifelong learning opportunities, as well as incentives to employers to invest in training.

. . . and, in the East, Economic Insecurity Is Manifested Differently

Unlike the experience of the western part of the region, the transition to a market economy in the eastern part of the region was associated with a rise in overall employment protection, especially among workers in temporary employment. The labor markets in the eastern part of the region, particularly in the former Soviet Union economies, were distinctly different from their Western European counterparts because of the lack of open unemployment and a persistently tight labor market. Thus, contrary to popular belief, pretransition employment protection was more flexible in the east than in the west in certain dimensions, such as the regulation of temporary contracts and collective dismissals, but more rigid in other dimensions, such as allowing or paying for overtime. In the early transition to a market-based economy, these gaps, especially in the protection for temporary contracts, were addressed, leading to greater employment protection (figure 3.6).

Reforms in the early 2000s to liberalize labor markets focused on narrowing the protections for permanent employment and thereby reducing labor market duality. Reforms that provided more flexibility in permanent employment were implemented in the Baltic States and the rest of the former Soviet Union economies, except for Azerbaijan and Ukraine, while protections for temporary employment were left untouched or were expanded, except in the Kyrgyz Republic, Russia, and Turkmenistan. As a result, average protections from 1990 to 2009 almost tripled for temporary contracts, while declining by 25 percent for permanent contracts. Thus, in contrast to Western Europe, the insider-outsider segmentation in the labor market was reduced in the eastern part of the region.

Likewise in contrast to the west, policy changes in the east were associated with a decline in nonstandard employment, although many workers were still vulnerable. The drop-off in nonstandard employment was led by the substantial shrinkage in the share of nonstandard employment in particular occupations, such as skilled agricultural workers, plant and machine operators, and, to a lesser degree, elementary occupations, likely indicating a shift to more standard forms of employment in these occupations. Unlike in the west, labor market reforms may have prevented the growth of temporary employment by reducing the difference in protection between temporary and permanent contracts.

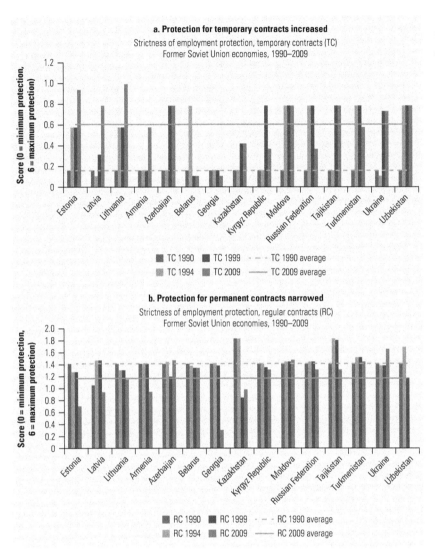

FIGURE 3.6
Employment protection, by
contract type, Eastern
Europe and Central Asia

Source: World Bank calculations based on data of Muravyev 2010.

Nonetheless, a gap still exists, which has the potential to contribute to a rise in nonstandard employment. Yet, while employment protection measures apply to formal workers only, most of these countries still have a sizable informal sector (figure 3.7). Changes in employment protection may not have had a large impact on the types of contracts, but may have affected the level of informality. For instance, the enhanced protection for both permanent and temporary contracts in Ukraine in the late 2000s likely contributed to the country's overall high informality rates.

While its manifestations are different in the east and the west, job insecurity is increasing across the region, and policies are not adequate to address it. Labor market reforms, in conjunction with technological change, have reduced job security in the west, especially among youth and low-paid workers. In the east, more highly skilled workers are losing ground in the face of declining skill premiums in the labor

FIGURE 3.7
Employment structure,
selected countries of
Eastern Europe and
Central Asia

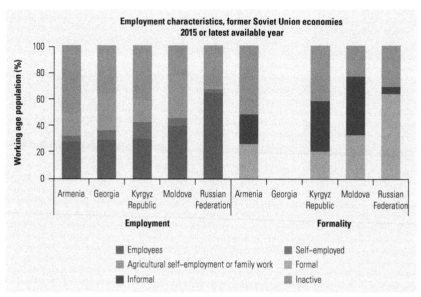

Source: World Bank calculations based on household survey data.

market. Spending on labor market interventions, particularly on active labor market measures, is lower in the east than in the west. As of 2016, the average spending on active measures was less than 0.05 percent of GDP in Armenia and Moldova and only about 0.10 percent of GDP in the Western Balkans, approximately one-fourth of the EU average (Numanović 2016). Moreover, programs reach only a fraction of individuals who are out of work, and access is particularly limited in rural or remote areas. While labor market regulations in most countries in the east provide basic protections, they fail to support most workers because of the significant informality. In both parts of Europe and Central Asia, growing insecurity will require changes in labor market policies to extend support to workers where possible; where this is impossible, other arrangements for support will need to be considered.

The Impact of Tax and Transfer Systems on Income Redistribution

Europe and Central Asia Is Achieving Substantial Income Redistribution

Government policies in the EU reduce income inequality substantially. Overall redistribution in the EU, measured as the difference between the Gini of market income and the Gini of disposable income, averages 21 Gini points. This is significantly larger than the corresponding difference in other high-income countries, such as Australia (15 Gini points), Japan (16), Korea (5), Switzerland (9), and the United States (11) (figure 3.8; see annex 3A for details on the methodology). The level of redistribution is also much larger in the region than in selected economies on which comparable data are available, such as Chile (3.2 Gini points), Mexico (1.9), and Russia (11.0). This reduction in inequality is achieved by taxes, social insurance contributions, public pensions, other social insurance, and social assistance transfers (both means tested and non–means tested). European countries have some of the highest taxes and the largest expenditures on social protection systems in the world. Much of the reduction derives from public pensions, which reduce inequality in market income by almost 12 Gini points (figure 3.9).[8] Direct taxes and transfers, including means-tested and non–means-tested benefits, are important, reducing inequality by an additional 9 Gini points.[9] However, the size of social protection systems and the extent of redistribution achieved by pensions versus transfers vary considerably across the EU (figure 3.10; see figure 3.9, where countries are ranked from the smallest redistribution to the broadest).

FIGURE 3.8 Gini index, market versus disposable income, non-EU countries

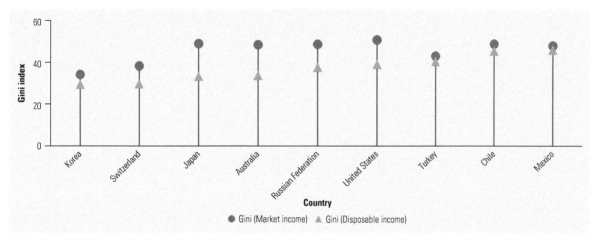

Source: Data of IDD (Income Distribution Database), Organisation for Economic Co-operation and Development, Paris, http://www.oecd.org /social/income-distribution-database.htm.
Note: In the case of Turkey, the Gini of market income is after taxes, but before transfers.

FIGURE 3.9 Gini index, various income concepts, EU28

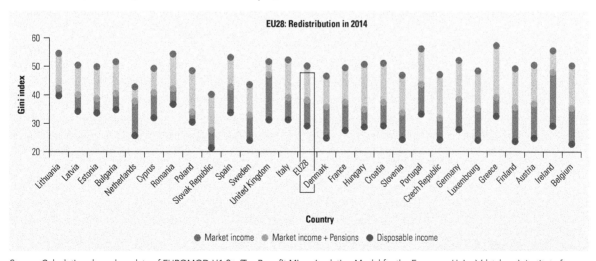

Source: Calculations based on data of EUROMOD H1.0+ (Tax-Benefit Microsimulation Model for the European Union) (database), Institute for Social and Economic Research, University of Essex, Colchester, UK, https://www.euromod.ac.uk/2017/12/13/euromod-h10-released.
Note: EU28 = average of the current country composition of the EU: Austria, Belgium, Bulgaria, Croatia, Cyprus, Czech Republic, Denmark, Estonia, Finland, France, Germany, Greece, Hungary, Ireland, Italy, Latvia, Lithuania, Luxembourg, Malta, Netherlands, Poland, Portugal, Romania, Slovak Republic, Slovenia, Spain, Sweden, and United Kingdom.

FIGURE 3.10 Nordic countries spend the most on social protection

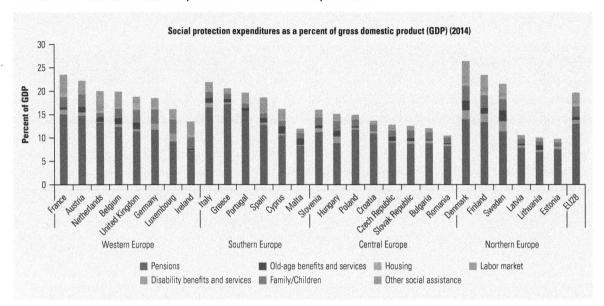

Source: Calculations based on data of ESSPROS (European System of Integrated Social Protection Statistics) (database), Eurostat, European Commission, Luxembourg, http://ec.europa.eu/eurostat/web/social-protection.
Note: EU28 = average of the current country composition of the EU: Austria, Belgium, Bulgaria, Croatia, Cyprus, Czech Republic, Denmark, Estonia, Finland, France, Germany, Greece, Hungary, Ireland, Italy, Latvia, Lithuania, Luxembourg, Malta, Netherlands, Poland, Portugal, Romania, Slovak Republic, Slovenia, Spain, Sweden, and United Kingdom.

The large expenditure on social protection in Europe is financed by high taxes and compulsory social contributions. These amounted to an average of 38.9 percent of GDP in the EU in 2015, significantly above the amounts in other high-income countries such as Japan (about 7 percentage points above) and the United States (about 12 percentage points above). The taxes collected vary greatly across the EU, ranging from 46.4 percent of GDP in Denmark in 2016 to 23.3 percent of GDP in Ireland (figure 3.11).

The structure of taxation and the structure of social protection expenditures differ across the EU because of different approaches to the organization of social protection. For instance, social security contributions represent 37.0 percent of overall tax revenue in France, while they are miniscule in Denmark (0.1 percent of overall taxes). This is because social protection in France is organized along the lines of a conservative-corporatist welfare state. This model relies on various social insurance arrangements that are typically tied to employment. Benefits are usually financed through contributions from both employers and employees. Risk pools are often formed around occupations and have historically excluded people outside the labor market. Social protection in Denmark is organized along the lines of a social-democratic welfare state, which aims to provide a basic level of services to each citizen. Benefits are typically financed through general taxation, which results in a more redistributive agenda and a substantive amount of risk sharing. Universal flat-rate benefits are often combined with earnings-related entitlements for the employed. Denmark achieves universal coverage of the poorest 40 percent of the population (the bottom 40) (figure 3.12). France also achieves high coverage rates of social protection, though not universal: 86 percent of the bottom 40.

FIGURE 3.11 Structure of taxation, European Union, 2016

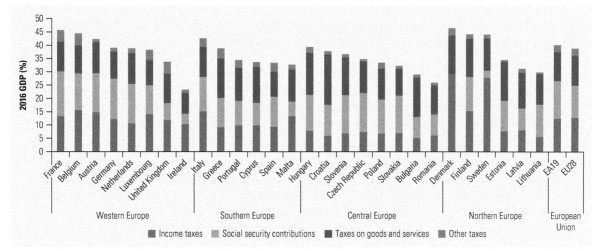

Source: Calculations based on data of TEDB (Taxes in Europe Database), Directorate-General for Taxation and Customs Union, European Commission, Brussels, https://ec.europa.eu/taxation_customs/economic-analysis-taxation/taxes-europe-database-tedb_en.
Note: EA19 = the euro area, that is, Austria, Belgium, Cyprus, Estonia, Finland, France, Germany, Greece, Ireland, Italy, Latvia, Lithuania, Luxembourg, Malta, Netherlands, Portugal, Slovak Republic, Slovenia, and Spain; EU28 = average of the current country composition of the EU: Austria, Belgium, Bulgaria, Croatia, Cyprus, Czech Republic, Denmark, Estonia, Finland, France, Germany, Greece, Hungary, Ireland, Italy, Latvia, Lithuania, Luxembourg, Malta, Netherlands, Poland, Portugal, Romania, Slovak Republic, Slovenia, Spain, Sweden, and United Kingdom.

FIGURE 3.12 Most EU15 countries achieve near universality in social protection coverage

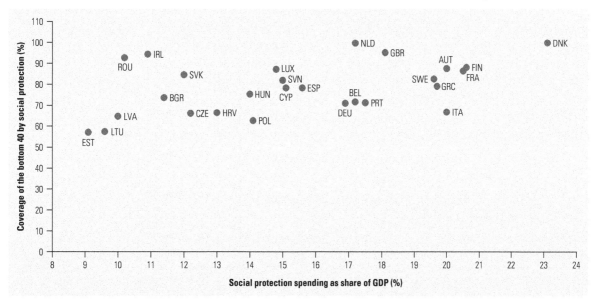

Source: Calculations based on data of EUROMOD H1.0+ (Tax-Benefit Microsimulation Model for the European Union) (database), Institute for Social and Economic Research, University of Essex, Colchester, UK, https://www.euromod.ac.uk/2017/12/13/euromod-h10-released.
Note: EU15 = Austria, Belgium, Denmark, Finland, France, Germany, Greece, Ireland, Italy, Luxembourg, Netherlands, Portugal, Spain, Sweden, and United Kingdom. GDP = gross domestic product.

The welfare state orientation influences the overall coverage and generosity of transfers. Southern euro area countries have established a Mediterranean welfare state, which has an extreme orientation toward social insurance and much greater segmentation in the labor market. A large share of social protection expenditures is allocated to pensions. Expenditures on pensions in Italy, Greece, Portugal, and Spain average 15.5 percent of GDP, compared with an average of 12.8 percent in continental Western European countries (Austria, Belgium, France, Germany, Luxembourg, and the Netherlands) and 12.9 percent in the Nordic countries (Denmark, Finland, and Sweden). Expenditures on social assistance programs, such as family benefits and benefits targeted on poverty, financed from general taxation and aimed at the general population, are quite small in most Mediterranean welfare states. In 2016, Italy spent nearly 22.0 percent of GDP on social protection, of which 16.5 percent represented pension expenditures. By contrast, Denmark spent 26.0 percent of GDP in 2016 on social protection, but only 14.0 percent on pensions. Denmark achieves almost universal coverage; Italy covers only 67.0 percent of the bottom 40 (see figure 3.12).[10]

The amount of spending on social assistance and the level of means testing also influence the overall coverage and generosity of benefits. A comparison between the Baltic States and Ireland illustrates this. Ireland is a liberal welfare state, characterized by markets that are allowed to operate with minimal government intervention. Liberal welfare states typically rely on greater targeting and provide lower social insurance benefits, compared with other EU15 countries. Ireland achieves almost universal coverage of the bottom 40 by spending substantially on social assistance (3.7 percent of GDP) and by targeting about half of social assistance based on income. By contrast, the Baltic States cover less than 70 percent of the bottom 40 (figure 3.13). They spend an average of only 2 percent of GDP on social assistance, and only 10 percent of social assistance is targeted based on income (figure 3.14). The coverage and average value of benefits for the bottom 40 are low. For instance, in Latvia, 35 percent of the bottom 40 receive no benefits at all, and another 39 percent receive social protection transfers that average less than 20 percent of the

FIGURE 3.13 The Baltic States, Central Europe, and the southern euro area: low benefits

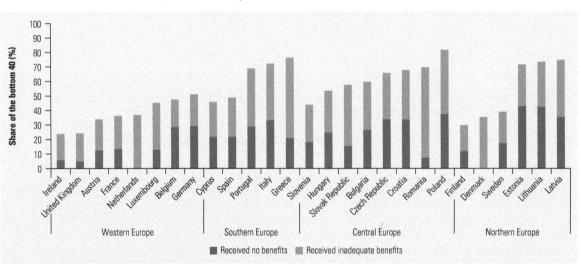

Source: Calculations based on data of EUROMOD H1.0+ (Tax-Benefit Microsimulation Model for the European Union) (database), Institute for Social and Economic Research, University of Essex, Colchester, UK, https://www.euromod.ac.uk/2017/12/13/euromod-h10-released.

FIGURE 3.14 The Baltic States: lowest means testing of nonpension benefits in the EU

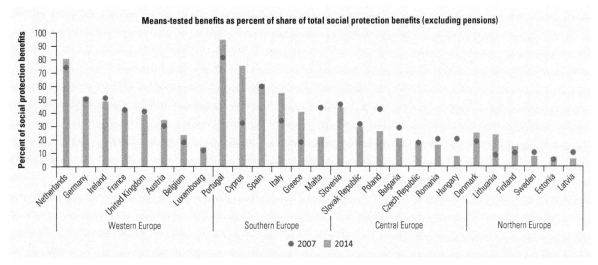

Source: Calculations based on data of EUROMOD H1.0+ (Tax-Benefit Microsimulation Model for the European Union) (database), Institute for Social and Economic Research, University of Essex, Colchester, UK, https://www.euromod.ac.uk/2017/12/13/euromod-h10-released.

poverty line. Ireland achieves one of the highest levels of redistribution in the EU, while the Baltic States achieve some of the lowest levels of redistribution (see figure 3.9).

A Long-Term Downward Trend in Tax Progressivity Is Impairing Redistribution

Changes in tax policy have exacerbated the effects of the growing share of the top 1 percent in total income in many countries in the region. The rise in top incomes is driven by many forces, including globalization, technological change that amplifies the rewards for skills, changes in regulations that may shelter specific groups from competition, and changes in the way top executives are compensated.[11] Changes in tax policy, including reductions in the top marginal tax rates and a reduction in tax rates on capital, have also contributed.

From the early 1980s until prior to the global recession, the share of top incomes grew, while the top personal income tax rates fell sharply. Top marginal tax rates were high in the early 1980s, at 84.4 percent in Portugal; 72.0 percent in Belgium, Italy, and the Netherlands; 65.1 percent in Spain; and 62.0 percent in Austria. Reforms undertaken in the next decade brought top tax rates down substantially in several counties (figure 3.15). By 1995, top tax rates in the EU averaged around 47 percent. Many countries reduced top income tax rates additionally between 1995 and 2008, and, in 2008, the average in the EU declined to 39 percent, where it has largely remained (figure 3.16). There have been large changes in specific countries since the financial crisis; most notably, Greece and Portugal increased the top rate by 15 percentage points, and Hungary lowered the top rate by 25 percentage points. However, the tax regimes in most countries have been much more stable than in previous decades.

FIGURE 3.15 Top personal income tax rates declined, Western Europe, 1981–95 . . .

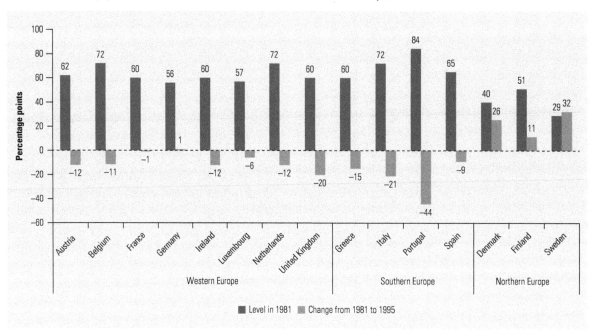

Source: Calculations based on data of TEDB (Taxes in Europe Database), Directorate-General for Taxation and Customs Union, European Commission, Brussels, https://ec.europa.eu/taxation_customs/economic-analysis-taxation/taxes-europe-database-tedb_en.

FIGURE 3.16 . . . and in 1995–2008, but stability returned after the 2008–09 recession

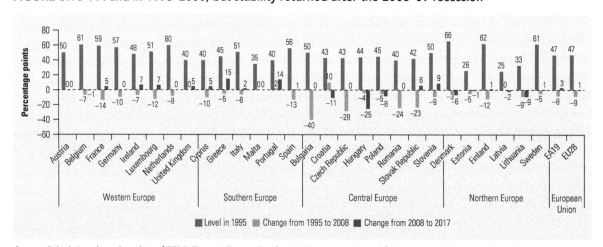

Source: Calculations based on data of TEDB (Taxes in Europe Database), Directorate-General for Taxation and Customs Union, European Commission, Brussels, https://ec.europa.eu/taxation_customs/economic-analysis-taxation/taxes-europe-database-tedb_en.
Note: EA19 = average of the euro area, that is, Austria, Belgium, Cyprus, Estonia, Finland, France, Germany, Greece, Ireland, Italy, Latvia, Lithuania, Luxembourg, Malta, Netherlands, Portugal, Slovak Republic, Slovenia, and Spain; EU28 = average of the current country composition of the EU: Austria, Belgium, Bulgaria, Croatia, Cyprus, Czech Republic, Denmark, Estonia, Finland, France, Germany, Greece, Hungary, Ireland, Italy, Latvia, Lithuania, Luxembourg, Malta, Netherlands, Poland, Portugal, Romania, Slovak Republic, Slovenia, Spain, Sweden, and United Kingdom.

Tax rates on capital income have declined, further contributing to a reduction in the progressivity of taxation. Corporate tax rates have been cut substantially since 1995, and even further in some countries since the global financial crisis in 2008–09 (figure 3.17). The average statutory corporate income tax rate declined from 47 percent in 1981 to 25 percent in 2013,

FIGURE 3.17 Corporate tax rates declined in Western Europe, 1995–2008 and 2008–16

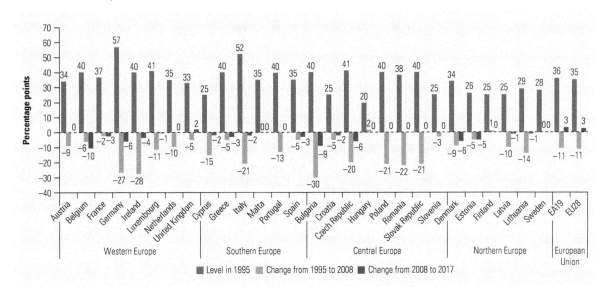

Source: World Bank computations based on data of TEDB (Taxes in Europe Database), Directorate-General for Taxation and Customs Union, European Commission, Brussels, https://ec.europa.eu/taxation_customs/economic-analysis-taxation/taxes-europe-database-tedb_en.
Note: EA19 = average of the euro area, that is, Austria, Belgium, Cyprus, Estonia, Finland, France, Germany, Greece, Ireland, Italy, Latvia, Lithuania, Luxembourg, Malta, Netherlands, Portugal, Slovak Republic, Slovenia, and Spain; EU28 = average of the current country composition of the EU: Austria, Belgium, Bulgaria, Croatia, Cyprus, Czech Republic, Denmark, Estonia, Finland, France, Germany, Greece, Hungary, Ireland, Italy, Latvia, Lithuania, Luxembourg, Malta, Netherlands, Poland, Portugal, Romania, Slovak Republic, Slovenia, Spain, Sweden, and United Kingdom.

and taxes on dividend income for distributions of domestic source profits fell from 75 percent to 42 percent (OECD 2014). This has benefited people at the top of the income distribution among whom the ownership of capital assets is concentrated.

Recent Changes in Redistribution Have Been Mixed

The extent of redistribution has increased in most countries in Western Europe, but in only about half the countries in Central and Eastern Europe. Assessing the change in redistribution caused by tax and transfer systems can shed light on how public policies are mitigating or exacerbating the distributional tensions described in chapter 2. The size of the redistribution rose in most Western European countries in 2007–14 (figure 3.18). The largest improvement, equivalent to 7 Gini points, occurred in Greece. In Eastern Europe, redistribution increased in about half the countries, but fell in the other half. Changes in the level of redistribution may arise because of policy changes by the government, for example, a rise in the benefit rates in public pension plans, or to changes in the underlying structure of the economy and in market incomes, but without policy change; for example, population aging raises the number of pension recipients and thus pension expenditures, without any change in benefit rates. Distinguishing between these two causes of changes in the redistributive impact of tax and transfer systems provides information on the reaction of public policy to emerging distributional tensions.

FIGURE 3.18
Changes in redistribution,
2007–14

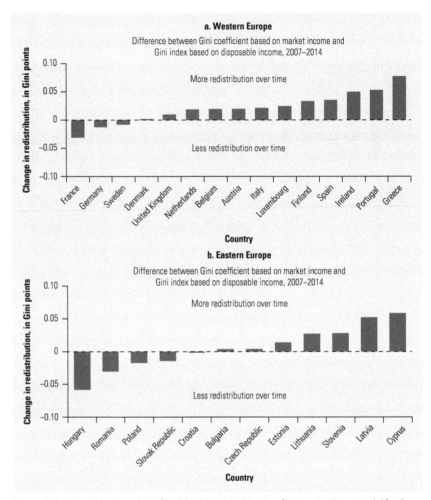

Source: Calculations based on data of EUROMOD H1.0+ (Tax-Benefit Microsimulation Model for the European Union) (database), Institute for Social and Economic Research, University of Essex, Colchester, UK, https://www.euromod.ac.uk/2017/12/13/euromod-h10-released.

Policy changes were the main reasons for the increase in redistribution in the EU15 from 2007 to 2014, with the exception of a few traditionally generous welfare systems, such as in Belgium, Denmark, and Sweden (figure 3.19, panel a).[12] The largest increase in redistribution caused purely by changes in tax and benefit policies was in Ireland, where changes in taxes and transfers reduced market income inequality by almost 2 Gini points. Ireland was followed closely by Luxembourg, Portugal, and the United Kingdom. In some countries, for example, the United Kingdom, changes in tax and transfer policies offset the negative effect of other changes, such as changes in income distribution caused by the interaction of changes in market incomes and the design of the system (labeled as market income component in figure 3.19). In other countries (for instance, France) policies only partially offset the deterioration in income redistribution driven by other forces. In many countries, the extent of redistribution derived from policy changes differs significantly from the overall change in

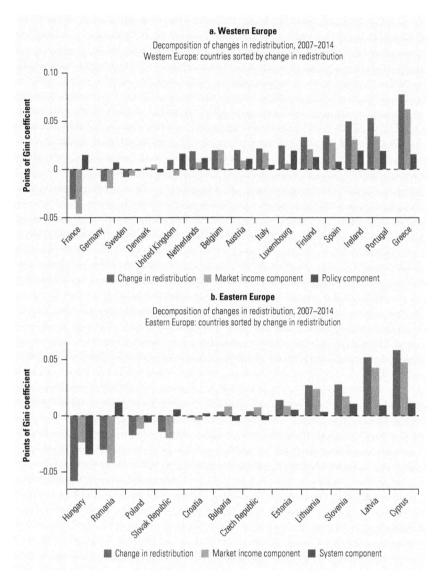

FIGURE 3.19
Decomposition of changes in redistribution, Western and Eastern Europe

redistribution. For example, Greece exhibited the largest rise in redistribution in 2007–14, but only the fifth largest increase in redistribution caused by policy changes. Annex 3B describes policy changes that had a significant impact on redistribution in selected countries.

In contrast to the EU15, changes in taxes and transfer policies in the EU13 reduced the amount of redistribution in half the countries (figure 3.19, panel b). The total amount of redistribution and the redistribution resulting from active policy changes rose in only a handful of countries. The change in the total amount of redistribution often differed substantially from the change in redistribution arising because of policy changes. Indeed, in several countries, the change in total distribution was much larger than the change in redistribution deriving from policy changes. Governments often did not compensate for the decline in redistribution driven by the structure of the system. For example, Romania exhibited the third-highest increase in redistribution arising from changes in taxes and transfers, but this was not sufficient to offset the decline in redistribution caused by changes in the underlying structure of the system. In a few countries, including Hungary and Lithuania and, to a minor extent, Bulgaria, the Czech Republic, and Poland, changes in tax and transfer policies actually reduced the amount of redistribution.

Changes in transfer policies did not have a significant positive impact on the change in redistribution in 2007–14. Figure 3.20 shows the share of pensions, means-tested benefits, non–means-tested benefits, and other transfers in gross income—defined as market income, plus total transfers—in selected countries for each income decile in 2007 and 2014 and a counterfactual scenario measuring the changes in the incidence of transfers that would have prevailed in 2014 if the benefits rules had remained as in 2007.[13] In Ireland and Romania, which had the largest increases in redistribution arising because of changes in policies in Western Europe and Eastern Europe, respectively, the share of transfers in gross incomes rose among the poorest deciles in 2007–14. However, the counterfactual distribution overlaps with the distribution observed in 2014, which implies that the incidence of transfers in 2014 is similar to the one that would have been observed if the 2007 system had still been in place. In France, despite policy changes that could have had a strong redistributive impact among the bottom deciles, the incidence of transfers declined slightly at the bottom (see annex 3C, figure 3C.2). There is no substantial difference between the counterfactual and the observed scenario in 2014. In Hungary, which exhibited the largest decline in redistribution induced by changes in tax and benefit policies, the incidence of transfers fell among the middle class and the top deciles and declined even more compared with the counterfactual scenario, which assumes that the tax-benefit system was the same as in 2007.

FIGURE 3.20 Incidence of transfers on gross income, by decile, 2007 and 2014

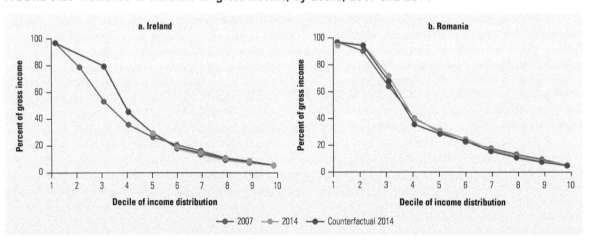

Source: Calculations based on data of EUROMOD H1.0+ (Tax-Benefit Microsimulation Model for the European Union) (database), Institute for Social and Economic Research, University of Essex, Colchester, UK, https://www.euromod.ac.uk/2017/12/13/euromod-h10-released.
Note: The blue line indicates the average incidence of transfers (means-tested, non–means-tested benefits, and pensions), calculated as a share of gross income in 2007. The green line indicates the same variable in 2014. The yellow line shows the counterfactual rate in 2014, assuming the tax and transfer system had been the same as in 2007.

By contrast, changes in tax policy and policies on social insurance contributions had an important impact on redistribution in some countries in Europe and Central Asia. Ireland is one of the few countries in the region in which the richest groups experienced a larger increase in taxes and social insurance contributions relative to the poorest groups (figure 3.21).

FIGURE 3.21 Impact of taxes and social insurance contributions on gross income, by decile

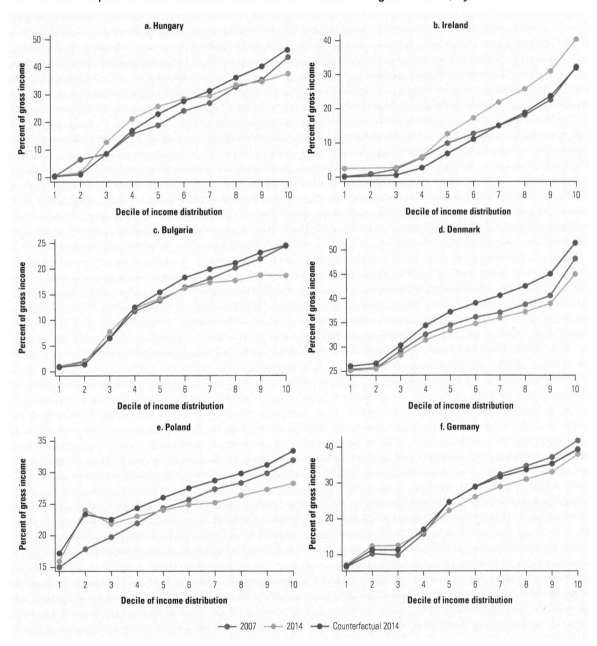

Source: Calculations based on data of EUROMOD H1.0+ (Tax-Benefit Microsimulation Model for the European Union) (database), Institute for Social and Economic Research, University of Essex, Colchester, UK, https://www.euromod.ac.uk/2017/12/13/euromod-h10-released.
Note: The blue line indicates the average incidence of transfers (means-tested, non–means-tested benefits, and pensions), calculated as a share of gross income in 2007. The green line indicates the same variable in 2014. The yellow line shows the counterfactual rate in 2014, assuming the tax and transfer system had been the same as in 2007.

Furthermore, the incidence of taxes was much greater in 2014 than in the counterfactual scenario; so, active policy changes seem to have led to greater progressivity. These trends might explain why Ireland is the top performer in the EU in the influence of policy change on redistribution. In several countries in which the size of the redistribution fell because of changes introduced through policies, including Bulgaria, Denmark, Hungary, and Poland, the incidence of taxes declined among the richest deciles much more than among the poorest ones. Moreover, tax incidence in these countries narrowed much more than if the rules on taxes and benefits had remained the same in 2014 as in 2007 (see information on individual countries in annex 3C, figure 3C.1).

These examples show that active changes in tax policies had a greater impact than changes in transfers on changes in redistribution and, in several countries, led to less rather than more redistribution.

Policy Changes Had a Mixed Effect on Income Distribution across Groups

This subsection considers how policy changes and the compensations automatically generated through the tax and transfer systems affected changes in income distribution across groups defined by age, occupation, or household type. The goal is to provide insights on how tax and transfer systems influenced the rise in distributional tensions described in chapter 2. Kanbur (2018) points out that, even if vertical redistribution improves, the distributional tensions among groups may worsen. If groups are defined by variables other than income, for example, age, and if these groups do not necessarily correlate perfectly with income, changes in vertical redistribution may not act in the same direction as changes in horizontal redistribution.

The Impact across Age-Groups

The impact of tax systems on the distribution of income across age-groups differs across Europe and Central Asia. The difference between the incomes of the young and the middle-aged is larger in Southern and Western Europe than in Central and Eastern Europe. In any progressive tax system, this would result in higher average tax rates among middle-age groups than among younger groups. This pattern is reproduced across Europe: the average tax rate across age-groups has the shape of an inverted U—low for the young and the elderly, high for the middle-aged—in most of Southern and Western Europe. The same profile is less steep in Central and Eastern Europe, where the elderly enjoy particularly low average tax rates. (See annex 3C, figure 3C.3, for the complete set of figures by country.)

In recent years, tax systems have been the least favorable for the young in Central and Eastern Europe, while they have compensated for the deterioration in incomes among younger generations in Southern and Western Europe. Several countries in Central and Eastern Europe have introduced flat-rate income tax systems in the last decade. The introduction of these systems has negatively affected particularly the young, while tax rates have been reduced among the middle-aged. This is illustrated by the case of

Hungary (figure 3.22, panel a). The average tax rate and the average social contribution among the 18–24 age-group jumped from around 26 percent in 2007 to 34 percent in 2014. The counterfactual simulation shows that, under the former pre–flat-rate tax system, the average rate among the 18–24 age-group in 2014 would have been 28 percent. Thus, the new system resulted in an increase of close to 7 percentage points in the average tax rate among the young. A similar calculation shows that the new system lowered the tax rate and social contributions among the 45–54 age-group to 35 percent from the counterfactual's 39 percent. These types of changes—beneficial for the middle-aged, but hard on the young—are also found in Bulgaria, Latvia, Lithuania, and Poland. Thus, in Central and Eastern Europe, market forces have resulted in improved prospects for younger generations, but tax policy changes have penalized these generations, potentially creating a source of distributional tension.

The opposite occurred in Southern and Western Europe, as illustrated by Greece (figure 3.22, panel b). Average tax rates rose between 2007 and 2014 among all age-groups, but particularly the middle-aged. The young saw almost no increase in the average tax rate affecting them, while the elderly experienced a rise that put them at the same level as the young. The counterfactual simulation shows that tax policy changes were the principle reason for the effective increase in tax rates. Cyprus, Portugal, and Spain followed a similar pattern. Because the younger generations in Southern and Western Europe suffered a decline in incomes with respect to the middle-aged and the elderly, the changes in the tax system partly offset the negative outcomes deriving from the market, potentially easing distributional tensions.

FIGURE 3.22 Tax changes: progressive in Southern Europe, regressive in Eastern Europe
Average tax rate and average social contribution on gross income, by age-group, 2007–14

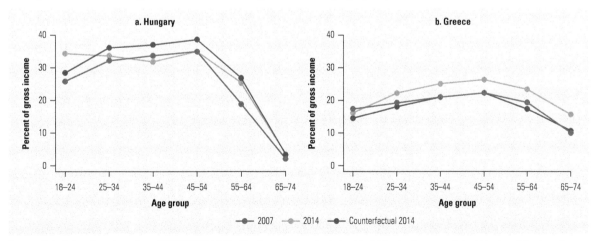

Source: Calculations based on data of EUROMOD H1.0+ (Tax-Benefit Microsimulation Model for the European Union) (database), Institute for Social and Economic Research, University of Essex, Colchester, UK, https://www.euromod.ac.uk/2017/12/13/euromod-h10-released.
Note: The blue line indicates the average tax rate and average social contribution in 2007 calculated as a share of gross income. The green line indicates the same variable in 2014. The yellow line indicates the counterfactual rate in 2014 had the tax and transfer system been the same then as in 2007.

Policy changes in Europe had little impact on the distribution of transfers across age-groups. As in the case of the share of transfers in incomes across income deciles, which remained roughly unchanged in 2007–14 (see above), the age profile associated with the incidence of transfers changed little over the period. Moreover, most of the observed change seems to be explained by changes in market incomes because the counterfactual simulation, wherein the transfer system of 2007 is applied to the market income structure of 2014, coincides closely in almost all countries with the actual outcome in 2014 (see annex 3C, figure 3C.4). Thus, changes in the incidence of transfers across age-groups in 2007–14 were not caused by changes in transfer systems, but by the compensations automatically generated by the systems in a context of changes in market incomes.

The Impact across Occupations

Tax systems in Europe and Central Asia are progressive across occupations. The least well-paid occupations, nonroutine manual-task–intensive occupations, pay the lowest average tax rates, while the most well-paid-occupations, nonroutine cognitive-task–intensive occupations, pay the highest average tax rates; routine-task–intensive occupations fall midway. In Germany and Spain, the difference between the highest and the lowest average tax rate in 2014 was around 10 percentage points, while, in Poland, the corresponding difference was closer to 4 percentage points, in line with the relatively flat tax profile of that country (figure 3.23; annex 3C, figure 3C.5).

However, the role of tax systems in the deterioration of incomes across occupational groups has been mixed. Germany, Poland, and Spain experienced job polarization, where market forces worsened the earnings of individuals in nonroutine manual-task–intensive occupations and routine-task–intensive occupations, while raising the relative wages paid to people in nonroutine cognitive-task–intensive occupations. In Germany, the average tax rate fell slightly among the three occupation groups, but more so among the most well-paid occupational group, workers in nonroutine cognitive-task–intensive occupations. The regressive nature of this outcome is a reflection of policy changes and market forces pulling in opposite directions. Policy changes alone would have resulted in a 3 percentage point reduction in average tax rates among workers in both routine and nonroutine manual-task–intensive occupations and a decline of 1 percentage point among workers in nonroutine cognitive-task–intensive occupations. Thus, policy changes partially offset the decline generated by market forces in the progressivity of Germany's tax structure across occupational groups. In this sense, the occupational groups negatively affected by job polarization appear to have been actively compensated by the tax system. Belgium, the Czech Republic, Finland, and Sweden also show a similar pattern.

In Poland, by contrast, policy changes exacerbated the decline in the progressivity of the tax system. Similar to the German experience, the average tax rate decreased among the three occupational groups. Workers in nonroutine cognitive-task–intensive occupations experienced the largest decrease. Unlike Germany, the counterfactual simulation shows that active changes in the tax system exacerbated the trend in Poland. Thus, changes in the tax system resulted in a decline by 4 percentage points in the tax rate among workers in nonroutine

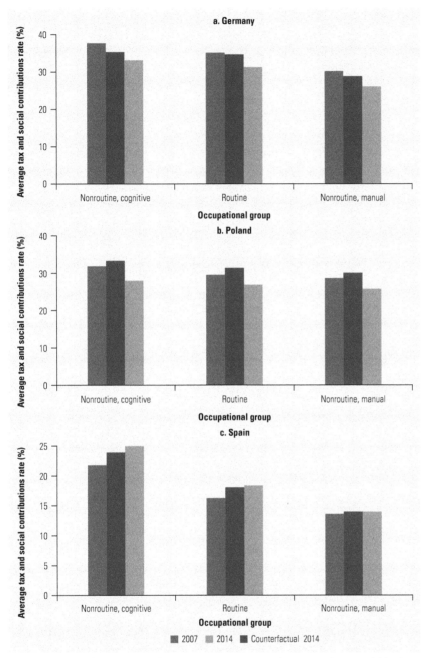

FIGURE 3.23

Differences in the reactions of tax systems to job polarization
Average tax rates and average social contributions, by occupational group, 2007–14

Source: Calculations based on data of EUROMOD H1.0+ (Tax-Benefit Microsimulation Model for the European Union) (database), Institute for Social and Economic Research, University of Essex, Colchester, UK, https://www.euromod.ac.uk/2017/12/13/euromod-h10-released.
Note: Occupational groups: nonroutine cognitive-task–intensive occupations (International Standard Classification of Occupations [ISCO] 08, major groups 1, 2, 3); routine-task–intensive occupations (ISCO 08, major groups 4, 7, 8); nonroutine manual-task–intensive occupations (ISCO 08, major groups 5, 6, 9).

cognitive-task–intensive occupations, a 3 percentage point decrease in the tax rate among workers in routine-task–intensive occupations, and a drop of only around 1 percentage point in the tax rate among workers in nonroutine manual-task–intensive occupations. Rather than alleviating the distributional tensions emerging from occupational change, the tax system in Poland appears to have added to the tensions. The same is true of tax systems in Bulgaria and Hungary.

In Spain, changes in the impact of the tax system on the distribution of income across occupational categories mainly reflect an automatic, market-driven reaction in the system. The average tax rate among workers in nonroutine cognitive-task–intensive occupations and routine-task–intensive occupations rose by nearly 2 percentage points in 2007–14, while the rate among workers in nonroutine manual-task–intensive occupations remained stable. Changes in tax policies do not explain any of the changes observed in the tax rate among the losers of job polarization, and they explain only half the increase in tax rates among workers in nonroutine cognitive-task–intensive occupations, the winners of occupational change. The reaction of the tax system to the policy changes appears to operate in the direction of somewhat alleviating the distributional tensions emerging from changes in the structure of occupations, but the policy changes did not contribute to this outcome. This pattern of automatic compensation is also evident in France, Romania, and Slovenia.

Policy changes in transfers have generated small, positive increases in transfers among workers in routine-task–intensive and nonroutine manual-task–intensive occupations (figure 3.24). Given that this analysis concerns workers who are employed, transfers make up only a small share of the gross income of these people. Over the sample of EU countries, the highest transfer values are found relative to nonroutine manual-task–intensive occupations in France, where transfers account for 12 percent of gross income. In Germany and Poland, policy changes in the transfer system increased the amount of transfers to workers in nonroutine, manual-task–intensive occupations by close to 1 percentage point of gross income. In Spain, policy changes explain practically none of the rise in the share of transfers in gross income across all occupational groups, that is, the change derives almost entirely from the automatic reaction of the system in the provision of compensations for changes in market incomes. Most other European countries show a similar pattern of small, positive policy-driven increases in transfers to the losers of occupational change (see annex 3C, figure 3C.6).

Most other European countries have shown small, positive policy-driven increases in transfers among workers in routine-task–intensive and nonroutine manual-task–intensive occupations. In Cyprus, for instance, workers in nonroutine manual-task–intensive jobs saw transfers increase from 8 percent to 14 percent of gross income in 2007–14. Of this 6 percentage point rise, almost 4 points are exclusively explained by policy changes in the transfer system. Only Hungary and Ireland have seen policy-driven declines in transfers.

Thus, the losers of job polarization—the shrinking routine-task–intensive occupations and the less well-paid nonroutine manual-task–intensive occupations—received a small compensation through transfers, but not much through tax systems, which, in some cases, even added to the tax pressure on these occupations relative to the winners of occupational change.

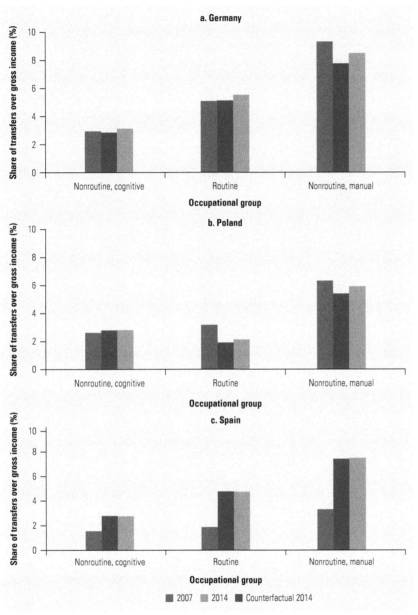

FIGURE 3.24
The limited role of policy changes in transfer systems across occupations
Total transfers as a share of gross incomes, by occupational group, 2007–14

Source: Calculations based on data of EUROMOD H1.0+ (Tax-Benefit Microsimulation Model for the European Union) (database), Institute for Social and Economic Research, University of Essex, Colchester, UK, https://www.euromod.ac.uk/2017/12/13/euromod-h10-released.
Note: Occupational groups: nonroutine cognitive-task–intensive occupations (International Standard Classification of Occupations [ISCO] 08, major groups 1, 2, 3); routine-task–intensive occupations (ISCO 08, major groups 4, 7, 8); nonroutine manual-task–intensive occupations (ISCO 08, major groups 5, 6, 9).

The Impact across Household Groups

Tax and transfer policies may also affect the distribution of income across types (or different groups) of households. Chapter 2 shows that the middle deciles of the income distribution have become more heavily populated by pensioners, while dual earner households are increasingly found at the top, and the traditional two-adult, one-earner male breadwinner households are now mostly found in the bottom deciles. Tax and transfer policies may benefit some types of households more than others. This subsection examines three types of households: (1) those consisting of adults entirely dependent on transfers for income; (2) those with two adults or more, only one of whom receives labor market income, while the others have no income (single-earner households); those with the typical male breadwinner household model; and (3) those with two adults, both of whom receive labor market earnings (the dual earner households).

Average tax rates across these household types differ between Western Europe and Central and Eastern Europe. For example, in all countries, transfer-dependent households enjoy the lowest average tax rate, but, in Central and Eastern Europe, this rate is zero or close to zero, while, in Southern and Western Europe, it is at least 10 percent. In both subregions, dual earner households have the highest average tax rates (see annex 3C, figure 3C.7). As in the case of age-groups, the difference in these average tax rates may not derive from differences in system characteristics, but different underlying income profiles. Households dependent on transfer income may be in lower income deciles in Central and Eastern Europe than in the rest of Europe, and this may be a reason for the difference in average tax rates. An analysis of changes can nonetheless provide some information on the causes of these static differences.

The impact of changes in tax policy on changes in income distribution across households have differed by country, but they have mostly benefited households dependent on transfers or dual earner households. For example, Belgium, Greece, and Poland had similar tax profiles in 2007. Average tax rates were lowest among transfer-dependent households, followed by two-adult, single-earner households (figure 3.25). In 2014, this profile was roughly the same, although average tax rates rose in Greece, but declined in Belgium and Poland. To the extent that single-earner households tended to face the greatest increase in vulnerability in recent years, understanding how tax systems reacted to this is relevant. Changes in tax policy in Belgium benefited transfer-dependent households, which tended to face a smaller rise in vulnerability; their tax rates would have been 5 percentage points higher had the system not been changed. Changes in tax policy in Finland, Ireland, and Latvia also benefited transfer-dependent households the most. In Greece, where all household types saw the tax rate go up, the size of the policy-driven increase was smallest among single-earner households (5 percentage points) and highest among dual earner households (more than 6 percentage points). Croatia and Lithuania were the only other countries in which single-earner households benefited the most in relative terms from changes in the tax system. In Poland, dual earner households reaped the largest benefits from changes in tax policy. Had the system not been changed, their average tax rate and average social contributions would have risen from around 29 percent in 2007 to over 30 percent in 2014, but system changes brought these down to close to 25 percent. As in Poland, tax system changes benefited in relative terms mostly dual earner households in Bulgaria, the Czech Republic, Hungary, and the United Kingdom. Overall, of the 27 EU countries on which the analysis was carried out, policy-driven changes in taxes benefited dual earner households in 13; they benefited transfer-dependent households in 11; and they benefited single-earner households in only 3, the ones facing the highest expansion in vulnerability.

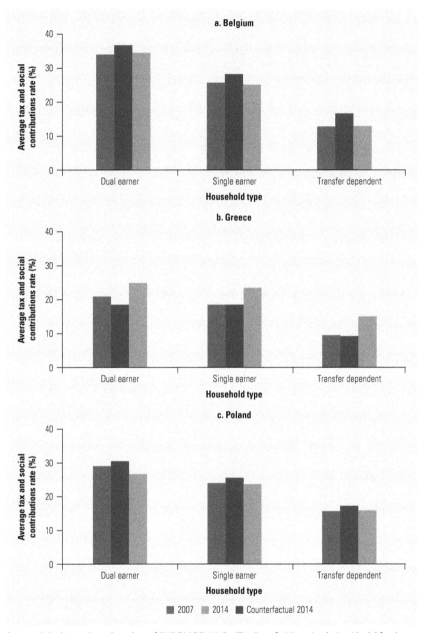

FIGURE 3.25

Three examples of changes in average tax rates by household type
Average tax rate and average social contributions 2007–14

Source: Calculations based on data of EUROMOD H1.0+ (Tax-Benefit Microsimulation Model for the European Union) (database), Institute for Social and Economic Research, University of Essex, Colchester, UK, https://www.euromod.ac.uk/2017/12/13/euromod-h10-released.
Note: The counterfactual scenario corresponds to the average rates that would have applied to each type of household in 2014 had the tax and transfer system been the same as in 2007.

There have been no significant changes in the profile of transfer incidence across the three household types. In all cases, the rates of transfer incidence are lowest among dual earner households (around 10 percent of gross income), while, among single-earners, they hover between 20 and 30 percent, and variation is limited across countries (see annex 3C, figure 3C.8).

The overall picture that emerges from the analysis of the effect of tax and transfer systems across household types in Europe is worrying. Changes in policy benefited the households that had experienced the largest rise in vulnerability in only a few countries. Most of the changes benefited those households that enjoy a greater degree of economic security, because they rely on either multiple sources of labor market income or a steady flow of public transfers.

Limited Labor Mobility Affects the Opportunities in High-Productivity Areas

Low labor mobility limits people's ability to use their productive capacity to access jobs by moving to thriving areas. A key aspect of inequality of opportunity is that the access of individuals to employment opportunities may be limited by their place of residence. Thus, promoting the ability of workers to migrate within a country or abroad can reduce inequality of opportunity. Moreover, the movement of workers from lower-productivity agricultural jobs in the countryside to higher-productivity manufacturing and service jobs in towns and cities is critical to raising productivity in developing countries. However, labor mobility is lower in Europe and Central Asia than in other regions, and it is particularly low in the eastern part of Europe and Central Asia (figure 3.26). People in the eastern part of the region appear to have a low appetite for migration whether within a country or abroad.

FIGURE 3.26 Labor mobility is low in Europe and Central Asia

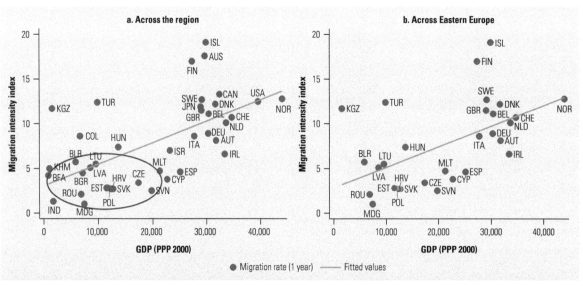

Sources: Bell et al. 2015; data of WDI (World Development Indicators) (database), World Bank, Washington, DC, http://data.worldbank.org /products/wdi.
Note: Migration intensity refers to around 2000–05, and GDP per capita PPP is an average of 2000 and 2005. Recognizing the absence of a central repository of internal migration data, Bell et al. (2015) pioneered in compiling internal migration data across countries based on census data and developed a comparable migration intensity index for a single year (statistics on changes of address in the previous year) and for five years (statistics on changes of address over the previous five years), although the five-year migration intensity index involves few observations. GDP = gross domestic product; PPP = purchasing power parity. Yellow circle indicates most of the countries in Europe and Central Asia.

Nearly 70 percent of unemployed respondents in the 2016 Life in Transition Survey (LiTS) in the Czech Republic, Estonia, and Uzbekistan said they were not willing to move to find employment. In these countries, fewer than 5 percent of all respondents were willing to move abroad.

Policies may contribute to low labor mobility in the region by raising migration costs or by failing to tackle the market failures that lead to low labor mobility. Many other issues may also prevent individuals from migrating to improve their job prospects. These include, for example, lack of resources, lack of information about job opportunities, lack of relatives or friends in areas of potential migration who can help reduce transition costs (for instance, two-thirds of respondents in the 2016 round of the LiTS who planned to migrate internally within 12 months said they had friends or relatives in the places where they planned to move), the desire not to lose support networks in the current area of residence, or difficulties facing spouses and children in relocating.[14]

The high cost of living in urban areas in some countries in the region may reduce labor mobility. Earnings are highly concentrated around the minimum wage in many Eastern European countries. If wage differentials between rural and urban areas are smaller than housing cost differentials, the economic return to moving may be low or negative. Here, the minimum wage is used to represent wage levels, while approximate housing costs in urban areas are proxied by monthly rents in the capital city. Countries with low within-country mobility tend to show high rent-to-wage ratios, for example, the Czech Republic, Estonia, Poland, and Romania (figure 3.27). Underdeveloped credit markets and the lack of affordable social housing also deter internal mobility, especially in countries with high homeownership rates, such as the Czech Republic, the Slovak Republic, and Ukraine (OECD 2004a, 2004b; World Bank 2015; see box 3.3 for an analysis on Kazakhstan).

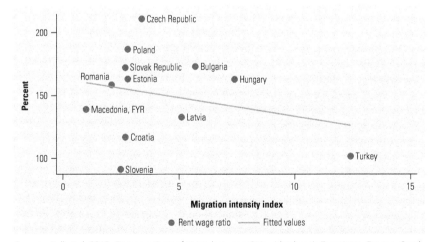

FIGURE 3.27

High housing costs in urban areas inhibit internal migration

Sources: Bell et al. 2015; Compare Cost of Living between Cities (database), Expatistan, Prague, Czech Republic, https://www.expatistan.com/cost-of-living.Expatistan.com; Global Housing Watch (database), International Monetary Fund, Washington, DC, http://www.imf.org/external/research/housing/.
Note: Housing costs refer to monthly housing rents for 85 square meters (furnished) in normal areas in each country's capital. Wage refers to the minimum wage.

BOX 3.3 Housing and Labor Mobility Constraints in Kazakhstan

Recognizing that cities are hubs of economic opportunity and prosperity, urbanization is one of the seven major systemic reforms envisioned in the Kazakhstan 2025 strategy (World Bank 2018b). But the pace of urbanization in Kazakhstan is slow. Internal migration flows in Kazakhstan in 2010–15 accounted for an average of only about 1.7 percent–2.3 percent of the population. In Canada, the comparable share is 14.0 percent; in Japan, it is 4.0 percent; and in the United States, it is 11.0 percent.

Recent research identifies two key constraints to urbanization in the country: the high cost of living in cities and a near absence of a rental housing market. Primarily because of the high cost of housing, the cost of living in Almaty, the largest city, and Astana, the capital, is 190 percent and 240 percent, respectively, of the national average. Real housing prices in Astana were three times higher in 2016 than in 2001, and prices more than quadrupled in Almaty over the same period (map B3.3.1). Along with significantly higher food costs, this means that Kazakhstan's cities are unaffordable for many rural residents who wish to relocate to places where job opportunities may be greater. At around 95 percent,

MAP B3.3.1 Housing price index
National average = 1

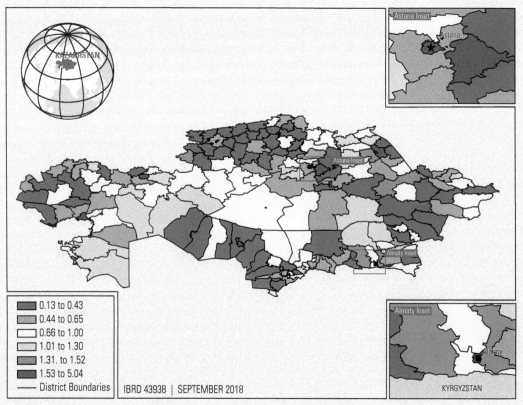

0.13 to 0.43	
0.44 to 0.65	
0.66 to 1.00	
1.01 to 1.30	
1.31. to 1.52	
1.53 to 5.04	
—— District Boundaries	IBRD 43938	SEPTEMBER 2018

Source: World Bank calculations based on household budget survey, Kazakhstan.

(continued)

BOX 3.3 **Housing and Labor Mobility Constraints in Kazakhstan** *(continued)*

Kazakhstan also has one of the highest homeownership rates in the world, but the rental market is small and targets mostly upper-income residents (figure B3.3.1). In the absence of affordable rental housing, most potential internal migrants in Kazakhstan are not able to move to urban areas for work.

A large body of research suggests that these kinds of barriers lead to exclusion of lower-income people and restrain economic growth. Disproportionate increases in housing prices can severely limit population flows to highly productive locations and sectors. In other countries, the rising cost of urban housing has been one of the primary causes of greater inequality.

FIGURE B3.3.1 Share of owner-occupied housing

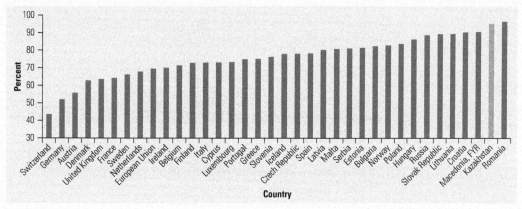

Source: World Bank calculations based on household budget surveys.

Cumbersome population registration requirements in some countries deter people from moving from lagging regions to leading ones. A Ukraine survey shows that the population registration system there is a key barrier to internal mobility (Koettl et al. 2014). In Kazakhstan, newcomers are required to submit a document proving that they have housing of at least 15 square meters for each resident and a rental agreement. Homeowners often may not provide such agreements to avoid taxes. In Albania, there was an influx of people to the capital and coastal cities after registration regulations were relaxed. The Albania case shows that less strict registration requirements enable people to move. In other cases, newcomers who do not register often lose eligibility for social benefits, including unemployment benefits, health care, and education, and, if they work, they must pay income taxes in the new jurisdiction. Income taxes, combined with potential forgone benefits, could reach up to around 90 percent of gross labor income among low-wage or part-time earners in the Czech Republic, Latvia, Lithuania, and Slovenia, where labor mobility is generally low. In Ukraine, the social benefits linked to proper residential registration discourage people who might otherwise relocate (Koettl et al. 2014).

The inadequate provision of education in rural areas may also be a barrier to mobility. Two issues are relevant. First, since the onset of the transition to a market economy, inequality in the caliber of education widened between rural and urban areas in countries in Eastern Europe. This has led youth to move to urban areas for a better education, as in Romania in recent years. Youth who cannot afford to migrate thus may continue to receive education of lower quality, which eventually hobbles them in meeting the demands of job markets in urban areas, which offer more jobs. Second, educational attainment generally tends to be lower in rural areas. Among the unemployed in Serbia, those with low educational attainment are less willing than those with higher educational attainment to relocate to find jobs. Individuals with low educational attainment represent about a third of the country's unemployed. This suggests that there is a need for active labor market policies that do more than provide passive mobility support. This might include transportation and relocation subsidies, as in Bulgaria. The policies should facilitate active employment services, subsidized on-the-job training and vocational training, paired with job search services.

Annex 3A. Decomposition Analysis: Drivers of Change in Redistribution

The European Union Tax-Benefit Microsimulation Model EUROMOD

The redistribution shown in figure 3.9 has been defined as the difference between the Gini index calculated on market incomes and the Gini index based on disposable incomes at a particular time *t*, as follows:

$$Redistribution_t = \left[Gini^{market} - Gini^{disposable} \right]_t \tag{3A.1}$$

This difference is a measure of the redistributive effectiveness of taxes and transfers at a given time. The larger this difference, the larger the impact of taxes and transfers on the reduction in inequality in market incomes. Market incomes include gross labor incomes, earnings from employment and self-employment (both permanent and temporary or irregular types of jobs), capital income (interest, dividends, profit, and so on), investment income, income from property, and private pension income. Disposable income equals market income, plus transfers (including public pensions, means-tested benefits, and non–means-tested benefits), less direct taxes and social insurance contributions (among employees and the self-employed). Direct taxes include, for example, personal income taxes, taxes on capital dividends and interest, and property taxes. Indirect taxes (for instance, consumption taxes and value added taxes) are excluded from the analysis. The Gini coefficients for market income; market income, plus pensions; and disposable income among countries of the European Union (EU) have been calculated using the microsimulation model EUROMOD.[15]

The analysis of the changes in redistribution in chapter 3 is based on the EU-wide tax-benefit static microsimulation model EUROMOD. EUROMOD simulates universal and targeted cash benefits, direct taxes, and social insurance contributions in the EU, based on the rules on taxes and benefits in each country and on the information available in the underlying input datasets. Components of tax-benefit systems that cannot be simulated, for example, the components depending on prior contributions or unobserved characteristics, are taken directly from the data, along with information on original incomes, that is, incomes before taxes and transfers. The model has been validated both at the microlevel and the macrolevel and tested across numerous applications. It is a consolidated tool widely used by policy makers and academics in distributional analysis of taxes and transfers and in the simulation of policy changes within and across EU countries. (See Sutherland and Figari 2013 for a comprehensive review.) Input data are typically harmonized based on either the EU-SILC User Database or the national EU-SILC surveys.[16] For the United Kingdom, the Family Resources Survey is used.[17] Details on which taxes and transfers are simulated and how and on which are taken from the data are available for each country in EUROMOD Country Reports.[18] These reports are updated annually. They also include relevant information on macro-validation statistics (for instance, the extent to which tax and benefit data included in the model match aggregate administrative data on benefit expenditure and the revenues from direct taxes).

EUROMOD enables the computation of the disposable incomes of individuals under different scenarios, taking account of the operation of tax-benefit systems and the way these interact with market incomes and personal or household characteristics. In this chapter, the underlying microdata for almost all countries are taken from EU-SILC 2008 and EU-SILC 2015. This means that the income reference years are generally 2007 for the earliest period considered and 2014 for the latest period of the analysis.[19] Indeed, the most recent tax-benefit system considered corresponds to 2014, while the earliest corresponds to 2007. In the EUROMOD jargon, 2007 and 2014 represent baseline years wherein reference income year and tax-benefit rules coincide, generating the best combination among input data, income year, and tax-benefit system. All simulations are carried out based on the tax-benefit rules in place on June 30 of the given policy year.

Decomposing Changes in Redistribution Using Counterfactual Simulations

A decomposition method proposed by Bourguignon and Ferreira (2005) makes possible a breakdown of the change in the size of redistribution over time into two components. The first component captures the change in market income inequality, discounted by the change in disposable income that would have occurred if the tax-benefit system had remained constant and only market income had changed. This component therefore isolates the effects of market forces in the change in redistribution. The second component captures the change in the redistribution that would have occurred if only the tax-benefit system had changed and the level of market income observed at the end of the period were kept constant.

To implement the decomposition, the Gini coefficient is first defined as a function of the distribution of income. The Gini coefficient of market income is a function of the distribution of market income (3A.2), and the Gini coefficient is a function of the distribution of disposable income (3A.3).

$$Gini_t^{market} = G\left(f\left(y_t^{market}\right)\right) \tag{3A.2}$$

$$Gini_t^{disposable} = G\left(f\left(y_t^{disposable}\right)\right) \tag{3A.3}$$

Disposable income is a function of market income and the tax and transfer system at a given time. So, equation 3A.3 can be rewritten as a function of the joint distribution of market income and the tax and transfer system, TB_t, as follows:

$$Gini_t^{disposable} = G\left(f\left(y_t^{market}, TB_t\right)\right) \tag{3A.4}$$

The redistribution at a given time is now defined as the difference between the Gini coefficient of the distribution of market income and the Gini coefficient of the distribution of disposable income:

$$Redistribution_t = Gini_t^{market} - Gini_t^{disposable} \tag{3A.5}$$

The change over time is simply the difference between redistribution in one period and the redistribution in another period, as follows:

$$\Delta\, Redistribution_{t_1-t_0} = \\ \left[Gini_{t_1}^{market} - Gini_{t_1}^{disposable}\right] - \left[Gini_{t_0}^{market} - Gini_{t_0}^{disposable}\right] \tag{3A.6}$$

The change in redistribution over time can be rewritten as the change in the Gini coefficient of market income over time and the change in the Gini coefficient of disposable income over time:

$$\Delta Redistribution_{t_1-t_0} = \\ \left[Gini_{t_1}^{market} - Gini_{t_0}^{market}\right] - \left[Gini_{t_1}^{disposable} - Gini_{t_0}^{disposable}\right] \tag{3A.7}$$

Equations 3A.2 and 3A.4 can be placed in equation 3A.7 to decompose further the change in the Gini coefficient of disposable income over time, as follows:

$$\Delta Redistribution_{t_1-t_0} = \left[G\left(f\left(y_{t_1}^{market}\right)\right) - G\left(f\left(y_{t_0}^{market}\right)\right)\right] \\ - \left[G\left(f\left(y_{t_1}^{market}, TB_{t_1}\right)\right) - G\left(f\left(y_{t_0}^{market}, TB_{t_0}\right)\right)\right] \tag{3A.8}$$

The change in the Gini coefficient of disposable income—the second term in brackets in equation 3A.8—will then depend on the change deriving from the changes in market income and the change deriving from changes in the tax and transfer system. In this sense, the change in the Gini coefficient of disposable income over time can be further decomposed into two components by making use of counterfactual simulations (Bourguignon and Ferreira 2005), as follows:

$$
\Delta Redistribution_{t_1-t_0} = \left[G\left(f\left(y_{t_1}^{market} \right) \right) - G\left(f\left(y_{t_0}^{market} \right) \right) \right]
$$

$$
- \left[G\left(f\left(y_{t_1}^{market}, TB_{t_0} \right) \right) - G\left(f\left(y_{t_0}^{market}, TB_{t_0} \right) \right) \right] \quad (3A.9)
$$

$$
- \left[G\left(f\left(y_{t_1}^{market}, TB_{t_1} \right) \right) - G\left(f\left(y_{t_1}^{market}, TB_{t_0} \right) \right) \right]
$$

The first term corresponds to the change in the Gini coefficient of market income. The second term corresponds to the difference in the Gini coefficient of disposable income arising because of changes in market income, that is, the change in the Gini coefficient of disposable income that would have been observed if the system had remained unchanged and only market income had changed over the period. The third term corresponds to the change in the Gini coefficient of disposable income arising from changes in the tax and transfer system, that is, the change in the Gini coefficient of disposable income that would have been observed if market income had remained unchanged and only the tax and transfer system had changed during the period. This decomposition of the change in the Gini coefficient of disposable income can be performed using two sets of counterfactuals: one in which the market component is calculated using the system in t_1 and the system component using market income in t_1 and another one in which the market component is calculated using the system in t_0 and the system component using market income in t_0. The results of the decomposition using either of the sets of counterfactuals will be different because this decomposition method is path dependent. To control for this, a common practice in the literature is to take the average of both decompositions for each component.

From equation 3A.9, one may see that a change in the distribution of market income from t_0 to t_1 affects the size of redistribution in two ways: (1) it affects the Gini coefficient of market income (the first term in brackets in 3A.9), and (2) it affects the Gini coefficient of disposable income absent any changes in the tax and transfer system (the second term in brackets in 3A.9). In this sense, the total effect of a change in the distribution of market income is the sum of the first two terms in brackets in equation 3A.9. The remaining term accounts for the changes in redistribution derived from changes in the tax and transfer system. Summing up, this yields:

$$
\Delta Redistribution_{t_1-t_0} =
$$

$$
\left[G\left(f\left(y_{t_1}^{market} \right) \right) - G\left(f\left(y_{t_0}^{market} \right) \right) \right]
$$

$$
- \left[G\left(f\left(y_{t_1}^{market}, TB_{t_0} \right) \right) - G\left(f\left(y_{t_0}^{market}, TB_{t_0} \right) \right) \right]
$$

$$
- \left[G\left(f\left(y_{t_1}^{market}, TB_{t_1} \right) \right) - G\left(f\left(y_{t_1}^{market}, TB_{t_0} \right) \right) \right]
$$

Change in redistribution

Market component

+

Policies component

Obtaining Counterfactual Income Distributions Using EUROMOD

To isolate the impact of the tax-benefit system on changes in disposable income versus market income over time, the following counterfactual exercise is run. Assume that $y_t^{disposable}$ is the distribution of disposable income in year t. A counterfactual distribution of disposable income in year t, denoted by $y_{t,t-j}^{*\,disposable}$, is calculated that would have been obtained if the country had kept the same tax-benefit system in place as in year $t-j$.

The distribution of disposable income is defined by a function $h()$:

$$y_t^{disposable} = h\left(y_t^{market}, TB_t, X_t\right), \qquad (3A.10)$$

where y_t^{market} is the market incomes; TB_t the tax-benefit rules; and X_t the population characteristics (sociodemographics, labor market, economic activity, and so on).

The counterfactual distribution is given by

$$y_{t,t-j}^{*\,disposable} = h\left(y_t^{market}, TB_{t-j}, X_t\right), \qquad (3A.11)$$

that is, the counterfactual distribution is obtained by employing the tax-benefit system from $t-j$ to the market incomes and population characteristics in year t.[20]

Implementation Steps in EUROMOD

The construction of the observed and counterfactual distributions is implemented for all EU countries using EUROMOD H1.0+ and the most recent EUROMOD data files.[21] For most countries, the observed distribution of disposable income in $t = 2014$ is compared with the counterfactual distribution constructed with the tax-benefit system in $t-j = 2007$.

The implementation is conducted in the following steps:
- The EUROMOD system cc_{t-j} (for example, at_2007 in the case of Austria) is copied, denoted as cc_{t-j}^*.
- The best fit data set is chosen to match the data set used by cc_t (at_2014), that is, system cc_{t-j}^* and system cc_t use the same data set.[22]
- To omit erroneous uprating, the reference year of system cc_{t-j}^* is set equal to the reference year of cc_t.
- Similarly, the exchange rate and currency parameters of cc_{t-j}^* are set equal to those of cc_t. This is relevant if there are currency changes between years $t-j$ and t.
- The cc_{t-j}^* and cc_t systems are run. There are no further changes in cc_{t-j} beforehand.

Annex 3B. Policy Changes That Have Contributed to Redistribution

In Italy, a number of policy changes were introduced between 2007 and 2014 that may explain the large redistributive effects of taxes and transfers: (1) the introduction of the new unemployment insurance scheme, the Assicurazione Sociale per l'impiego (social employment insurance), in 2013, renamed la Nuova Assicurazione Sociale per l'Impiego (the new social employment insurance) in 2015, which was designed to achieve greater coverage among workers who have lost their jobs involuntarily, including temporary workers with flexible contracts, and providing more generous replacement rates compared with the existing indennità di disoccupazione (unemployment benefit); (2) the introduction of a solidarity contribution on top incomes among employees earning above €300,000 a year, high-wage public sector employees, and high-income pensioners with labor (pension) income above €90,000 a year, equal to 3 percent of taxable income above the respective thresholds; (3) the introduction in 2014 of an in-work income tax credit (Bonus 80 euro) for employees, workers with temporary contracts, and recipients of unemployment benefits, with annual incomes between €8,174 and €24,600; and (4) an increase in the tax rate on capital dividends and interest on bonds, from 12.5 percent to 26.0 percent, and a rise in the tax rate on income from private pensions, from 11.0 percent to 20.0 percent.

In France, policies introduced during the period may explain the increase in redistribution deriving purely from changes in taxes and transfers. First, in 2009, the means-tested guaranteed minimum income (GMI) and the single-parent benefit were replaced by solidarity labor income. The GMI was not compatible with labor income because 100 percent of the income from employment was deducted from the amount of the GMI. In the case of solidarity labor income, only 38 percent of labor income is deducted from the benefit amount. The GMI was considered to be susceptible to poverty traps and was blamed for creating work disincentives. Solidarity labor income was designed to allow a beneficiary to combine social assistance with income from work up to a threshold, after which the beneficiary would lose eligibility. Other policies potentially leading to greater redistribution are the exceptional contribution on high incomes introduced in 2013 for incomes above €250,000 (€500,000 in the case of couples), and the abolishment of a tax cap or tax shield in 2011, according to which taxes paid by individuals could not exceed 50 percent of their income.

In Latvia, the positive redistributive effects attributable purely to policy changes may probably be explained by a series of policies introduced to mitigate the effects of the 2008–09 financial crisis, including the extension in coverage of the GMI benefit, the introduction of large public works schemes for the unemployed, and the extension of the coverage of unemployment benefits.

In Hungary, one of the most likely factors explaining the reduction in the size of the redistribution as a result of changes in tax-benefit policies was the introduction of flat-rate taxation in 2013. In 2007, the personal income tax schedule had two brackets: for incomes below Ft 1.7 million (around US$9,290 at the time), the tax rate was 18 percent, and, above that threshold, the tax rate was 40 percent. In 2014, however, the unique income tax rate was set at 16 percent. This change implied a greater reduction in the average tax rate for high earners. For someone earning slightly above the threshold (for instance, US$15,000), the average tax rate would drop from 26.4 percent to 16.0 percent, while, for someone earning four times as much (say, US$60,000), the average tax rate would drop from 36.6 percent to 16.0 percent.

Annex 3C. The Impact of Taxes and Transfers on Redistribution

Using EUROMOD to build counterfactual scenarios, the analysis in this annex compares the incidence of taxes and transfers across income groups and other groups in the population in 2007 and the corresponding incidence in 2014 as a means of measuring the impact of changes in tax and transfer policies on redistribution in Europe.[23] The main counterfactual scenario consists of estimating the incidence of taxes and transfers across income groups and other groups in the population in 2014 as if tax and transfer policies had remained unchanged relative to the initial situation in 2007. Comparing this counterfactual with the initial situation facilitates an explanation of the changes in incidence that arise from changes in market incomes given that, in the counterfactual and the initial situation, tax and transfer policies are the same. Differences between the counterfactual and the final situation derive from changes in tax and transfers policies because market incomes are the same in the scenario and in the final year distributions.

The annex presents two set of figures. The first set, figures 3C.1 and 3C.2, assesses the impact of the changes in tax and transfer systems on vertical inequality. Thus, it considers how groups are affected by the redistribution system if these groups are formed according to income. The second set, figures 3C.3 to 3C.8, considers how redistribution systems affect groups that are formed according to nonincome characteristics, such as age and occupation. This second set assesses the impact on horizontal inequality.

Figure 3C.1 presents the incidence of tax and social security contributions, calculated as the share of taxes and social security contributions paid over gross income (market income, plus transfers) for each decile of equivalized household income under the three scenarios in the 27 countries considered here. The progressivity of the incidence of tax and social security contributions is a common feature. The shape of this progressivity varies, however. In some countries, the incidence curve is convex. that is, the marginal tax rate is rising, as in Cyprus, Denmark, France, Italy, and Spain, while, in others, it is concave, that is, the marginal tax rate is not increasing, as in Bulgaria, Estonia, Hungary, Latvia, Lithuania, and the Slovak Republic. Most Central and Eastern European countries have flat income tax systems, while the countries of Southern Europe and Western Europe have progressive income tax systems. The introduction of flat tax systems flattens the incidence curve, particularly at the top of the income distribution. This can be seen in the cases of Bulgaria and Hungary, which introduced flat-rate tax

FIGURE 3C.1 Incidence of tax and social security contributions, by income decile

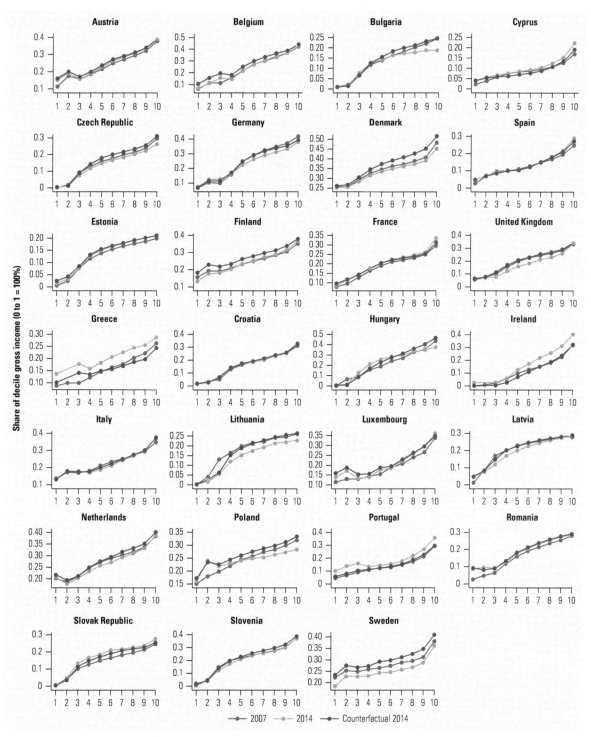

Source: Calculations based on data of EUROMOD H1.0+ (Tax-Benefit Microsimulation Model for the European Union) (database), Institute for Social and Economic Research, University of Essex, Colchester, UK, https://www.euromod.ac.uk/2017/12/13/euromod-h10-released.
Note: The blue line indicates the average tax rate and average social contribution in 2007 (2011 for Croatia) calculated as a share of gross income. The green line indicates the same variable in 2014. The yellow line indicates the counterfactual rate in 2014 had the tax and transfer system been the same then as in 2007.

FIGURE 3C.2 Incidence of transfers, by income decile

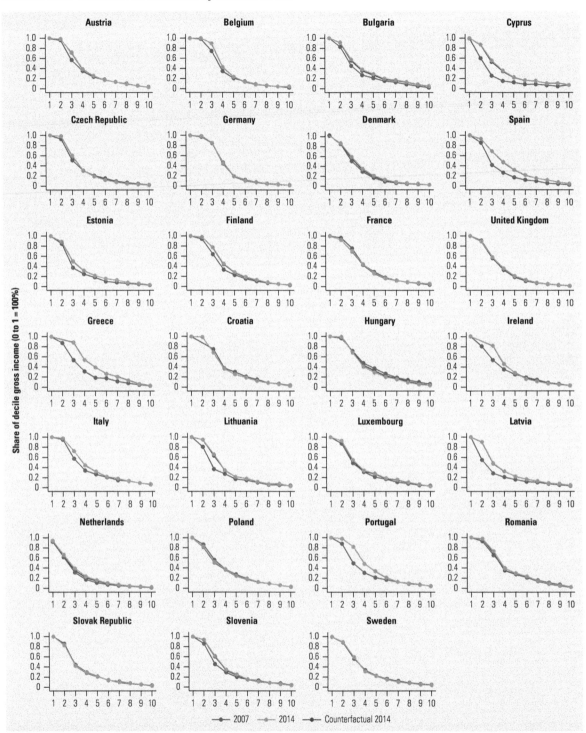

Source: Calculations based on data of EUROMOD H1.0+ (Tax-Benefit Microsimulation Model for the European Union) (database), Institute for Social and Economic Research, University of Essex, Colchester, UK, https://www.euromod.ac.uk/2017/12/13/euromod-h10-released.
Note: The blue line indicates the average tax rate and average social contribution in 2007 (2011 for Croatia) calculated as a share of gross income. The green line indicates the same variable in 2014. The yellow line indicates the counterfactual rate in 2014 had the tax and transfer system been the same then as in 2007.

income systems during the period under analysis. In these two countries, the slope of the incidence curve flattens for deciles 7 and above in 2014, and it is notably lower than in 2007. The counterfactual scenario shows that this flattening would not have occurred if the tax and transfer policies in 2014 were the same as those in 2007.

Figure 3C.2 presents the incidence of transfers (pensions and means-tested and non–means-tested benefits) as a share of gross equivalized income in the different scenarios. As expected, in all countries, transfers represent almost the entirety of income among the lowest deciles, that is, nontransfer income is close to zero among these income groups. For the median, decile 5, transfers represent around 20 percent of gross income, and, for the top decile, the incidence is close to zero. The profile of the transfer incidence curve is similar across Europe. It is downward sloping and convex in all cases. The differences that emerge in comparing the initial year and the final year are almost entirely derived from the underlying changes in market income. This is the case, for instance, in Cyprus and Greece, where the transfer incidence curve of 2014 lies entirely over that of 2007. The counterfactual scenario, in which the transfer policies of 2007 are left unchanged, overlaps the curve of 2014, meaning that there was practically no change in policies. If the market income distribution of 2014 is used, the transfer policies of 2007 and of 2014 result in the same incidence curve. This means that the change between 2007 and 2014 is entirely explained by changes in market income. In the case of Cyprus and Greece, where the market income levels of 2014 were lower than those of 2007 because of the ongoing economic crisis in those countries, this resulted in a higher transfer incidence.

Figure 3C.3 shows the incidence of tax and social security contributions on gross income across six age-groups, covering ages 18 to 74.[24] There is considerable heterogeneity across countries. In some countries, notably, countries in Western, Northern, and Southern Europe, the incidence across ages has an inverted U shape. In Central and Eastern Europe, the incidence is flat among groups of working age, from 18 to 55, but drops dramatically among the oldest age-groups. There are two main reasons for the difference in these profiles. First, the income of the older age-groups relative to the young and the middle age-group is lower in Central and Eastern Europe than in the rest of Europe, where older age-groups enjoy higher levels of income relative to the young. In any progressive tax scheme this would result in a lower tax rate among the elderly in Central and Eastern Europe relative to the elderly in Western, Northern, and Southern Europe. Another source of difference is the income tax scheme. Flat-rate income tax systems result in flat age-tax profiles. The introduction of this type of income tax scheme, as in the case of Bulgaria and Hungary, hurts the youngest age-group especially. The tax rates of these age-groups under the counterfactual scenario, that is, the market incomes of 2014 and the tax scheme of 2007, are lower than the tax rates found in 2014, when the flat-rate tax scheme was in place.

The average incidence of transfers on the gross income of age-groups is shown in figure 3C.4. A common and expected feature of the transfer incidence curve in all countries is the high incidence among the oldest age-groups, which is mainly explained by pensions. Some countries, however, show a U curve, that is, the youngest age-groups receive a nonnegligible amount of transfers. In Denmark,

FIGURE 3C.3 Incidence of taxes and social security contributions, by age-group

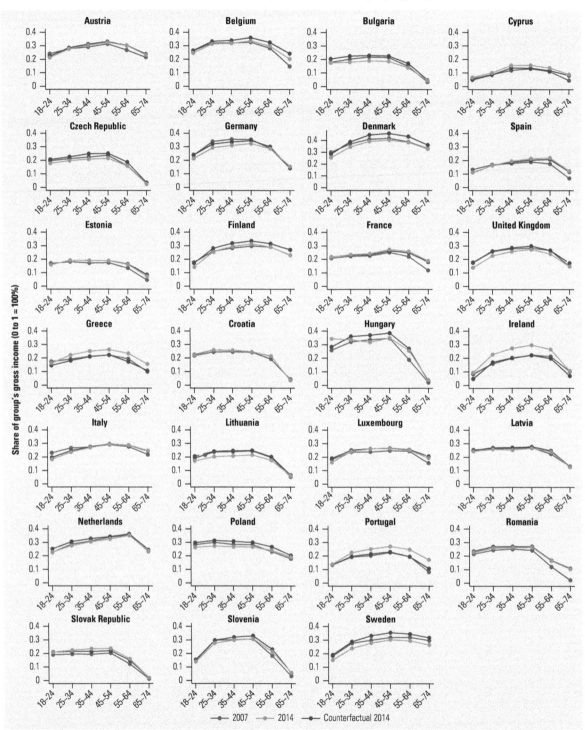

Source: Calculations based on data of EUROMOD H1.0+ (Tax-Benefit Microsimulation Model for the European Union) (database), Institute for Social and Economic Research, University of Essex, Colchester, UK, https://www.euromod.ac.uk/2017/12/13/euromod-h10-released.
Note: The blue line indicates the average tax rate and average social contribution in 2007 (2011 for Croatia) calculated as a share of gross income. The green line indicates the same variable in 2014. The yellow line indicates the counterfactual rate in 2014 had the tax and transfer system been the same then as in 2007.

FIGURE 3C.4 Incidence of transfers, by age-group

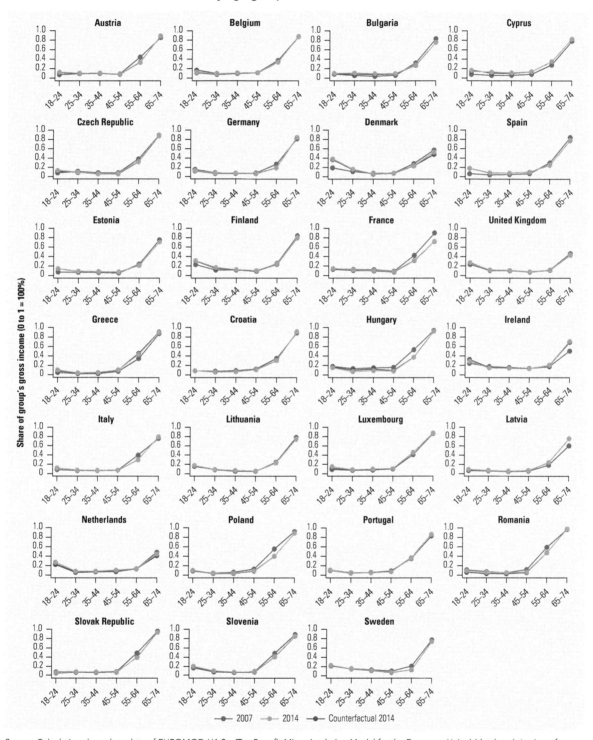

Source: Calculations based on data of EUROMOD H1.0+ (Tax-Benefit Microsimulation Model for the European Union) (database), Institute for Social and Economic Research, University of Essex, Colchester, UK, https://www.euromod.ac.uk/2017/12/13/euromod-h10-released.
Note: The blue line indicates the average tax rate and average social contribution in 2007 (2011 for Croatia) calculated as a share of gross income. The green line indicates the same variable in 2014. The yellow line indicates the counterfactual rate in 2014 had the tax and transfer system been the same then as in 2007.

for instance, transfers represent about 40 percent of the gross income of the 18–24 age-group. In Finland and Ireland, the corresponding share is around 30 percent, and, in Hungary, the Netherlands, Slovenia, Spain, Sweden, and the United Kingdom, the incidence is 20 percent. In all countries, the incidence is lowest among middle-aged groups, and little change is observed over time.

In figures 3C.5 and 3C.6, the analysis across occupational categories is presented. The first of these figures looks at the effects of the average tax rate and social security contributions on gross income. The common pattern across all countries, which is linked to the underlying distribution of income across occupations, consists in higher rates in nonroutine cognitive-task–intensive occupations and lower rates in nonroutine manual-task–intensive occupations, while the rate for routine-task–intensive occupations is in the middle. Comparing the counterfactual with the initial and final situations shows that, in some countries, the role of changes in tax policies was limited; this is reflected in the similarity of the rates in 2014 and in the counterfactual scenario. This is the case in Austria, Estonia, France, Romania, and Spain. In other countries, tax rates fell across the board proportionally. This is the case of the Czech Republic, Denmark, Finland, Lithuania, the Netherlands, and Sweden. Rates fell more in the case of nonroutine cognitive-task–intensive occupations in Bulgaria and Hungary, and they have increased significantly among that occupational group in Greece, Ireland, and Portugal.

Figure 3C.6 shows the average share of transfers over gross income for the three occupational categories. Because these are working-age individuals, the transfer incidence is especially low given that pensions are close to zero, and only means-tested and non–means-tested benefits are the transfers received. Incidence rates above 10 percent are observed in a few countries. Workers in nonroutine manual-task–intensive occupations, usually the lowest paid in the economy, register the highest rates, reaching a maximum of 15 percent of gross income in the United Kingdom. Countries that have seen policy-driven increases in transfer incidence are Cyprus, France, Luxembourg, and the Netherlands. Policy-driven decreases are seen in Hungary, Ireland, and Portugal. Overall, however, there is little variation in transfer incidence across occupations over time.

Figures 3C.7 and 3C.8 show the analysis across household types.[25] In particular, three household types are taken into consideration: (1) transfer-dependent households, composed of one or more adults, all of whom receive only transfer income; (2) single-earner households, composed of at least two adults, one of whom is employed and reporting labor income, while the other is not employed; and (3) dual earner households, composed of at least two adults, both of whom receive labor income.

Figure 3C.7 shows the average tax rate and social contributions for each of the three household types. As expected, dual earner households show the highest rates because their incomes are higher. In general, single-earner households follow, and transfer-dependent households exhibit the lowest rates. However, in Bulgaria, Croatia, the Czech Republic, Estonia, Hungary, Lithuania, the Slovak Republic, and Slovenia, the tax rate paid by this last group is close to zero. This difference may arise because of the nature of income distribution across household types. Over time, some policy-driven changes can be seen. Particularly among dual earner households, there were increases in Cyprus, Greece, Ireland,

FIGURE 3C.5 Incidence of tax and social security contributions, by occupational category

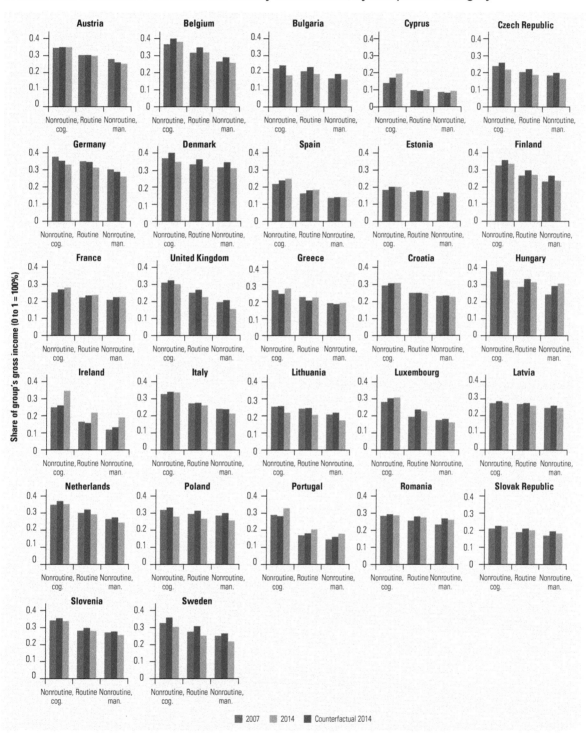

Source: Calculations based on data of EUROMOD H1.0+ (Tax-Benefit Microsimulation Model for the European Union) (database), Institute for Social and Economic Research, University of Essex, Colchester, UK, https://www.euromod.ac.uk/2017/12/13/euromod-h10-released.
Note: The blue line indicates the average tax rate and average social contribution in 2007 (2011 for Croatia) calculated as a share of gross income. The green line indicates the same variable in 2014. The yellow line indicates the counterfactual rate in 2014 had the tax and transfer system been the same then as in 2007.

FIGURE 3C.6 Incidence of transfers, by occupational category

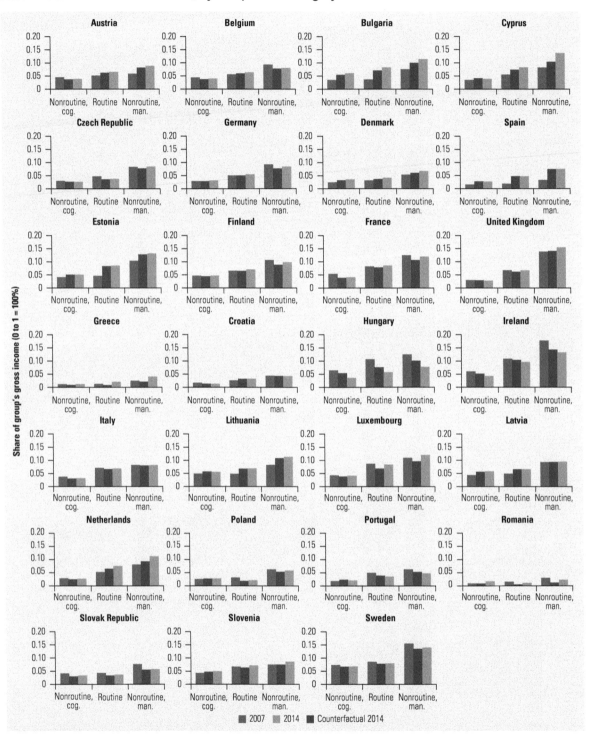

Source: Calculations based on data of EUROMOD H1.0+ (Tax-Benefit Microsimulation Model for the European Union) (database), Institute for Social and Economic Research, University of Essex, Colchester, UK, https://www.euromod.ac.uk/2017/12/13/euromod-h10-released.
Note: The blue line indicates the average tax rate and average social contribution in 2007 (2011 for Croatia) calculated as a share of gross income. The green line indicates the same variable in 2014. The yellow line indicates the counterfactual rate in 2014 had the tax and transfer system been the same then as in 2007.

FIGURE 3C.7 Incidence of tax and social security contributions, by household type

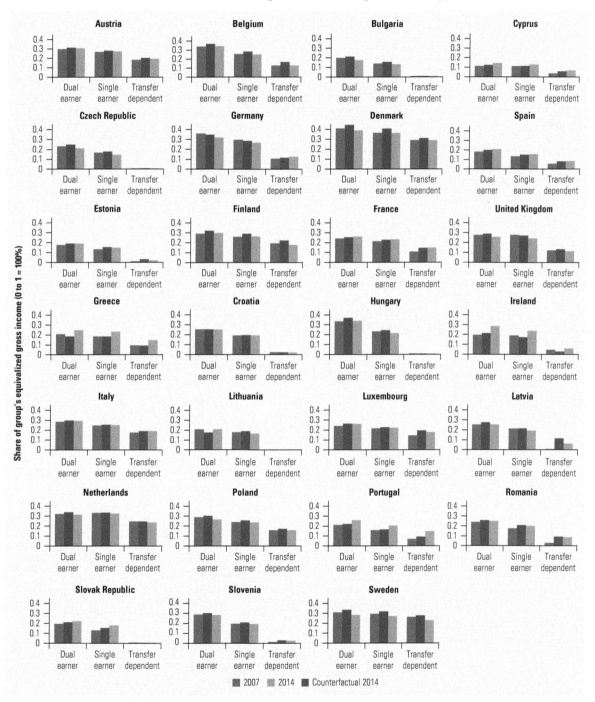

Source: Calculations based on data of EUROMOD H1.0+ (Tax-Benefit Microsimulation Model for the European Union) (database), Institute for Social and Economic Research, University of Essex, Colchester, UK, https://www.euromod.ac.uk/2017/12/13/euromod-h10-released.
Note: The blue line indicates the average tax rate and average social contribution in 2007 (2011 for Croatia) calculated as a share of gross income. The green line indicates the same variable in 2014. The yellow line indicates the counterfactual rate in 2014 had the tax and transfer system been the same then as in 2007.

FIGURE 3C.8 Incidence of transfers, by household type

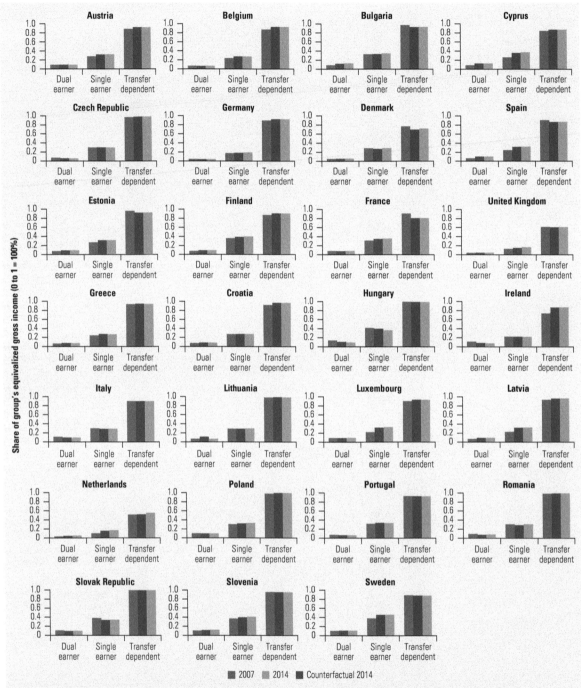

Source: Calculations based on data of EUROMOD H1.0+ (Tax-Benefit Microsimulation Model for the European Union) (database), Institute for Social and Economic Research, University of Essex, Colchester, UK, https://www.euromod.ac.uk/2017/12/13/euromod-h10-released.
Note: The blue line indicates the average tax rate and average social contribution in 2007 (2011 for Croatia) calculated as a share of gross income. The green line indicates the same variable in 2014. The yellow line indicates the counterfactual rate in 2014 had the tax and transfer system been the same then as in 2007.

and Lithuania, but decreases among dual earner households in Bulgaria, the Czech Republic, Denmark, Hungary, Poland, and Sweden. Transfer-dependent households experienced policy-driven tax rate declines in Belgium, Finland, Latvia, and Sweden. The situation among single-earner households changed little, and policy-driven tax changes that benefited this type of household the most in relative terms occurred only in Greece, where tax rates rose among all household types, but least among single-earners, and, in Croatia and Lithuania, where single-earner households saw a tax rate decrease.

Transfer incidence in gross income is shown in figure 3C.8. As expected, transfer-dependent households had the highest incidence, almost by definition. Single-earner households had a higher rate (between 20 percent and 30 percent of gross income) than dual earner households (around 10 percent of gross income). Little change was observed, and most of this is explained by changes in market income. The counterfactual scenario is mostly coincident with the actual scenario of 2014.

Notes

1. Based on data of ICTWSS (Database on Institutional Characteristics of Trade Unions, Wage Setting, State Intervention, and Social Pacts), Amsterdam Institute for Advanced Labour Studies, University of Amsterdam, Amsterdam, http://uva-aias.net/en/ictwss.

2. The comparisons are based on measurements using (a) an employment protection index constructed from doing business indicators for all countries on which raw data on each indicator were available as of 2017 and (b) the Organisation for Economic Co-operation and Development (OECD) employment protection legislation index. The constructed employment protection index covers a broader set of labor market regulation and protection indicators relative to the OECD employment protection legislation and also a wider set of countries, which allows more comprehensive comparisons. However, doing business indicators are only available for the last decade, limiting the analysis of trends in employment protection, while OECD employment protection legislation data are available for a longer period, but for a smaller set of countries. This chapter utilizes these two measures in a complementary manner. For doing business, see Doing Business (database), International Finance Corporation and World Bank, Washington, DC, http://www.doingbusiness.org/data.

3. Job quality is measured through a subindex constructed using principal components analysis and relevant doing business indicators, such as the annual leave associated with different job tenures, parental leave and wage replacement rate for parental leave, equal enumeration for equal work and gender nondiscrimination in hiring, unemployment protection, and so on. See Doing Business (database), International Finance Corporation and World Bank, Washington, DC, http://www.doingbusiness.org/data.

4. While informality exists to a larger extent in these countries compared with Japan or Korea, the majority of workers are active in the formal sector following the increases in formalization rates in recent years. For instance, in 2012, 70 percent of workers reported that they contributed to social security, and, as of 2016, 80 percent of employment is reportedly in the formal sector. See Albania: Living Standards Measurement Survey 2012 (dataset), World Bank, Washington, DC, http://microdata.worldbank.org/index.php/catalog/1970; World Bank 2018a.

5. The EU13 is Bulgaria, Croatia, Cyprus, the Czech Republic, Estonia, Hungary, Latvia, Lithuania, Malta, Poland, Romania, the Slovak Republic, and Slovenia.

6. Only temporary and part-time employment can be reliably identified in the EU-LFS data. Nonstandard employment is thus defined as part-time or temporary contract employment. While data on temporary agency workers exist on recent years, their unavailability for earlier years limits their value in the analysis of trends. The data are thus omitted. See EU-LFS (European Union Labour Force Survey) (database), Eurostat, European Commission, Luxembourg, http://ec.europa.eu/eurostat/statistics-explained/index.php/EU_labour_force_survey_%E2%80%93_data_and_publication.

7. Although most countries in Europe and Central Asia supply unemployment benefits, the coverage rates tend to be low in the eastern part of the region because of the high degree of informality.

8. The impact of pensions on the Gini is captured by the green line segments in figure 3.9, that is, the distance between the blue points (market income) and the green points (indicating that public pensions are added to market income).

9. The impact of direct taxes and transfers is captured by the yellow line segments in figure 3.9, representing the distance between the green points and the yellow points (indicating that direct taxes are being deducted from market income, plus pensions, while social assistance transfers are added to arrive at disposable income).

10. Coverage of the poorest 20 percent is similarly low in Italy, at 65 percent.

11. Between 1980 and the late 2000s, the income share of the top 1 percent rose by 70 percent in Finland, Norway, and Sweden, reaching around 7 percent–8 percent (OECD 2014).

12. This decomposition analysis is based on the methodology developed by Bourguignon and Ferreira (2005) and described in detail in annex 3A. The policy component measures the share of redistribution that derives from active policy changes, but these changes do not necessarily imply an explicit intention to redistribute. For example, a country may have to reduce the fiscal deficit (this is the intentional policy objective), and, to do so, it increases tax rates. This may generate a redistribution, but this was not the primary objective of the policy change.

13. Annex 3C shows the results for the EU and for various components of taxes and transfers.

14. See LiTS (Life in Transition Survey) (database), European Bank for Reconstruction and Development, London, http://www.ebrd.com/what-we-do/economic-research-and-data/data/lits.html.

15. See EUROMOD H1.0+ (Tax-Benefit Microsimulation Model for the European Union) (database), Institute for Social and Economic Research, University of Essex, Colchester, UK, https://www.euromod.ac.uk/2017/12/13/euromod-h10-released.

16. See EU-SILC (European Union Statistics on Income and Living Conditions) (database), Eurostat, European Commission, Luxembourg, http://ec.europa.eu/eurostat/web/microdata/european-union-statistics-on-income-and-living-conditions; Longitudinal–User Database of EU-SILC (European Union Statistics on Income and Living Conditions) (database), Eurostat, European Commission, Luxembourg, http://ec.europa.eu/eurostat/web/microdata/european-union-statistics-on-income-and-living-conditions.

17. See FRS (Family Resources Survey) (database), Department for Work and Pensions, London, https://www.gov.uk/government/collections/family-resources-survey--2.

18. See EUROMOD Country Reports (database), Institute for Social and Economic Research, University of Essex, Colchester, UK, https://www.euromod.ac.uk/using-euromod/country-reports.

19. Because of data limitations, the earliest income year is 2006 for France, 2008 for Malta and the United Kingdom, and 2011 for Croatia. The final income year is 2013 for Germany. See EU-SILC (European Union Statistics on Income and Living Conditions) (database), Eurostat, European Commission, Luxembourg, http://ec.europa.eu/eurostat/web/microdata/european-union-statistics-on-income-and-living-conditions.

20. Additionally, a corresponding counterfactual distribution is obtained wherein the income year is kept constant instead of the tax-benefit system, that is,

$$y_{t-j,t}^{* \, disposable} = f\left(y_{t-j}^{market}, TB_t, X_{t-j} \right).$$

21. The most recent data files are from April 6, 2018.

22. For most countries, the input dataset refers to the income year of the previous year (that is, the 2015 input data refer to the 2014 income year). Whenever possible, the observed distributions are constructed using the income year that is equivalent to the tax-benefit system year (that is, the 2015 input data, which contain information on the 2014 incomes, are used for the 2014 system).

23. The exceptions are Croatia, for which the initial year is 2011, and Germany, for which the initial year is 2008. For EUROMOD, see EUROMOD H1.0+ (Tax-Benefit Microsimulation Model for the European Union) (database), Institute for Social and Economic Research, University of Essex, Colchester, UK, https://www.euromod.ac.uk/2017/12/13/euromod-h10-released.

24. Unlike the case of the income groups analyzed above, the analysis of other groups is performed using unequivalized individual incomes. This is because, rather than grouping individuals into households, they are grouped according to individual characteristics such as age and occupation. The gross individual income and the individual tax, social security contributions, and transfers of all individuals belonging to each group are summed up, and the relationship among them is calculated.

25. Because the unit of analysis is the household rather than the individual, gross income is calculated equivalized across households.

References

Aguirregabiria, Victor, and César Alonso-Borrego. 2014. "Labor Contracts and Flexibility: Evidence from a Labor Market Reform in Spain." *Economic Inquiry* 52 (2): 930–57.

Albertini, Julien, Jean Olivier Hairault, François Langot, and Thepthida Sopraseuth. 2017. "A Tale of Two Countries: A Story of the French and US Polarization." IZA Discussion Paper 11013 (September), Institute of Labor Economics, Bonn, Germany.

Autor, David H., Alan Manning, and Christopher L. Smith. 2010. "The Contribution of the Minimum Wage to U.S. Wage Inequality over Three Decades: A Reassessment." NBER Working Paper 16533, National Bureau of Economic Research, Cambridge, MA. http://www.nber.org/papers/w16533.

Bell, Martin, Elin Charles-Edwards, Philipp Ueffing, John Stillwell, Marek Kupiszewski, and Dorota Kupiszewska. 2015. "Internal Migration and Development: Comparing Migration Intensities around the World." *Population and Development Review* 41 (1): 33–58.

Bentolila, Samuel, and Juan J. Dolado. 1994. "Labour Flexibility and Wages: Lessons from Spain." *Economic Policy* 9 (18): 53–99.

Betcherman, Gordon. 2015. "Labor Market Regulations: What Do We Know about Their Impacts in Developing Countries." *World Bank Research Observer* 30 (1): 124–53.

Blanchard, Olivier, and Augustin Landier. 2002. "The Perverse Effects of Partial Labour Market Reform: Fixed Duration Contracts in France." *Economic Journal* 112 (480): F214–F244.

Boeri, Tito, and Pietro Garibaldi. 2007. "Two Tier Reforms of Employment Protection: A Honeymoon Effect?" *Economic Journal* 117 (521): F357–F385.

Bourguignon, François, and Francisco H. G. Ferreira. 2005. "Decomposing Changes in the Distribution of Household Incomes: Methodological Aspects." In *The Microeconomics* of *Income Distribution Dynamics in East Asia and Latin America*, edited by François Bourguignon, Francisco H. G. Ferreira, and Nora Lustig, 17–46. Washington, DC: World Bank.

Bussolo, Maurizio, Damien Capelle, and Hernan Winkler. 2018. "Job Tenure: Labor Market Policies, Globalization, and the Growing Intergenerational Divide." Paper presented at the Institute of Labor Economics, the World Bank, and the Network on Jobs and Development's "2018 Jobs and Development Conference," Bogotá, Colombia, May 11–12.

Causa, Orsetta, Mikkel Hermansen, and Nicolas Ruiz. 2016. "The Distributional Impact of Pro-Growth Reforms." Economics Department Working Paper 1342 (November 17), Organisation for Economic Co-operation and Development, Paris.

Checchi, Daniele, and Cecilia García-Peñalosa. 2010. "Labour Market Institutions and the Personal Distribution of Income in the OECD." *Economica* 77 (307): 413–50.

European Commission. 2010. *Employment in Europe 2010*. October. Brussels: Directorate-General for Employment, Social Affairs and Equal Opportunities, European Commission.

———. 2014. "Income Inequality: Wage Dispersion in the European Union." Study IP/A/EMPL/2013–05 (November), Policy Department A: Economic and Scientific Policy, Directorate General for Internal Policies, European Commission, Brussels.

Fries-Tersch, Elena, Tugce Tugran, and Harriet Bradley. 2017. *2016 Annual Report on Intra-EU Labour Mobility*. May. Brussels: European Commission.

Gatti, Roberta V., Matteo Morgandi, C. Oriolo, and S. Wojciech. 2017. "The Reform of the Labor Code to Reduce Dualism in the Labor Market; the Italian Labor Market Reform: Design and Process of Relevance to Poland." World Bank, Washington, DC.

Kanbur, Ravi. 2018. "On the Volume of Redistribution: Across Income Levels and across Groups." CEPR Discussion Paper DP12816 (March), Centre for Economic Policy Research, London.

Karacsony, Sandor, Frieda Vandeninden, and Mirey Ovadiya. 2017. "Portraits of Labor Market Exclusion 2.0: Country Policy Paper (CPP) for Bulgaria." July, World Bank, Washington, DC.

Katz, Lawrence F., and Alan B. Krueger. 2016. "The Rise and Nature of Alternative Work Arrangements in the United States, 1995–2015." NBER Working Paper 22667 (September), National Bureau of Economic Research, Cambridge, MA.

Koettl, Johannes, Olga Kupets, Anna Olefir, and Indhira Santos. 2014. "In Search of Opportunities? The Barriers to More Efficient Internal Labor Mobility in Ukraine." *IZA Journal of Labor and Development* 3 (1): 1–28.

Millán, Natalia, Mirey Ovadiya, and Aylin Isik-Dikmelik. 2017. "Portraits Of Labor Market Exclusion 2.0: Country Policy Paper (CPP) for Greece." July, World Bank, Washington, DC.

Muravyev, Alexander. 2010. "Evolution of Employment Protection Legislation in the USSR, CIS, and Baltic States, 1985–2009." IZA Discussion Paper 5365 (December), Institute of Labor Economics, Bonn, Germany.

Numanović, Amar. 2016. "Weak Labour Markets, Weak Policy Responses: Active Labour Market Policies in Albania, Bosnia and Herzegovina, and Macedonia." With Blagica Petreski, Elena Polo, and Despina Tumanoska, Analitika: Center for Social Research, Sarajevo, Bosnia and Herzegovina.

OECD (Organisation for Economic Co-operation and Development). 2004a. *OECD Territorial Reviews: Czech Republic*. Paris: OECD.

———. 2004b. *OECD Economic Surveys: Slovak Republic*. Paris: OECD.

———. 2014. "Focus on Top Incomes and Taxation in OECD Countries: Was the Crisis a Game Changer?" May, Directorate for Employment, Labour, and Social Affairs, OECD, Paris.

———. 2015. *In It Together: Why Less Inequality Benefits All*. May 21. Paris: OECD.

Ovadiya, Mirey, and Frieda Vandeninden. 2017. "Portraits Of Labor Market Exclusion 2.0: Country Policy Paper (CPP) for Croatia." July, World Bank, Washington, DC.

Pontusson, Jonas, David Rueda, and Christopher R. Way. 2002. "Comparative Political Economy of Wage Distribution: The Role of Partisanship and Labour Market Institutions." *British Journal of Political Science* 32 (2): 281–308.

Sutherland, Holly, and Francesco Figari. 2013. "EUROMOD: The European Union Tax-Benefit Microsimulation Model." EUROMOD Working Paper EM 8/13 (March), Institute for Social and Economic Research, University of Essex, Colchester, UK.

Wallerstein, Michael. 1999. "Wage-Setting Institutions and Pay Inequality in Advanced Industrial Societies." *American Journal of Political Science* 43 (3): 649–80.

World Bank. 2002. "Globalization, Growth, and Poverty: Building an Inclusive World Economy." Report 23591 (January). Policy Research Report Series. World Bank, Washington, DC.

———. 2015. "Ukraine: Urbanization Review." World Bank, Washington, DC.

———. 2017. "Portraits of Labor Market Exclusion 2.0." Synthesis Note. World Bank, Washington, DC.

———. 2018a. "Job Dynamics in Albania: A Note Profiling Albania's Labor Market." Report 127217 (May), World Bank, Washington, DC.

———. 2018b. "A New Growth Model for Building a Secure Middle Class: Kazakhstan Systematic Country Diagnostic." Report 125611-KZ (April). World Bank, Washington, DC.

The Social Contract: Do Distributional Tensions Matter?

Introduction

A social contract is stable if there is a sustainable equilibrium among the outcomes of market forces, public policies, and people's preferences. Chapter 2 discusses the distributional tensions emerging in Europe and Central Asia from changes in market forces. Chapter 3 shows that the region's public systems reduce vertical inequality, but do not always effectively address new distributional tensions. Because these tensions are not likely to disappear and may even rise and that redistribution systems are not catching up sufficiently quickly, the social contract may be under pressure.

This chapter focuses on two main issues. First, it analyzes the remaining hinge in the social contract: what determines the preference of individuals for equity or, more generally, the nature of the society in which they would like to live. Because preferences are not directly observable, one must rely on examining the related demand for redistribution. Second, the chapter shows whether the signs of an unstable social contract, such as voting polarization, can be linked to unreleased distributional tensions.

Views about the extent to which government should raise taxes to redistribute income to poorer citizens or address other kinds of distributional tensions are based on several concerns. People may favor income redistribution because they consider themselves poor and thus anticipate an increase in their own incomes from the measures, even if they take the higher taxes into account. They may also prefer the redistribution because they anticipate benefiting from a general decline

in inequality (arising from lower crime rates, for instance) or because they hold strong opinions about equity and social justice.

Choices among redistributive policies will depend on the perceptions of individuals about the overall level of inequality and, often, on where they place themselves in the distribution of income. Indeed, perceptions of inequality are associated more closely than objective indicators of inequality with demands for redistribution. Thus, subjective perceptions of inequality are linked to voting behavior even when they are inconsistent with objective measures of inequality.

Subjective perceptions of inequality are often based on widely available macroeconomic variables imperfectly associated with inequality, such as the unemployment rate or the poverty rate, or variables related to economic opportunity and thus future inequality, such as government expenditures on education. Specific circumstances of individuals, such as age, skill level, access to a stable job, or whether one expects to achieve a higher income than one's parents, influence which macroeconomic variable is more relevant to form perceptions of inequality. For example, relative to less well-educated people, well-educated people tend to pay more attention to expenditures on education. People who are unemployed or in poor health and receive public transfers tend to consider themselves lower in the distribution than people who have the same incomes, but who are employed or in good health. This implies that unemployment insurance, for example, may not be as effective in sustaining the social contract as one might believe based on its success in supporting incomes.

There are several signs that the social contract is weakening in Europe and Central Asia. More people are voting for extremist parties that reject the current social order, or they are not voting at all. Separatist movements, for example, in Catalonia and Scotland, are gaining popularity. Trust in the region's political institutions is declining. The aspirations of workers for a middle-class lifestyle marked by stable, secure employment are being frustrated as technological progress and globalization roil labor markets. People increasingly believe that a good job and success in life depend on one's connections rather than ability or hard work.

These signs of the fraying social fabric in the region are related to the distributional tensions discussed in chapter 2. In some countries, support for extremist political parties has grown especially among workers who carry out routine tasks or nonroutine manual tasks and who have experienced a decline in the demand for their skills. Support for extremist parties has also expanded among individuals living in regions with higher shares of households at risk of poverty or larger gaps in inequality. The satisfaction of individuals with their lives varies by location, even after accounting for income. Declining trust in institutions is associated with widening inequality.

The next section shows that economic security and fairness may be more important than objective indicators of inequality in determining subjective perceptions of inequality and preferences for redistribution. The subsequent section describes fissures of the social contract, such as polarization of the voting, and declining trust in public institutions, and shows that they can be linked to an imbalance between the demand for equity, in particular, from those on the losing side of the distributional tensions, and the level of equity achieved in the current environment.

The Third Component of the Social Contract: The Preference for Equity

Relative to countries in other regions, the countries of Europe and Central Asia redistribute income on a larger scale and have more extensive state welfare systems, more progressive taxation, and more generous social protection. Most individuals dislike inequality, but not with the same intensity. Cultural differences and experiences explain the large variations in the aversion to inequality across countries and across time. A large literature has shown that in experimental settings and in representative population surveys, self-reported satisfaction or well-being is reduced by inequality (Clark and D'Ambrosio 2015; Ferrer-i-Carbonell and Ramos 2014). However, the same level of inequality or a similar increase in inequality may be tolerated by some, but not by others. One reason for the large welfare states in Europe is the high degree of inequality aversion among populations (Alesina and Angeletos 2005; Alesina and Glaeser 2004). This inequality aversion or preference for equity is the third element in the descriptive framework of the social contract (chapter 1).

The aversion to inequality is not the simple distaste for a substantial dispersion in incomes, but a convinced opinion that the process generating income dispersion should be fair and that unregulated markets do not always reward effort fairly. Europeans seem to believe more strongly than North Americans, for instance, that misfortune can affect anybody and that government should act as both an insurer and a redistributor of income. Alesina and Angeletos (2005), using data from the World Values Survey, show that about 70 percent of the U.S. population believe that the poor are able to escape poverty, while, in Western Europe, the share is only around 40 percent.[1] The World Values Survey also highlights differences between the eastern and western parts of Europe and Central Asia.[2] In the eastern transition countries, only 24 percent of survey respondents believe that the poor can escape poverty.

These opinion survey results suggest that differences in the aversion for inequality is partly determined by differences in life experience. Giuliano and Spilimbergo (2014) show, for instance, that growing up during a period of recession causes individuals to become more risk averse and more prone to demand substantial redistribution. By the same token, the radical transformations of countries in the east during the transition must have shaped beliefs and expectations in complex ways. Grosfeld and Senik (2010) document that, in Poland, individuals were quite tolerant of the widening inequality at the beginning of the transition because it was interpreted as a signal of greater opportunities. But the situation changed after a few years; the authors identify a turning point around 1996, when significant inequality aversion emerged. In this case, a simple measure of correlation between changes in inequality and inequality aversion would have an unexpected negative sign. The rapidly widening inequality during the initial phase of the transition was accompanied by low aversion. Later, stable or narrowing inequality was associated with growing aversion.

Preferences for equity are important because they influence the demand for redistribution (box 4.1).[3] However, the link between the preference for equity and the demand for redistribution, that is, political support for an extensive welfare

BOX 4.1 Preferences for Equity and Demand for Redistribution, a Brief Digression

In democratic societies, greater inequality is likely to be associated with a demand for greater redistribution of income.[a] Even without assuming that equity provides utility to individuals, that is, postulating that self-interest is the only motivation for the actions of individuals, economists have built models that link the level of inequality to the demand for redistribution. The model of Meltzer and Richard (1981) is a well-known example. In their framework, redistribution policy consists of a flat income tax rate and an equal lump sum transfer to all individuals. In this scheme, for a given tax rate, the higher one's income, the greater the probability one will be on the giving side, rather than the receiving side. Thus, the higher one's income, the lower the preferred income tax rate. If the tax rate is determined by majority vote, then the median voter is the decider. The median voter will support a higher tax rate if her income is below the income of the average voter because she would be a net beneficiary of the tax and transfer system. The reverse would occur, and a low tax rate would be chosen, if the income of the median voter is above the income of the average voter.

In this model, the equilibrium income tax rate depends on the degree of inequality, measured as the distance between the median income and the average income. Equity does not affect welfare directly or indirectly. Welfare simply depends on the current level of consumption, and self-interest motivates individuals.

There have been many extensions of this model. One of these considers not only current consumption, but also expectations about future consumption. Bénabou and Ok (2001) propose a model in which prospects of upward mobility, rather than current incomes, determine the preference for redistribution. They show that individuals who are poorer than average and oppose redistribution are acting rationally if they expect to have incomes in the future that are above average. This view is closely related to Hirschman's tunnel effect whereby the prospects of mobility influence the demand for redistribution (Hirschman and Rothschild 1973). Ravallion and Lokshin (2000) find empirical support for this effect in data on the Russian Federation, and Cojocaru (2014), using data of the Life in Transition Survey (LiTS), confirms the hypothesis in a subset of transition economies.[b]

The demand for redistribution may depend on the views of individuals on the implications of inequality for society, rather than their own pocketbooks. Individuals may care about inequality in society because inequality can indirectly affect their welfare or because of their views of what constitutes a just society. For example, unequal societies tend to have higher crime rates; so, some people may support more extensive redistribution to reduce the likelihood of robbery. Or an individual's productivity may be greater if the overall level of education in society is higher. Workers might therefore support higher tax rates to fund education in the interest of raising their own incomes. Individuals may worry about inequality on its own, apart from its impact on their welfare. They may have views about social justice, that is, on justifiable levels of inequality or poverty as a moral or ideological concept (Alesina and La Ferrara, 2005). Alesina and Giuliano (2011) review the large literature dealing with these issues and emphasize the distinction that individuals make between fair and unfair inequality, that is, the concept of inequality of opportunity.

a. Acemoglu and Robinson (2006, 36) argue that similar dynamics can affect autocratic regimes, as higher "inter-group inequality makes revolution more attractive for the citizens," because, if the poor overthrow the dictator, they "get a chance to share the entire income of the economy (minus what is destroyed in the revolution)." Acemoglu and Robinson (2012) develop a full theory whereby inclusive political systems and inclusive economic development reinforce each other, while a vicious cycle is generated if elitist political structures generate income concentration that supports and perpetuates the concentration of political power.
b. See LiTS (Life in Transition Survey) (database), European Bank for Reconstruction and Development, London, http://www.ebrd.com/what-we-do/economic-research-and-data/data/lits.html.

system or, in the case of this report, for changing the social contract, is not simple and direct for a number of reasons. First, other factors, beyond dislike of income inequality, influence the demand for redistribution. Trust, the efficacy of the state, and corruption have been shown to explain variations in the demand for redistribution for the same level of inequality or for the same growth in inequality (Ferrer-i-Carbonell and Ramos 2014). Second, individuals compare their preferred or desired level of inequality with their perception of inequality. This perception of inequality may deviate from the inequality measured by the Gini coefficient on the distribution of incomes, for example, because individuals have different reference groups. They care about the differences across incomes with their neighbors, peers at work, or age-group (Clark and D'Ambrosio 2015). Thus, they care about horizontal inequalities. Another reason that perceived inequality may differ from objectively measured inequality is that the concept of inequality that individuals may have may include ideas of fairness and security.[4] In these cases, simply redistributing income from the rich to the poor may not meet people's preferences for enhancements in equity.

Perceptions of Inequality Are Key in Explaining the Demand for Redistribution

Focusing only on measures of income inequality across *individuals* can miss important distributional tensions across *groups*. Similarly, focusing only on *objective* measures of dispersion of income distribution can miss the main drivers of dissatisfaction with the inequality in a society. *Subjective* measures and perceptions of inequality are important because they affect the demand for redistribution and the political participation of citizens, which has major implications for the stability of the social contract.

"We suggest that most theories about political effects of inequality [demand for redistribution, the political participation of citizens, democratization] need to be reframed as theories about effects of perceived inequality," note Gimpelson and Treisman (2018, 27), highlighting the significance of perceptions. There are two main reasons for this shift in perspective (Chambers, Swan, and Heesacker 2014; Cruces, Perez-Truglia, and Tetaz 2013; Kuhn 2011, 2016; Niehues 2014; Norton and Ariely 2011):

- Perceptions of inequality and objective inequality often differ.
- The demand for redistribution correlates much more closely with perceptions of inequality than with objective measures of inequality.

Opinion surveys have relied on two approaches to measure perceptions of inequality. One involves asking individuals to place themselves on an income ladder that represents the distribution of incomes, while the other asks for direct assessments of the degree of inequality in their societies. Following the first approach, the Life in Transition Survey (LiTS) finds that 57 percent of respondents place themselves in the middle of the distribution, that is, steps 4, 5, or 6 of the 10-step income ladder that represent the middle deciles of the distribution; by definition, more than 30 percent of the population cannot be on these steps (Bussolo and Lebrand 2018).[5]

Inconsistencies between perceptions of inequality or trends in inequality relative to objective measurements appear to be common in Europe and Central Asia. While the Gini coefficients for roughly half the countries sampled in the 2016 round of the LiTS declined in 2008–13, indicating a narrowing in inequality, a majority of the respondents in each country said that income inequality had widened (figure 4.1).[6]

Perceptions about inequality and the demand for redistribution are strongly correlated (Niehues 2014). This is confirmed by data of the International Social Survey Program, which asks respondents whether they agree with the statement "it is the responsibility of the government to reduce income differences between people with high incomes and those with low incomes."[7] A country's Gini coefficient of income inequality, poverty and unemployment rates, and data on government education expenditure explain only 12.9 percent of the variation in responses (figure 4.2). However, perceptions of inequality alone explain close to 15 percent of the variation (figure 4.3). Thus, individual perceptions of inequality alone explain more of the demand for redistribution than objective measures of inequality.[8]

The association of perceptions and the demand for redistribution also varies by education, employment, and the degree of mobility. Individuals with tertiary educational attainment appear much more reactive than those with lower educational attainment. A rise in inequality is accompanied by an increase in the demand for redistribution among the more well educated that is 50 percent greater than the corresponding increase in demand among people with less than upper-secondary educational attainment. For any growth in the perception of inequality, the demand for redistribution rises by 60 percent more among the employed than among the unemployed. Perceptions of inequality also have a greater impact on the demand

FIGURE 4.1
Perceptions of inequality differ systematically from objective measures

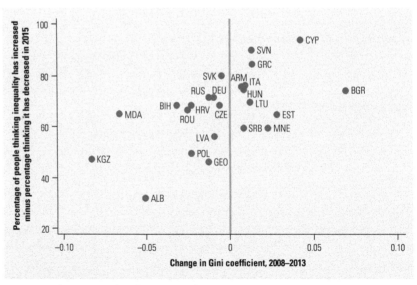

Source: Bussolo, Ferrer-i-Carbonell, Giolbas, and Torre 2018.
Note: The vertical axis indicates a net percentage, that is, the difference between the share of the population that thought inequality had increased and the share that believed it had decreased. Thus, in Albania, 32 percent of the population did not think that inequality had increased; rather, 44 percent believed it had risen, and only 12 percent thought it had declined.

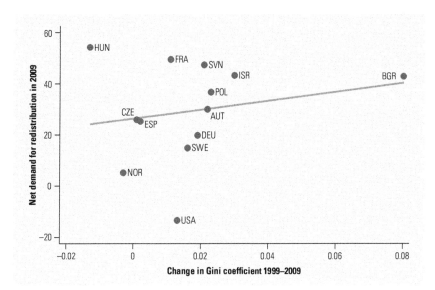

FIGURE 4.2
Measured changes in inequality explain little of the demand for redistribution

Source: Bussolo, Ferrer-i-Carbonell, Giolbas, and Torre 2018.

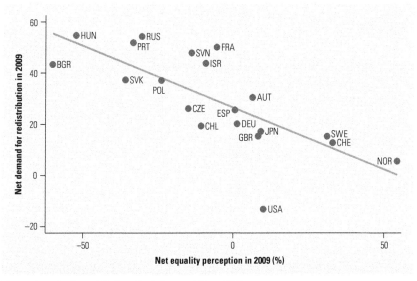

FIGURE 4.3
Perceived inequality correlates strongly with the demand for redistribution

Source: Bussolo, Ferrer-i-Carbonell, Giolbas, and Torre 2018.
Note: Net equality perception is defined as the difference between the share of people believing their country is equal and the share of people believing their country is unequal.

for redistribution among survey respondents who say they hold lower-status jobs relative to their parents than among respondents who say they hold higher-status jobs relative to their parents.

That the demand for redistribution among highly skilled and employed individuals is more sensitive to changes in perceived inequality is understandable because such individuals are probably more on the giving side than the receiving side of any progressive redistribution scheme. They would therefore be willing to pay higher taxes only if inequality is high. If inequality declines, then their willingness to pay higher taxes to reduce inequality would also decline. This finding is expected also because mobility is, in practical terms, more evident whenever inequality is high.

Perceptions of Inequality Are Influenced by Disparities in Income but Also by Insecurity and Unfairness

The importance of preferences for equity within the framework of the social contract is clear. If the level of inequality in a country is not in line with the preferences of the population because it deviates from an ideal level, is considered unfair, or produces negative externalities, such as crime, that reduce welfare, the population will demand corrective action. The government may respond by undertaking redistributive policies. However, the perceptions of inequality may deviate from objective measures of inequality, or the area of inequality targeted by the policies may not be the same as the area of inequality that is the focus of the perceptions. In both cases, the policies may fail, leading to more highly polarized voting outcomes and greater pressure on the social contract.

Understanding which factors influence perceptions is therefore fundamental to this study of the social contract. The literature on perceptions of inequality has focused mainly on the ability of individuals to predict correctly the dispersion in income distribution or the place the individuals occupy within the distribution. This report broadens this view and, rather than assuming that gaps between objective and subjective assessments of inequality are due to misperceptions, investigates how these perceptions are formed.

People use various indicators to form perceptions of the level of inequality in a society. Perceptions of inequality may depend on objective measures of inequality (the Gini coefficient), other macroeconomic variables that are correlated with inequality and are more widely reported than the Gini (unemployment and poverty rates, for instance), or variables that are correlated with equality of opportunity and thus future inequality (government expenditure on education). Along with variables that account for influences specific to an individual country or year, these four macroeconomic variables—the Gini coefficient, the unemployment rate, the poverty rate, and government expenditure on education—explain 24.4 percent of the variation in the perceptions of individuals on inequality.[9]

However, individual circumstances may generate a different impact from these aggregate factors on each person's perceptions about the prevailing degree of inequality in a society:[10]

- Across all groups defined by educational attainment, high unemployment rates appear to be strongly correlated with perceptions that inequality is high. Objective measures of inequality, such as the Gini coefficient, are correlated with perceptions of inequality, particularly among individuals with lower educational attainment. High public expenditure on education, meanwhile, is correlated with perceptions of low inequality, especially among the more well educated.
- Higher poverty rates are associated with perceptions of higher inequality among the 24–34 age-group, while, among the group over age 45, lower public expenditure on education is associated with higher perceived inequality.
- Employment status is also key to the formation of perceptions. The perception of inequality among the employed is correlated with the level of education expenditures, while this is not the case among the unemployed.
- Perceived intergenerational mobility is associated with differences in the perception of inequality. Among people who believe their job status is worse than

that of their fathers, that is, that they have experienced downward mobility, objective measures, such as the Gini coefficient or the poverty rate, are positively correlated with perceptions of inequality. Among people who think their job status is the same or better than that of their fathers, there is no such correlation.

These results highlight the importance of the horizontal inequality approach. Because the distributional tensions described in chapter 2 reflect inequality between specific groups, rather than inequality amongst individuals, perception of inequality may become more negative even if objective vertical inequality has not changed. For example, in the aftermath of the financial crisis of 2008–09, a reduction in government expenditure on education because of the adoption of austerity policies would have been associated with perceptions of higher inequality by the employed, the over 45 age-group, and individuals with higher degrees in education. Increases in the unemployment rate would affect perceptions of inequality especially among youth.

The perceptions of individuals about their position in the distribution of income is also influenced by the nonmonetary aspects of life and by individual circumstances. At a given level of objective monetary income (or consumption, as shown on the horizontal axis of figure 4.4), individuals who are not in stable, full-time employment are more likely to report that they feel poor compared with those who have stable, full-time employment. Indeed, the difference in the probability that one feels poor across individuals in the sixth decile between those who have worked during the previous 12 months and those who have not is equivalent to the difference in the level of consumption between the sixth decile and the third decile (figure 4.4). Thus, in assessing their position in the distribution, individuals value the impact of a change in employment status as if there were a three-decile difference in consumption. Similarly, at a given level

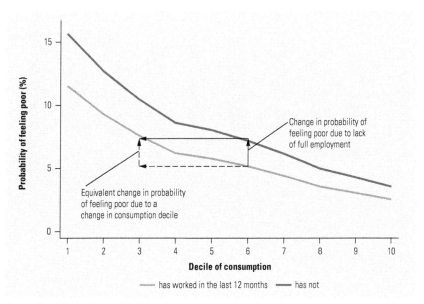

FIGURE 4.4
Individuals more likely feel poor when they are not in full-time employment

Source: Bussolo and Lebrand 2017.

of income, people who report that they are in good health are less likely to state that they feel poor than people who report they are in bad health.[11]

The strong preferences for public sector jobs in Europe and Central Asia also demonstrate the great demand for stable, long-term employment, job security, and regular earnings (figure 4.5). The value placed on economic security can be illustrated by evidence from the 2010 round of the LiTS showing that, on average, 71 percent of people would prefer a secure job with limited prospects for advancement to a more well-paying job with less security (figure 4.6).

FIGURE 4.5

A large share of people in the region prefer a public sector job . . .
Share of the population, by preferred type of job (percent)

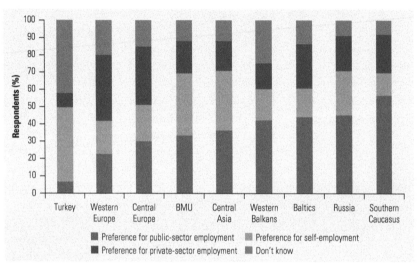

Source: Data of the 2010 round, LiTS (Life in Transition Survey) (database), European Bank for Reconstruction and Development, London, http://www.ebrd.com/what-we-do/economic-research-and -data/data/lits.html.
Note: The figure shows population-weighted regional averages. Central Asia excludes Turkmenistan. BMU = Belarus, Moldova, and Ukraine; Western Europe = France, Germany, Italy, and the United Kingdom.

FIGURE 4.6

. . . Linked to the value placed on job stability and economic security
Share of the population, by preferred type of job; a safe average salary and low prospects or high salary and good job prospects, but less secure (percent)

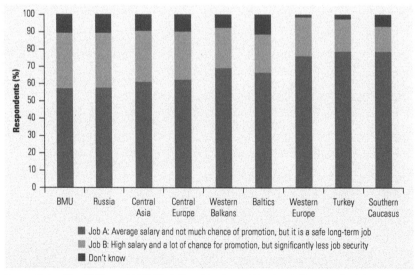

Source: Data of the 2010 round, LiTS (Life in Transition Survey) (database), European Bank for Reconstruction and Development, London, http://www.ebrd.com/what-we-do/economic-research-and -data/data/lits.html.
Note: The figure shows population-weighted regional averages. Central Asia excludes Turkmenistan. BMU = Belarus, Moldova, and Ukraine; Western Europe = France, Germany, Italy, and the United Kingdom.

"If your job isn't stable, your income isn't stable either," said a man in Tajikistan (Dávalos et al. 2016, 14).

The high value placed on stable employment indicates the limits of unemployment compensation schemes. If individuals lose their jobs, but receive unemployment insurance, their position in the income distribution may not change substantially, but their perceived position may be heavily affected. Because perceptions influence voting, citizen engagement, the demand for redistribution, and other participatory actions among individuals, the effectiveness of policy in sustaining support for the social contract may be less than its success in supporting incomes.

Comparisons within a reference group, rather than the entire country, are also important in determining perceptions about income distribution. A large literature inspired by the Easterlin (1974) paradox is analyzing the role of relative income, that is, the incomes of others in reference groups, rather than absolute income levels, in an effort to explain subjective well-being. Reference groups tend to be groups of people with similar ages, with the same level of education, living in nearby neighborhoods, or other comparable peer groups. In a format similar to figure 4.4, figure 4.7 compares the probability of feeling poor (that is, of declaring belonging to deciles 1 or 2) for two groups of people who are in different positions with respect to their reference groups. For example, among all the people who belong to the sixth decile in the countrywide distribution of consumption, there is one group of people who are in the bottom ventile in their own reference group (or below the 25th percentile, the blue line in the figure) and a group of people who are in the top ventile of their reference group (or above the 75th percentile, the green line in the figure). The probability of feeling poor is greater among the first group. So even if the two groups have the same ranking in the whole distribution, the different positions in their own reference group influence their perception. This difference in relative position is equivalent to the monetary distance between two deciles of overall consumption.

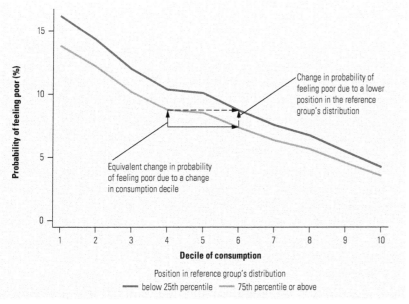

FIGURE 4.7
Their position in a reference group affects whether individuals feel poor

The importance of reference groups in influencing the views of individuals about income distribution underlines the usefulness of the horizontal approach adopted in this report. Differences across groups matter. In this specific context, it matters in terms of the support for income redistribution and social protection systems. Because individuals may not have accurate information about the full distribution, they make inferences using the information about their reference group to which they have ready access. In their experiment, Cruces, Perez-Truglia, and Tetaz (2013) show that individuals use reference groups to form views about their position in the overall distribution, and, based on these views, they support or do not support measures of redistribution. They also show that, once individuals are informed about their true position, they correct their demand for redistribution. For example, people who "overestimated their relative position and thought that they were relatively richer than they were tend to demand higher levels of redistribution" than those in the control group (Cruces, Perez-Truglia, and Tetaz 2013, 100).

Moreover, perceptions of inequality have shifted considerably. Perceptions of changes in societal inequality and fairness and of one's position in the income distribution are critical in determining demand for policies toward redistribution and social equity. So even with stable preferences for equity, people's choices in terms of support for redistributive policy or voting may change because perceptions shift. Survey data of the International Social Survey Program indicates that the share of people who view European society as less equal has increased since the 1990s.[12] In particular, individuals were asked to classify their country in a range with two extremes. At one end, a highly unequal society is represented as having a small elite at the top, a few people in the middle, and the great majority at the bottom. At the other end, a highly equal society is represented as having most people in the middle.[13] Figure 4.8 shows the difference between the share of people who believe they are living in a highly equal society minus the share of people who think they are living in a highly unequal society. In Eastern Europe, the share of people indicating the former is up to 60 percentage points smaller than the share indicating the latter. This highlights a pervasive perception of inequality. The share of individuals who believe they are living in a highly unequal society grew considerably during the 1990s, coinciding with the big increase in inequality recorded during the transition (chapter 1). It fell slightly during the 2000s. Interestingly, these "net" perceptions of inequality are stronger in Eastern Europe than in Western and Southern Europe, where objective measures of inequality—the Gini coefficient, for instance—are actually higher. In these last two subregions, too, there has been an increase in perceptions of inequality. The share of people indicating they live in a highly equal society has shrunk across all countries in the subregions included in the International Social Survey Program during the 2000s. Overall, these figures show clearly that there have been large shifts in perceptions. In the case of Poland, for example, close to 30 percent of the population changed views on the degree of inequality affecting the country.

Perceptions of unfairness in the access to jobs are also becoming more widespread. People in the region perceive that unequal access to connections and networks gives rise to unequal access to economic opportunities.

"Jobs, that's what you need connections for," explained a man in the former Yugoslav Republic of Macedonia through a qualitative survey (Dávalos et al. 2016, 15).

"Anywhere you go, connections matter, at a medical school or a kindergarten," echoed a man in Kazakhstan (Dávalos et al. 2016, 15). Similarly, the share of people

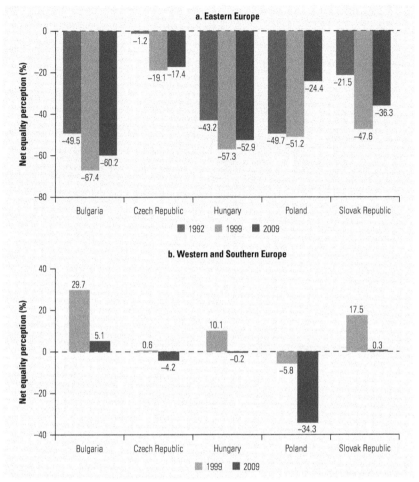

FIGURE 4.8
Perceptions of inequality have increased throughout Europe

Source: Bussolo, Ferrer-i-Carbonell, Giolbas, and Torre 2018.
Note: The panels plot the difference between the share of respondents answering "type D" (very equal society) and the share of respondents answering "type A" (very unequal society) when asked "which type do you think describes your country the best?" A negative value indicates that there are more individuals believing their society is unequal than equal, while a positive value indicates that there are more individuals believing their society is equal than unequal.

who agree that connections matter in obtaining a private or public sector job has grown across the region (figure 4.9).

In the Baltic States, for instance, the share of respondents saying that connections were essential or very important in obtaining public sector jobs rose from 59 percent in 2010 to 69 percent in 2016. The corresponding shares were 51 percent and 62 percent, respectively, for private sector jobs. Countries in the South Caucasus also experienced growth in perceptions of the importance of connections. Moreover, the share of people across the region saying that political connections matter for succeeding in life rose from 13 percent in 2010 to 22 percent in 2016, while the share saying that effort and hard work were driving success fell (see figure 4.9, panel c).

The shift in perceptions of social equity and fairness, along with changes in distribution caused by market forces and changes in the ability of governments to effect the desired income redistribution, may lead to a deterioration in people's acceptance of the social contract.

FIGURE 4.9
The value placed on connections in obtaining a job is rising

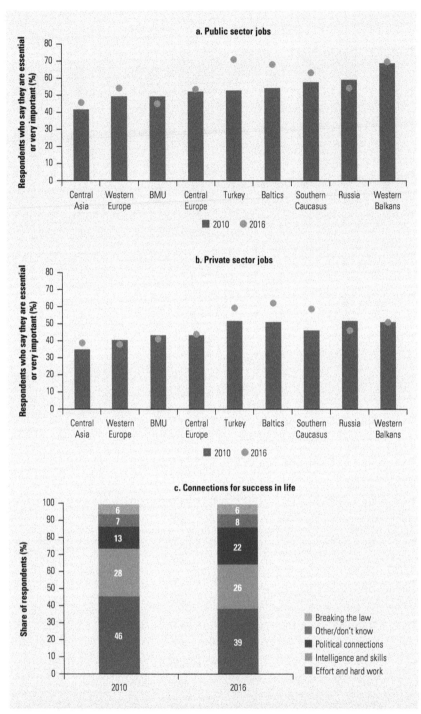

Source: Calculations based on data of the 2010 and 2016 rounds, LiTS (Life in Transition Survey) (database), European Bank for Reconstruction and Development, London, http://www.ebrd.com/what -we-do/economic-research-and-data/data/lits.html.
Note: The figure shows population-weighted regional averages. BMU = Belarus, Moldova, and Ukraine. Central Asia excludes Turkmenistan. Western Europe = Germany and Italy.

There Are Fissures in the Social Contract in the Region

The social contract—understood as the equilibrium among market forces, preferences, and redistribution systems—is sustainable only if most of a population adheres to the rules of the game. Refusal by a sufficiently large group to accept these rules threatens the underlying consensus required for civil peace and economic growth. This report documents how redistribution systems in Europe and Central Asia have not been effective in protecting important segments of the population from the rise in social tensions driven by market forces (chapters 2 and 3). This means that level of equity has been shrinking. However, the demand for equity—evident in people's assessments of the impact of the changes on their welfare and on their preferences for fairness—has been increasing. Is this imbalance threatening the social contract? This section provides evidence of the imbalance by describing two manifestations: (1) the growing polarization in voting and (2) the decline in trust in institutions.[14] The section also considers whether a direct link can be detected between the distributional tensions and the imbalance.

More people in Europe and Central Asia are refusing to accept the current system by voting for extreme parties. This is not a new phenomenon. Calculations show there has been a rise in the share of votes going to extreme parties in Europe since the beginning of this century (figure 4.10). Rodrik (2018) finds that, across countries with at least one populist party, the global share of votes for populist movements of the right or the left rose from around 2 percent in 1976–80 to only slightly under a quarter in 2011–15. He attributes the growing support for populism to the loss in income among workers in advanced countries that is driven by globalization, particularly because the competition from workers in poorer countries with

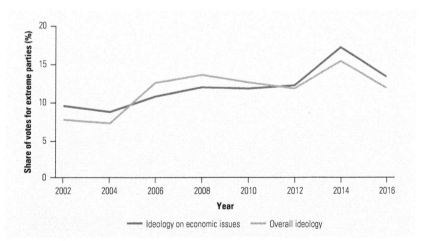

FIGURE 4.10

Voting for extreme parties has increased in recent years

Sources: Estimates based on 2002–16 data of Chesdata (Chapel Hill Expert Survey) (database), Center for European Studies, University of North Carolina at Chapel Hill, Chapel Hill, NC, https://www.chesdata.eu/; ESS (European Social Survey) (database), European Research Infrastructure Consortium, London; Norwegian Centre for Research Data, Bergen, Norway, http://www.europeansocialsurvey.org/.
Note: The European Social Survey asked respondents which party they voted for during the last elections. If this information was missing, responses to the question "Which political party do you feel closest to?" were used. Data of the Chapel Hill Expert Survey were used to assign each party a score from 1 (extreme left) to 10 (extreme right) based on rankings by experts of each party's overall ideological stance and stance on economic issues. The survey reports the average score assigned by experts, which can take any value between 1 and 10. The figure shows the percent of voters who voted for parties with ranks of less than 3 or more than 7.

lower labor and environmental standards is perceived as unfair. Similarly, Autor et al. (2017), for the United States since 2000, and Colatone and Stanig (2017), for Western Europe since the 1990s, find that locations more highly exposed to a surge in imports from China tend to add their support to more radical politicians.

Extreme parties have achieved growing electoral success in Europe over the past couple of years. Examples include the victory of the Five Star Movement, which has advocated holding a referendum on Italy's commitment to the euro, in the latest elections; the ascension of the Freedom Party of Austria, which has steadily gained seats in the legislature and has come close to overtaking the Austrian People's Party and the Social Democratic Party; the success of the Swedish Democrats in the 2018 general election; the rising popularity of Marine Le Pen, who, with 34 percent of the vote in the second round of the presidential election, accumulated more votes than any extremist candidate in French postwar history; and the ability of the right-wing nationalist Alternative for Germany, previously unrepresented in the Bundestag, to gain 13 percent of the vote in the September 2017 federal elections to become the third-largest party in the country. Political conflict is perhaps even more intense in the eastern part of the region, manifested in violent efforts to change political systems or boundaries. Examples include the smoldering conflict in Armenia and Azerbaijan, the attempted coup in Turkey, the conflict in Ukraine, and uneasiness in Central Asian countries, where political leaders have expressed concern over the possibility of a local resurgence of Islamic parties and social unrest.

Workers penalized by recent shifts in the demand for skills appear to be voting more regularly for extremist parties. Workers in jobs that are intensive in routine tasks are facing a growing risk of unemployment, while workers in jobs intensive in nonroutine manual tasks are experiencing a decline in wages relative to other workers (chapter 2). The share of votes for extremist parties among these groups of workers rose by 4.5 percentage points in 2002–16 (figure 4.11, panel a).[15]

FIGURE 4.11
Workers facing less demand for their skills tend to vote for extreme parties

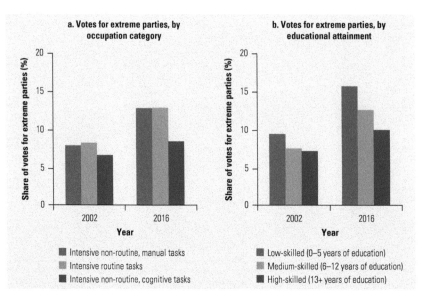

Source: Calculations based on 2002–16 data of ESS (European Social Survey) (database), European Research Infrastructure Consortium, London; Norwegian Centre for Research Data, Bergen, Norway, http://www.europeansocialsurvey.org/.
Note: Extreme parties are those defined as having an ideology score higher than 7 (far right) or lower than 3 (far left) according to the Chapel Hill Expert Survey.

Similarly, in Europe, earnings by low- and medium-skilled workers, defined as 13 years of education or less, declined relative to the earnings of high-skilled workers (more than 13 years of education). Meanwhile, the share of votes for extremist parties by low- and medium-skilled workers rose by about 6 percentage points in 2002–16, compared with an increase of only 2 percentage points among high-skilled workers.

There is also evidence that voting for extreme parties is related to regional welfare disparities. Differences in income and poverty rates across regions are related to differences in the share of votes for extreme parties, adding another dimension to the importance of territorial inequalities (Kanbur and Venables 2005). In Hungary, for example, the correlation between the regional share of people living on less than 60 percent of the median income—the European Union (EU) at-risk-of-poverty measure—and the regional share of votes for extreme parties was around 0.63 in terms of both levels and changes in 2002–14 (maps 4.1 and 4.2). In Poland, these correlations reached 0.71 during a similar period. In France, the correlation between the change in the share of votes for extreme parties and the at-risk-of-poverty measure was 0.48 in 2011.[16]

Voting for extreme parties is also motivated by local changes in inequality. Winkler (2017) finds that a 5-point Gini increase in local income inequality boosts the likelihood that a voter will support a far-left or far-right party by 4 percentage points. Moreover, a rise in local inequality drives a rise in the support for far-right political parties and intensifies the anti-immigrant sentiment among older voters. Because political participation by older voters is typically high, while that of younger voters is falling, this can potentially explain the shift to the right in many European countries.

The expansion of separatist movements also indicates a refusal to accept the social contract. While not necessarily extremist in ideological terms, separatist movements represent a break from the existing system. The electoral success of the Scottish National Party, ideologically on the center left, paved the way for a Scottish independence referendum in September 2014. The outcome—45 percent for independence, 55 percent against—showed that a considerable portion of Scottish society was ready to break the 300-year political union with England. In June 2016, 53.4 percent of English voters (51.9 percent of all British voters) chose to leave the EU after more than 40 years of political and economic integration with the continent. Since the early years of the 2010s, Catalan voters have increasingly supported parties advocating for independence from Spain; the political class has reacted by regrouping along the independence-union axis, rather than on the left-right axis traditional in Catalonia. The results in the several elections over the past few years have shown that the electorate is split almost evenly between independence and anti-independence, causing a political deadlock in the region.

Some people opt out of the system by not voting. Voter turnout has been declining across Europe, especially among younger generations (figure 4.12). This phenomenon is likely related to growing dissatisfaction with the political system. By contrast, turnout was at record highs when citizens had the opportunity to vote for dramatic changes, as in the Scottish independence referendum, the Brexit referendum, and the Catalan regional elections of December 2017. This suggests that voters desert the polls only if there is no viable exit option on offer.

MAP 4.1

The expansion in voting for extremist parties

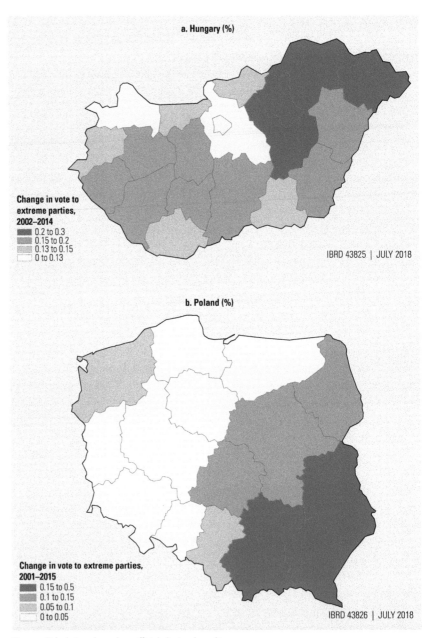

a. Hungary (%)

Change in vote to extreme parties, 2002–2014

- 0.2 to 0.3
- 0.15 to 0.2
- 0.13 to 0.15
- 0 to 0.13

IBRD 43825 | JULY 2018

b. Poland (%)

Change in vote to extreme parties, 2001–2015

- 0.15 to 0.5
- 0.1 to 0.15
- 0.05 to 0.1
- 0 to 0.05

IBRD 43826 | JULY 2018

Source: Calculations based on official electoral results.
Note: Extreme parties are those defined as having an ideology score higher than 7 (far right) or lower than 3 (far left) according to the Chapel Hill Expert Survey.

Trust in political institutions appears to be shrinking. The share of survey respondents reporting that they completely distrust most major institutions, particularly parliaments and the heads of state, rose sharply across the Europe and Central Asia region from 2010 to 2016 (figure 4.13). Yet, trust is the cement that binds people and institutions in a society and is critical for growth. A large body of literature demonstrates the importance of interpersonal trust to economic performance. For example, Algan and Cahuc (2010) show the causal effect that a measure of trust has on income in several European countries, while Algan and Cahuc (2013)

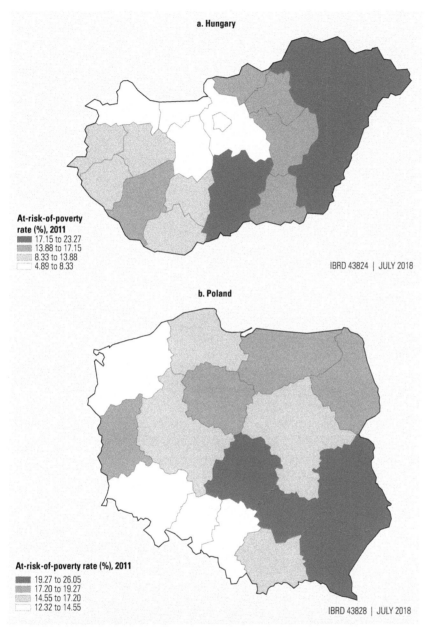

MAP 4.2
The at-risk-of-poverty measure, 2011

a. Hungary

At-risk-of-poverty
rate (%), 2011
- 17.15 to 23.27
- 13.88 to 17.15
- 8.33 to 13.88
- 4.89 to 8.33

IBRD 43824 | JULY 2018

b. Poland

At-risk-of-poverty rate (%), 2011
- 19.27 to 26.05
- 17.20 to 19.27
- 14.55 to 17.20
- 12.32 to 14.55

IBRD 43828 | JULY 2018

Source: 2011 EU poverty maps; for instance, see Simler 2016.

show that one-fifth of the cross-country variation in income per capita across the world is explained by differences in generalized trust, and this correlation is also found across regions within countries. Trust and economic performance are mutually dependent. Trust in institutions can improve efficiency in an economy, while a disappointing performance can undermine trust in institutions. For example, Stevenson and Wolfers (2011) show that countries experiencing a big rise in unemployment have also witnessed a decrease in the trust of the population in government and the finance sector. Similarly, Algan et al. (2017) find that the rise in

FIGURE 4.12
Voter turnout has declined among the young, but not among the old

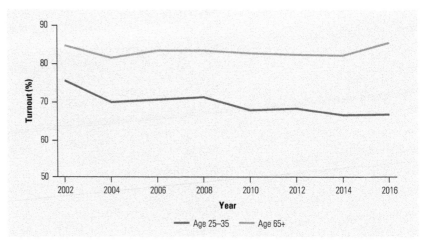

Sources: Calculations based on 2002–16 data of ESS (European Social Survey) (database), European Research Infrastructure Consortium, London; Norwegian Centre for Research Data, Bergen, Norway, http://www.europeansocialsurvey.org/.

FIGURE 4.13
Distrust in institutions has increased across Europe and Central Asia

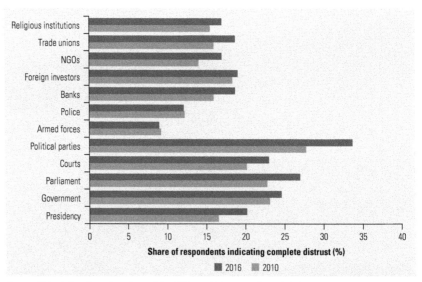

Source: Calculations based on data of the 2010 and 2016 rounds, LiTS (Life in Transition Survey) (database), European Bank for Reconstruction and Development, London, http://www.ebrd.com/what -we-do/economic-research-and-data/data/lits.html.
Note: The countries included are Albania, Armenia, Belarus, Bosnia and Herzegovina, Bulgaria, Croatia, the Czech Republic, Estonia, FYR Macedonia, Georgia, Hungary, Kazakhstan, the Kyrgyz Republic, Latvia, Lithuania, Moldova, Montenegro, Poland, Romania, the Russian Federation, Serbia, Slovenia, Tajikistan, Turkey, Ukraine, and Uzbekistan. NGOs = nongovernmental organizations.

unemployment related to the business cycle—rather than changes in unemployment driven by other causes, for example, changes in the rules governing worker protections—during the financial crisis of 2008–09 explains a significant amount of the decrease in trust toward EU political institutions, such as national and European parliaments, courts, and political parties.

Increases in inequality may be contributing to the decrease in trust. The decline in trust in government institutions is explained by changes in unemployment and income, but also by changes in inequality (Algan et al. 2017). Reductions in the share of respondents indicating that they trust government are correlated with increases in inequality (figure 4.14). Thus, a more unequal society is associated with a more distrustful citizenry. This suggests that, at least in Europe and Central Asia, people may view the pursuit of economic equality as one of the main objectives of government.

In Europe, the increase in the distrust of government institutions is greater among population groups that have lost out on income distribution. Data of the European Social Survey enable a deeper look into the nature of the rising distrust toward government institutions.[17] In particular, individuals who have lost out because of changes in labor markets in the EU showed the largest increase in distrust of national and European parliaments (figure 4.15) in line with the evidence presented by Dustmann et al. (2017). The share of individuals in routine-task–intensive occupations (the losers of occupational change) reporting distrust of the parliament of their countries rose from 18 percent in 2002 to 23 percent in 2016, while, among individuals in nonroutine cognitive occupations (the winners of occupational change), the share increased from 12 percent to 15 percent. An analysis of the data on the distrust toward the European Parliament shows that the difference is even greater. Among workers in routine-task–intensive occupations, the share of those reporting complete distrust of the parliament in Brussels and Strasbourg rose from 19 percent to 31 percent, while, among workers in nonroutine cognitive-task occupations, the rise was from 15 percent to 22 percent. Similar differences are found if individuals are grouped according to years of education (figure 4.15, panel b).

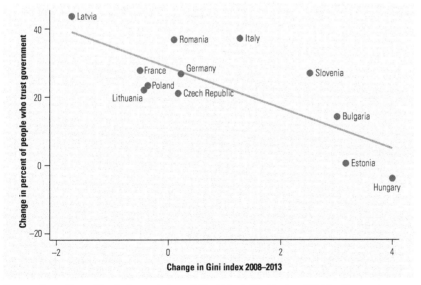

FIGURE 4.14
Greater inequality is associated with a rise in distrust of government

Sources: Data of PovcalNet (online analysis tool), World Bank, Washington, DC, http://iresearch .worldbank.org/PovcalNet/; 2006, 2010, and 2016 rounds, LiTS (Life in Transition Survey) (database), European Bank for Reconstruction and Development, London, http://www.ebrd.com/what-we-do /economic-research-and-data/data/lits.html.

FIGURE 4.15 Distrust of institutions has risen among the losers of occupational change

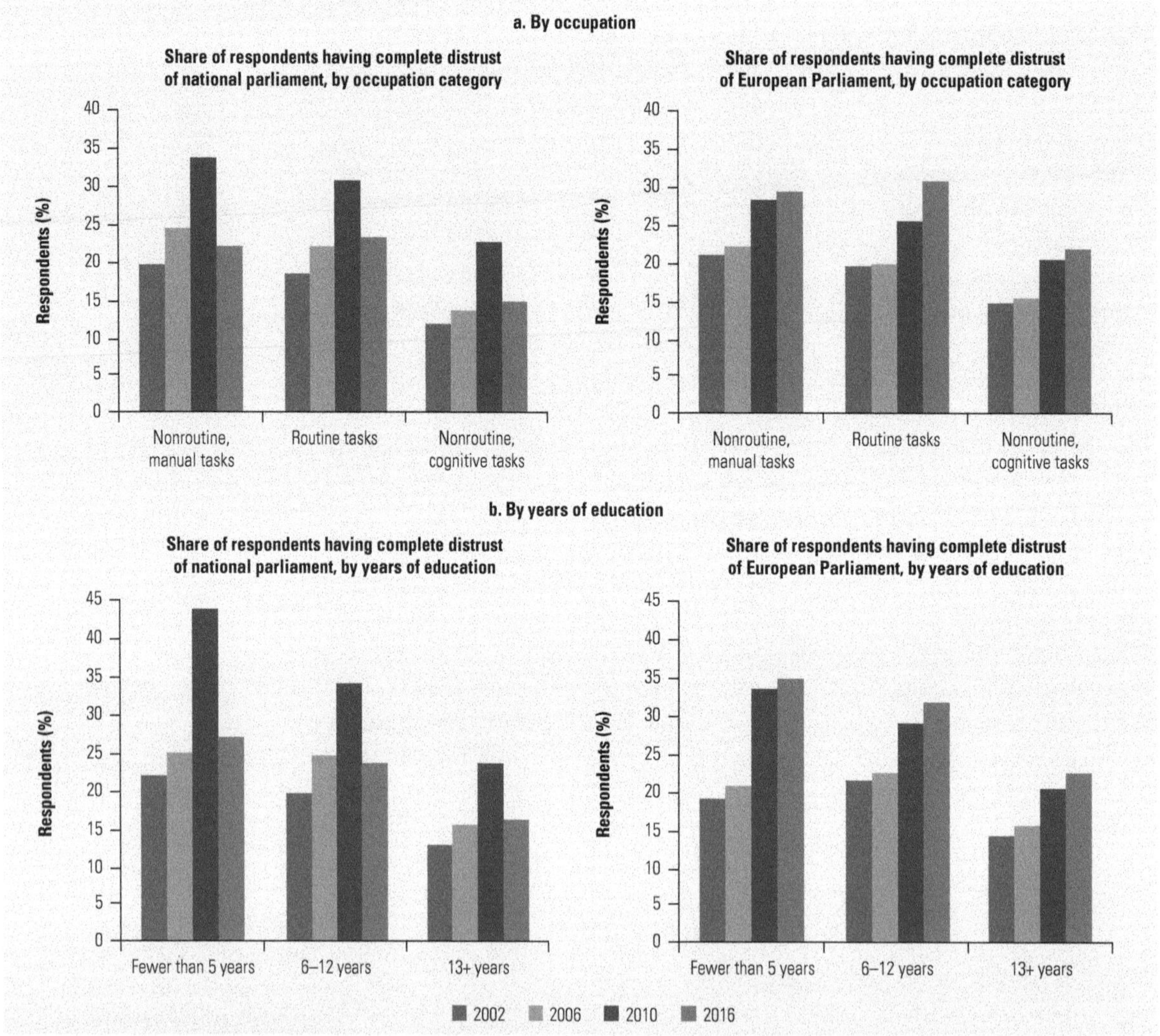
a. By occupation
Share of respondents having complete distrust of national parliament, by occupation category
Share of respondents having complete distrust of European Parliament, by occupation category
Respondents (%)
Nonroutine, manual tasks
Routine tasks
Nonroutine, cognitive tasks
b. By years of education
Share of respondents having complete distrust of national parliament, by years of education
Share of respondents having complete distrust of European Parliament, by years of education
Fewer than 5 years
6–12 years
13+ years
2002
2006
2010
2016

Sources: Calculations based on data of ESS (European Social Survey) (database), European Research Infrastructure Consortium, London; Norwegian Centre for Research Data, Bergen, Norway, http://www.europeansocialsurvey.org/.
Note: Complete distrust corresponds to values of 0–2 on a 0–10 scale of trust as originally recorded in the survey data.

Notes

1. See WVS (World Values Survey) (database), King's College, Old Aberdeen, United Kingdom, http://www.worldvaluessurvey.org/wvs.jsp.
2. The fifth wave (1995–99) of the World Values Survey contains a specific question about escaping poverty. The countries covered in this wave are Albania, Armenia, Azerbaijan, Belarus, Bosnia and Herzegovina, Bulgaria, Croatia, the Czech Republic, Estonia, Finland, Georgia, Germany, Hungary, Latvia, Lithuania, the former Yugoslav Republic of Macedonia, Moldova, Montenegro, Norway, Poland, Romania, the Russian Federation, Serbia, the Slovak Republic, Slovenia, Spain, Sweden, Switzerland, Turkey, Ukraine, and the United Kingdom. See WVS (World Values Survey) (database), King's College, Old Aberdeen, United Kingdom, http://www.worldvaluessurvey.org/wvs.jsp.

3. In this section, the terms inequality aversion, dislike of inequality, and equity preference are used synonymously.

4. "The term inequality is used perhaps rather loosely in the empirical literature," Clark and D'Ambrosio (2015, 1148) state at the outset of their extensive survey. "It is of interest to ask which measures of the distribution of income are the most important (to individuals) in this context: Is it (as is commonly assumed) the Gini coefficient, or rather something else?"

5. See LiTS (Life in Transition Survey) (database), European Bank for Reconstruction and Development, London, http://www.ebrd.com/what-we-do/economic-research-and-data/data/lits.html.

6. The objective Gini indicator shown in figure 4.1 is measured based on survey data, which do not include the top income earners. Nonetheless, individuals may have information about the richest people in the country and use that information to form their perceptions of inequality.

7. See ISSP (International Social Survey Program) (database), Leibniz Institute for the Social Sciences, Mannheim, Germany, http://issp.org/data-download/by-year/.

8. Since both demand for redistribution and perceptions of equality are subjective variables, they are bound to depend on the same unobservable individual characteristics, such as political opinions or noncognitive skills. For example, one's perceptions on equality as well as one's demand for redistribution might be both shaped by the type of media the individual reads. Unobservables may be behind the strong correlation amongst these two subjective variables. This also means that problems of endogeneity would affect a regression approach which tries to explain demand for redistribution using equality perceptions and other controls, since the independent variable equality perception would be correlated with the error term. To correct for this correlation, Bussolo, Ferrer-i-Carbonell, Giolbas and Torre (2018) adopt a two-step approach. First they estimate the perceptions of equality as a function of a series of controls (measured Gini, unemployment, poverty, government expenditures, as well as individual characteristics). Then, they re-estimate the demand for redistribution equation including the predicted error term obtained from the first regression. This corrects endogeneity as the predicted error term already includes those unobservable characteristics that explain individuals' equality perceptions. The results from this two-step approach confirm that demand for redistribution still depends on the "corrected" perceptions of inequality.

9. The variables that account for influences specific to an individual country or year are dummy variables set equal to zero or one across all observations of each variable. A constant is also included in the regression.

10. This is the same heterogeneity analysis reported above with respect to the demand for redistribution. There, individual characteristics, such as educational attainment or labor market status, are shown to affect how a given change in the perception of inequality is translated into a group-specific demand for redistribution. Here, individual characteristics influence the translation of the impact of an aggregate variable, such as unemployment, into a group-specific perception.

11. A stable job and good health not only confer economic security (a monetary evaluation), but also economic status. People may also consider permanent income rather than current income in their perceptions.

12. See ISSP (International Social Survey Program) (database), Leibniz Institute for the Social Sciences, Mannheim, Germany, http://issp.org/data-download/by-year/.

13. The International Social Survey Program surveys asks individuals if the society in which they live is one of four types shown in a diagram. The four types are the two extremes (type A, the most unequal, and type D, the most equal) and two additional intermediate types (types B and C). There is an additional fifth option (type E), which is not included in the analysis because the diagram is not clear in terms of inequality. See ISSP (International Social Survey Program) (database), Leibniz Institute for the Social Sciences, Mannheim, Germany, http://issp.org/data-download/by-year/.

14. A clear link is evident in what political scientists have been labeling democratic decon-solidation (Foa and Mounk 2016). In particular, authors are emphasizing the worrisome trend of the decline in support for democracy among younger generations.

15. Establishing causality is quite difficult in these contexts. Autor et al. (2017) and Colantone and Stanig (2017) use an exogenous rise in imports from China to study the electoral consequences of trade exposure.

16. For France and Hungary, the results are aggregated at the Nomenclature of Territorial Units for Statistics–3 level. For Poland, the results are aggregated at the Nomenclature of Territorial Units for Statistics–2 level. To capture the preferences of voters, the focus in the case of France is on the results of the first round of national legislative elections, and, in the case of Hungary and Poland, the focus is on the party list vote for legislative elections. Ideologically, extreme parties are those with a general ideology score in the Chapel Hill Expert Survey below 3 (extreme left) or above 7 (extreme right). See Chesdata (Chapel Hill Expert Survey) (database), Center for European Studies, University of North Carolina at Chapel Hill, Chapel Hill, NC, https://www.chesdata.eu/.

17. See ESS (European Social Survey) (database), European Research Infrastructure Consortium, London; Norwegian Centre for Research Data, Bergen, Norway, http://www.europeansocialsurvey.org/.

References

Acemoglu, Daron, and James A. Robinson. 2006. *Economic Origins of Dictatorship and Democracy.* Cambridge, UK: Cambridge University Press.

———. 2012. *Why Nations Fail: The Origins of Power, Prosperity, and Poverty.* New York: Crown Business.

Alesina, Alberto F., and George-Marios Angeletos. 2005. "Fairness and Redistribution." *American Economic Review* 95 (4): 960–80.

Alesina, Alberto F., and Paola Giuliano. 2011. "Preferences for Redistribution." In *Handbooks in Economics*, vol. 1A, *Handbook of Social Economics*, edited by Jess Benhabib, Alberto Bisin, and Matthew O. Jackson, 93–132. San Diego: North-Holland.

Alesina, Alberto F., and Edward L. Glaeser. 2004. *Fighting Poverty in the US and Europe: A World of Difference.* Oxford, UK: Oxford University Press.

Alesina, Alberto F., and Eliana La Ferrara. 2005. "Ethnic Diversity and Economic Performance." *Journal of Economic Literature* 43 (3): 762–800.

Algan, Yann, and Pierre Cahuc. 2010. "Inherited Trust and Growth." *American Economic Review* 100 (5): 2060–92.

———. 2013. "Trust, Growth and Well-Being: New Evidence and Policy Implications." IZA Discussion Paper 7464 (June), Institute of Labor Economics, Bonn, Germany.

Algan, Yann, Sergei Guriev, Elias Papaioannou, and Evgenia Passari. 2017. "The European Trust Crisis and the Rise of Populism." Brookings Papers on Economic Activity, BPEA Conference Drafts, September 7–8, Brookings Institution, Washington, DC.

Autor, David H., David Dorn, Lawrence F. Katz, Christina Patterson, and John Van Reenen. 2017. "Concentrating on the Fall of the Labor Share." *American Economic Review: Papers and Proceedings* 107 (5): 180–85.

Bénabou, Roland, and Efe A. Ok. 2001. "Social Mobility and the Demand for Redistribution: The Poum Hypothesis." *Quarterly Journal of Economics* 116 (2): 447–87.

Bussolo, Maurizio, and Mathilde Sylvie Maria Lebrand. 2017. "Feeling Poor, Feeling Rich, or Feeling Middle Class: An Empirical Investigation." Working paper (May 29), World Bank, Washington, DC.

Bussolo, Maurizio, Ada Ferrer-i-Carbonell, Anna Giolbas, and Iván Torre. 2018. "Perceptions, Reality and Demand for Redistribution." Background paper, World Bank. Washington, DC.

Chambers, John R., Lawton K. Swan, and Martin Heesacker. 2014. "Better Off than We Know: Distorted Perceptions of Incomes and Income Inequality in America." *Psychological Science* 25 (2): 613–18.

Clark, Andrew E., and Conchita D'Ambrosio. 2015. "Attitudes to Income Inequality: Experimental and Survey Evidence." In *Handbook of Income Distribution*, vol. 2A, edited by Anthony B. Atkinson and François Bourguignon, 1147–1208. *Handbooks in Economics*. Amsterdam: North-Holland.

Cojocaru, Alexandru. 2014. "Prospects of Upward Mobility and Preferences for Redistribution: Evidence from the Life in Transition Survey." *European Journal of Political Economy* 34: 300–14.

Colantone, Italo, and Piero Stanig. 2017. "The Trade Origins of Economic Nationalism: Import Competition and Voting Behavior in Western Europe." Baffi-Carefin Working Paper 2017–49 (January), Centre for Applied Research on International Markets, Banking, Finance, and Regulation, Bocconi University, Milan.

Cruces, Guillermo, Ricardo Perez-Truglia, and Martin Tetaz. 2013. "Biased Perceptions of Income Distribution and Preferences for Redistribution: Evidence from a Survey Experiment?" *Journal of Public Economics* 98 (February): 100–12.

Dávalos, María Eugenia, Giorgia DeMarchi, Indhira V. Santos, Barbara Kits, and Isil Oral. 2016. "Voices of Europe and Central Asia: New Insights on Shared Prosperity and Jobs." World Bank, Washington, DC.

Dustmann, Christian, Barry Eichengreen, Sebastian Otten, André Sapir, Guido Tabellini, and Gylfi Zoega. 2017. *Europe's Trust Deficit: Causes and Remedies*. Centre for Economic Policy Research. London, UK.

Easterlin, Richard A. 1974. "Does Economic Growth Improve the Human Lot? Some Empirical Evidence." In *Nations and Households in Economic Growth: Essays in Honor of Moses Abramovitz*, edited by Paul A. David and Melvin W. Reder, 89–125. New York: Academic Press.

Ferrer-i-Carbonell, Ada, and Xavier Ramos. 2014. "Inequality and Happiness." *Journal of Economic Surveys* 28 (5): 1016–27.

Foa, Roberto Stefan, and Yascha Mounk. 2016. "The Danger of Deconsolidation: The Democratic Disconnect." *Journal of Democracy* 27 (3): 5–17.

Gimpelson, Vladimir, and Daniel Treisman. 2018. "Misperceiving Inequality." *Economics and Politics* 30 (1): 27–54.

Giuliano, Paola, and Antonio Spilimbergo. 2014. "Growing Up in a Recession." *Review of Economic Studies* 81 (2): 787–817.

Grosfeld, Irena, and Claudia Senik. 2010. "The Emerging Aversion to Inequality: Evidence from Subjective Data." *Economics of Transition* 18 (1): 1–26.

Hirschman, Albert, and Michael Rothschild. 1973. "The Changing Tolerance for Income Inequality in the Course of Economic Development." *Quarterly Journal of Economics* 87 (4): 544–66.

Kanbur, Ravi, and Anthony J. Venables, eds. 2005. *Spatial Inequality and Development*. UNU-WIDER Studies in Development Economics Series. Helsinki: United Nations University–World Institute for Development Economics Research; New York: Oxford University Press.

Kuhn, Andreas. 2011. "In the Eye of the Beholder: Subjective Inequality Measures and Individuals' Assessment of Market Justice." *European Journal of Political Economy* 27 (4): 625–41.

———. 2016. "The Subversive Nature of Inequality: Subjective Inequality Perceptions and Attitudes to Social Inequality." CESifo Working Paper 6023, Center for Economic Studies and Ifo Institute, Munich.

Meltzer, Allan H., and Scott F. Richard. 1981. "A Rational Theory of the Size of Government." *Journal of Political Economy* 89 (5): 914–27.

Niehues, Judith. 2014. "Subjective Perceptions of Inequality and Redistributive Preferences: An International Comparison." IW-Trends Discussion Paper 2, Cologne Institute for Economic Research, Cologne, Germany.

Norton, Michael I., and Dan Ariely. 2011. "Building a Better America, One Wealth Quintile at a Time." *Perspectives on Psychological Science* 6 (1): 9–12.

Ravallion, Martin, and Michael Lokshin. 2000. "Who Wants to Redistribute? The Tunnel Effect in 1990s Russia." *Journal of Public Economics* 76: 87–104.

Rodrik, Dani. 2018. "Populism and the Economics of Globalization." *Journal of International Business Policy* 1 (1–2): 12–33.

Simler, Kenneth. 2016. "Pinpointing Poverty in Europe: New Evidence for Policy Making." Poverty and Equity Global Practice, World Bank, Washington, DC.

Stevenson, Betsey, and Justin Wolfers. 2011. "Trust in Public Institutions over the Business Cycle." NBER Working Paper 16891, National Bureau of Economic Research, Cambridge, MA.

Winkler, Hernan. 2017. "The Effect of Income Inequality on Political Polarization: Evidence from European Regions, 2002–2014." Working paper, World Bank, Washington, DC.

How Can the Stability of the Social Contract Be Restored?

Introduction

The countries of Europe and Central Asia have made dramatic progress since World War II in improving growth and inclusion and enabling people to achieve a middle-class lifestyle. However, people, institutions, and policy makers are struggling to adapt to changes in the nature of inequality that threaten to undermine the commitment to the social contract. In addition to the widening gap between the rich and the poor, inequality is growing across groups defined by age, occupation, and household type. Moreover, demographic background and connections, rather than abilities and effort, appear to be increasingly important in gaining access to economic opportunity. Expanding horizontal inequality and a deepening sense of unfairness are adding to the discontent with economic and political institutions. Reducing social tensions may require the redesign of institutions that have been key to supporting growth and equity in the region over recent decades. These challenges are likely to require a far-reaching response to restore stability to the social contract and meet the aspirations of populations for fairness, access to public services, and adequate, reliable incomes.

The goal of this report is not to propose specific policies. Rather, the aim is to make a broad contribution to the debate over the sort of society in which people might wish to live. A crucial question revolves around whether, financed by a progressive tax structure, universal approaches to income support, social insurance, and government services, which are critical to the access to economic opportunities, could improve equity and growth and thus address the distributional tensions that have been troubling society. A universal approach to social assistance might be compared with an approach that emphasizes means testing, whereby assistance is based on income. A universal approach to social insurance might be compared with an approach that links benefits to employment relationships. The impact of a universal approach, the form it should take, and the desirable pace of change will differ dramatically across countries, depending on the country context and political economy considerations.

There is a strong case for a comprehensive approach that addresses numerous problems at once because reforms in one area may affect reforms in other areas. It is also possible to build a coalition for change by recognizing the trade-offs between the winners and losers in each area. For example, improving labor market flexibility by easing stringent employment protection rules, primarily on permanent contracts, could be accompanied by an expansion of the access to social protection so everyone has adequate incomes able to meet needs. Given the many possible profiles of employment and the rapid transition among individuals across types of employment and between standard and nonstandard employment and unemployment, decoupling participation in essential social insurance programs from specific employment relationships would simplify the provision of access to insurance against risks. Raising the revenues necessary to financing robust social protection and, even more importantly, restoring equity in the tax systems can be achieved through more progressive taxation. Enhancing international coordination and cooperation in the taxation of capital would help limit the tax avoidance associated with shifting capital to alternative jurisdictions. Such an enhancement is a prerequisite for tax progressivity and improving equality of opportunity.

Recognizing the significance of rising distributional tensions highlights the need for more public investment in information. In particular, the collection and public dissemination of data on inequality across groups (workers, age-generations, residents of regions) and of perceptions of inequality, fairness, and intergenerational mobility are a high priority to monitor the distributional impact of policy changes and to improve social cohesion via an open debate (World Bank 2005).

Promoting Growth and Protecting People

The labor market is at the center of the distributional tensions that threaten the social contract in Europe and Central Asia. Labor is the predominant source of income of most households, and, in many countries, access to social insurance benefits, such as pensions and high-quality, affordable health insurance, is linked to employment. A stable, good-quality job confers status and often a degree of autonomy and a sense of control that are important to well-being and social inclusion. Europe and Central Asia's considerable record in providing robust employment protection and good-quality jobs has been supported by well-functioning labor markets. However, the decline in job security because of greater reliance on nonstandard employment contracts and large shifts in the demand for skills is undermining these achievements.

Policies in most countries of Europe and Central Asia provide significant job protections, which can support growth and welfare. Job security is important to well-being. Stable employment encourages workers and firms to invest in skills, and job protections help balance uneven power relationships between employers and workers. However, overly strict employment protection can severely constrain labor mobility, which contributes to productivity by enabling individuals and firms to achieve the best possible job matches. Excessive protection can also extend unemployment duration and boost long-term unemployment rates (box 5.1). The partial deregulation of the labor market (mainly for new entrants) in Europe during the late 1990s was an attempt to improve labor market flexibility. However, some studies find that the reforms contributed to a proliferation of contract types with wide variation in benefits and encouraged the substitution of permanent with temporary work. The reforms also contributed to a proliferation of contract types with wide variation in benefits. The reforms thus led to erosion in job security and reduced access to social insurance systems, which, together, have been partly responsible for distributional tensions. Decoupling access to social insurance from specific employment relationships would enable societies to realize labor market flexibility without impairing access to critical benefits.

Reducing differences in protection across types of contracts and in the number of types of contracts could promote more equitable treatment of workers. In some countries, permanent contracts are associated with excessive protections, while temporary contracts are more lightly regulated. Reducing these differences would provide incentives for employers to pick the appropriate type of contract based on economic necessity (is the nature of the task truly temporary?), rather than because one contract provides less protection or fewer benefits. Italy and Slovenia have pursued this approach. As part-time work becomes more common in countries in the region, partly because some workers value flexibility, the benefits supplied

---

BOX 5.1 **The Perils of Excessive Employment Protection**

Moderate employment protection can promote investment in good job matches and higher productivity, but overly burdensome employment protection impairs labor mobility. In France in 2011, 78 percent of hires and 71 percent of separations occurred because of the start or the end of a fixed-term contract (Dares 2012). Excessive employment protection also affects transitions between temporary and permanent employment, cementing the cleavage between insiders and outsiders. For instance, in 2016, the three-year average of transitions was 11 percent in France and Spain and 22 percent in Poland.[a] By contrast, the rate was more than 40 percent in Austria, Denmark, Estonia, Latvia, and the United Kingdom. High levels of temporary employment among youth, combined with low transition rates, can foster greater resentment both toward other youth sufficiently lucky to have found open-ended contracts (reflecting that inequality within cohorts has been rising) and toward the older generation that enjoys greater job protections and more benefits. Strict employment protection reduces job creation and job destruction, leading to increases in unemployment duration and long-term unemployment rates.

a. Data of Eurostat Statistics (database), Eurostat, European Commission, Luxembourg, http://ec.europa.eu/eurostat/web/main/home.

through employment, for instance, sick leave and vacation, should be prorated according to hours worked. Managing the proliferation in the types of contracts can help governments ensure that all contracts offer core protections and can also facilitate enforcement. This is desirable from the point of view of workers, given the information asymmetries that may enable firms to pick the type of contract most advantageous to them at the expense of workers.

Simpler and more predictable dismissal procedures would improve equity and efficiency. Excessively uncertain and complex dismissal procedures significantly raise the cost of firing and can add enormously to any monetary compensation related to dismissal. Specialized courts could handle unfair dismissal cases, thereby reducing litigation bottlenecks and ensuring greater uniformity in the application of the law. Many reform programs since 2008 focus on aspects of employment protection law that affect labor mobility and job-to-job transition, including limitations imposed on reinstatement in the case of unfair dismissals and on extensions of the duration of job probationary periods. The gaps in protection between temporary and permanent employment with respect to dismissals could be narrowed by treating a worker whose temporary contract is repeatedly renewed as a permanent employee for the purposes of dismissal. This could discourage companies from using serial short-term contracts for jobs that should be open-ended employment relationships.

Active labor market programs can be critical in assisting dismissed workers in finding new jobs.[1] The standard services that are offered as part of active labor market measures include counseling, training, job search assistance, intermediation, and various wage subsidies. The level and composition of spending on active labor market programs vary widely within Europe and Central Asia. Even in countries with reasonable expenditure allocations, such programs are not tailored to the needs of people transitioning between jobs.

The shift should be made from ad hoc single-issue interventions to integrated packages of services. Evidence shows that active labor market programs are much more effective if they offer integrated services that can be adapted to the profile of the individual worker and the nature of any shocks that might have been experienced. For instance, the package of services needed to help workers in a large and thriving metropolis who lose their jobs if a single firm downsizes is different from the package of services needed by the same workers displaced from the same jobs by trade liberalization or technological change affecting entire industries. Many studies have documented that adjustment in local labor markets in which industries are exposed to foreign trade can be remarkably slow, and depressed wages, lower labor force participation, and high unemployment rates may follow a shock for at least a decade.

Systems to profile workers and monitor and evaluate programs can improve the effectiveness of active labor market programs. Service providers in such programs can apply profiling systems to investigate the constraints individuals face and thus adapt programs to needs. Monitoring and evaluation are essential in assessing results. Examples of best practice can be a useful input in program design, but information on the impact of programs is necessary in determining effectiveness in each case. As demonstrated by examples of success, program services need not be financed by government alone, nor do they need to be provided by governments alone (box 5.2).

BOX 5.2 Helping Displaced Workers through Active Labor Market Programs

Workers displaced by structural changes, such as trade and technological change, often must upgrade their skills. They may also require support in moving to a new location and active encouragement and coaching to learn about and take advantage of opportunities for redeployment and reinsertion into work. The intervention required often costs more and is higher intensity than the interventions called for to help people who have experienced a transient shock.

Countries can learn from examples of success. A program of the Austrian Steel Foundation has assisted displaced workers in finding new work after the privatization of the steel industry by offering vocational orientation, small business start-up assistance, extensive training and retraining, formal education, and job-search assistance. The program is financed by the trainees, firms, and local government through unemployment benefits, and by workers in the steel industry who pay a solidarity portion of their gross wages to the foundation. The program boosted the probability of employment among participants (Winter-Ebmer 2001). The German moving subsidy for unemployed job-seekers has been effective in promoting labor mobility. Beneficiaries frequently find higher wages in more stable jobs, mainly because of enhanced job matching (Caliendo, Künn, and Mahlstedt 2017). Similarly, Romania's program for the reimbursement of unemployed individuals for expenses associated with migration has been effective in improving labor market outcomes (Rodríguez-Planas and Benus 2010).

In Sweden, job security councils are important institutions supporting workers affected by collective redundancy, which typically refers to layoffs of more than 10 percent of a workforce by an employer. The first job security councils were established in the early 1970s during deteriorating economic conditions and the 1973 oil crisis. The councils receive no direct state funding, but are financed through membership fees that are assessed as a percentage of the total payroll of each affiliated member company. The objective of the councils is to ensure that workers have substantial moral, financial, and professional support early on in the wake of dismissal. They often become involved as soon as an employee receives a notification of dismissal during the notice period and offer early risk services, such as goal-setting, activity planning, and personal consultations, to prepare the employee for the dismissal. They also provide transition services, which include labor market information, training and education, counseling, advisory seminars, business start-up support, and guidance meetings (Eurofound 2018). The councils further support redundant employees with financial compensation, which is supplied in addition to the general unemployment benefit. In 2015, the job security council for public sector employees found a new job for 9 active job-seekers in 10 within seven months; 70 percent of the clients found new jobs with equal or better pay relative to the previous jobs.

Source: Adapted from Diedrich and Bergström 2006; Eurofound 2018; World Bank 2018.

Extending Social Protection to Everyone[2]

Countries in Europe and Central Asia have a long history of delivering substantial social protection. The welfare systems and institutions that developed alongside industrialization have been a success. The share of formal employment rose even as labor market institutions and social protection systems conferred greater security, including protection from dismissal (unfair or otherwise), income support for the poor, more generous pensions, and well-financed sickness and disability protections. However, shifts in demand for skills, declining job security, and widening inequality among groups highlight the need for an overhaul in these arrangements. This agenda is more urgent in countries in the western part of the region that are in the front line in terms of labor market polarization and where aging trends are more mature. Yet, the general principles apply to all countries in the region.

Social protection systems in most of the region may not be sufficient to address emerging distributional tensions. Social insurance is currently provided mainly through employment. The trend toward more nonstandard employment and reduced employment tenure among the youngest generations is impairing the access to social insurance in the western part of the region, while significant informality is limiting access in the eastern part of the region. Likewise, although most countries in the region run extensive social assistance programs, these have not been designed to provide economic security, particularly among individuals of working age. Social assistance is typically organized around the life cycle. Family and child benefits cover individuals under 18; targeted last resort social assistance programs and heating and housing benefits support the poor and are the main programs available for individuals of working age; and noncontributory social pensions are aimed at the elderly. In many Western European countries, the coverage of overall social assistance among the poorest 40 percent of the population (the bottom 40) is nearly universal (see chapter 3, figure 3.12). In several countries, a large share of social assistance expenditures is allocated to programs in which targeting is not based on income (see chapter 3, figure 3.14). Despite the existence of such extensive social protection, the systems in these countries have been less effective in providing security in the face of rising distributional tensions.

Framework of Revamped Social Protection Policy

The basic framework presented in figure 5.1 illustrates a revamped social protection policy package that may help in responding to looming challenges and to changes in the way people work. Under ideal circumstances, such a framework would include two systems to cover two sets of risks, as follows:

- Programs to prevent poverty and protect against catastrophic losses (the bottom circle in figure 5.1) would include cash transfers, typically financed through general revenue (that is, social assistance), and insurance against catastrophic loss because of health care costs, disability, premature death, extreme longevity, or the need for long-term care (that is, social insurance). Such events have the potential to impoverish most households along the income spectrum. Key differences between social insurance and social assistance are outlined in table 5.1.
- Additional mandated programs can meet consumption smoothing objectives (the middle circle in figure 5.1). To help households smooth consumption over the lifetime of the members and because myopia may result in people saving less than they need, governments can mandate contributions to finance programs that provide benefits beyond the guaranteed minimum core.

Programs in the guaranteed minimum core would cover everyone, no matter whether or how they are engaged in the labor market. They would be provided by the government to all citizens or residents. Programs in the second circle are mandated by the government and would cover all individuals in the formal sector, including the self-employed and their dependents. The top circle in figure 5.1 shows

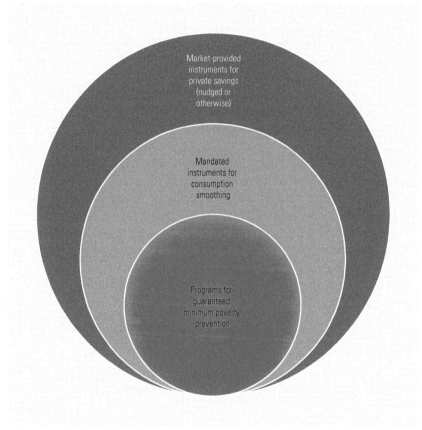

FIGURE 5.1
Social protection policy
package

Source: Adapted from World Bank 2018.

TABLE 5.1 Main Differences in Social Protection Pillars

Features	Social insurance	Social assistance
Entitlement	On basis of contributions	Categorical (that is, child benefits and social pensions) or poverty targeted (on the basis of current resources)
Eligibility condition	Depends on labor market status	Largely independent of labor market status[a]
Unit of assessment	Individual, possibly with extra payments to dependents	Individual (typically for categorical benefits) or household unit, that is, the nuclear family or the household, for poverty targeted programs
Finance	Largely by contributions; more recently, several countries have large deficit financing from the state budget	General taxation
Risks covered	Protect against large losses and help smooth consumption across work and unemployment, sickness and health, youth and old age	Prevent poverty; provide protections to vulnerable groups, such as children, people with disabilities, the elderly

Source: Adapted from Atkinson 2015.
a. Conditions may be added concerning the extent of job search or participation in active labor market programs as part of eligibility.

market-provided instruments that individuals may purchase privately, that is, there is no mandate. This set of instruments should be regulated by the government.

In the face of rising uncertainty and insecurity, it is important that the government provide guaranteed minimum poverty prevention as part of the revamped social protection policy package. In addition to social assistance programs, coverage financed through general government revenue to protect against large catastrophic losses as part of the core policy package can advance the goal of supplying basic social insurance to everyone. This insurance is currently offered in most European countries mainly through employment-related social insurance programs. Recent progress toward universal health coverage in several countries throughout the world has involved government payments for part or all of the premiums for health coverage among the poor. This approach is less common in the case of other sorts of catastrophic loss, and workers in nonstandard employment or with a weak attachment to the labor market remain vulnerable. Beyond ensuring core poverty prevention, the size of the first layer of social protection, financed through general government revenues and provided to all citizens and residents, varies by country. For instance, some Nordic countries already provide pensions, sickness and parental benefits to everyone based on financing through general revenues.

Additional mandated programs can meet consumption smoothing objectives. Because basic income needs are covered in the core and financed through general tax revenues, the size of mandatory savings and insurance can be reduced, while continuing to guarantee the same levels of consumption smoothing and risk protection. Overall payroll contributions can thus be reduced. This lowers the tax wedge placed on labor, thereby cutting labor costs, and can stimulate greater labor demand, including at the lower end of the skills distribution.

The revamped social protection policy package also helps clarify and distinguish between the poverty prevention and consumption smoothing objectives. Most social insurance systems, particularly old-age pensions, currently have two distinct goals: to prevent poverty among target groups, such as the elderly, the disabled, and survivors of individuals who have died prematurely, and to enable people to smooth consumption across employment status and unemployment, sickness and health, and youth and old age. In many social insurance systems in Europe and Central Asia, a single pillar is designed to meet both functions and is financed through payroll-based social insurance contributions alone. However, government budget transfers are often required to finance pension system deficits. This makes it difficult to determine the extent to which society or beneficiaries are financing program benefits and whether various categories of workers are receiving reasonable benefits in relation to the contributions the workers are paying into the system. Separating out the poverty prevention objective and including it in the guaranteed minimum poverty prevention core would enable the objective to be met effectively (the bottom circle in figure 5.1). An additional layer of contributions could be mandated to achieve adequate savings or insurance to support consumption smoothing beyond the basic minimum (the middle circle in figure 5.1).

Technological Options to Extend Coverage

In countries where the current coverage of open-ended full-time work contracts is high, reorganizing social protection according to the scheme shown in figure 5.1 is less urgent. An alternative option for expanding coverage and reducing the impact on work incentives might then involve technological approaches to ensuring the coverage of workers with nonstandard employment contracts. It has traditionally been more difficult to collect contributions from and pay benefits to farmers, the self-employed, entrepreneurs, workers in microenterprises, and workers with temporary or part-time contracts. In many programs in Europe and Central Asia, these types of nonstandard workers are covered through separate voluntary pension systems or through the establishment of social pensions, that is, pensions paid on a universal or means-tested basis directly through the state budget. Recent changes in technology and the wider use of national identity systems based on biometric data make covering these types of workers easier through standard national social security systems. Technology has made mandating and collecting contributions easier even in the absence of a standard open-ended employment contract. The use of mobile technologies, swipe cards, automated teller machines, and other methods of payment now allow nonstandard workers to make contributions easily and cheaply through mobile phones and other points of contact located close to their residences, even in remote parts of a country. The costs of collection have dropped dramatically, and payment of contributions has become easier, more flexible, and more convenient for a wider array of workers. Similarly, governments may make payments to workers more easily through digital channels, whether they are linked or not to bank accounts, regardless of where the workers live and work and regardless of the type of employment or employment contract. Governments in countries in which the use of technology is well established and at an advanced stage can now mandate contributions for the middle circle of the social protection policy package shown in figure 5.1 even among workers without traditional standard open-ended employment contracts.

The Debate on Universalism

An important debate has emerged on the relative advantages of a more universal approach in the provision of social assistance as part of guaranteed minimum poverty prevention. Several Western European countries have already achieved nearly universal coverage of households among the bottom 40. Child benefits are provided universally, and most of the elderly are covered through social insurance systems or noncontributory social pensions. The debate now centers on the coverage of the active-age population through more universal means. If they are poor, individuals in this group currently receive some support through housing and heating allowances and through last resort social assistance programs that are income and asset tested. It is among the active-age population that insecurity and uncertainty are growing because of the distributional tensions manifested through labor markets. *World Development Report 2019* advocates progressive universalism in addressing this insecurity and uncertainty (World Bank 2019; box 5.3).

To situate the debate on universalism, it is useful to compare the key design features of the various social assistance cash transfer instruments currently available in countries of Europe and Central Asia and listed in box 5.4. Table 5.2 describes the cash transfer instruments, such as unconditional cash transfers (UCTs), including child benefits and social pensions; guaranteed minimum income (GMI) programs, which are narrowly targeted on the poor; and conditional cash transfer (CCT) programs, which provide income support in exchange for the

BOX 5.3   Progressive Universalism

Achieving universal needs-based access to income support and universal access to social insurance cannot be accomplished overnight. Both the ultimate goal and the transition to the goal need to be considered. *World Development Report 2019* argues for progressive universalism in income support according to four key principles (World Bank 2019). First, the expansion in social assistance coverage depends on the country context, including preferences for redistribution, the available fiscal space, the political economy, and implementation capacity. Second, a gradual approach to scaling up social assistance is likely to be more successful than a sudden, sharp increase, especially in countries in which administrative capacity is limited.

Third, higher social assistance expenditures should be devoted first to the poor, many of whom are more difficult to reach than higher-income groups. Fourth, people at the bottom of the income distribution are likely to require more support relative to other groups.

These principles have major implications for social assistance program design. For example, avoiding targeting errors that lead to the exclusion of poor recipients is more important than ensuring that more well-off households that should not be eligible are excluded. This places a premium on comprehensive, efficient information systems that can be used to identify the people in greatest need.

Source: World Bank 2019.

BOX 5.4   Types of Social Assistance Cash Transfers

Universal basic income (UBI) is the provision of a minimum cash benefit for all individuals. The specific objectives of the UBI are to provide a cash transfer for all individuals to (a) give them basic or minimum income support and (b) help cushion them from labor market trends and fluctuations. Variations of the UBI include the following:

- The pure UBI (PUBI): a minimum income transfer to all individuals, where universal refers to all individuals
- PUBI for adults only (PUBI-AO)
- Progressive realization of a UBI (PRUBI): a minimum income transfer to all, but, first, to the poorest, plus other vulnerable groups
- Tapered version of a UBI or PRUBI (TUBI) whereby (a) benefits are not flat, but means-tested (say, according to income); or (b) there is a

gradual reduction or tapering of benefits toward the top of the distribution, such as a clawback of benefits among the rich either directly or through taxation, which presumes progressive taxation

Unconditional cash transfers (UCTs) are a widely applied social assistance instrument that provides a cash benefit to an intended population. Variations of the UCT include the following:

- A categorical UCT (C-UCT), whereby cash benefits are granted to all individuals in a specific category, such as all children (child allowances), the disabled, the elderly (social pensions), or the unemployed
- A poverty-targeted UCT (PT-UCT), whereby cash benefits are granted to all households or individuals based on an assessment of their

(Continued)

BOX 5.4 **Types of Social Assistance Cash Transfers** *(continued)*

(household) means (incomes, assets, proxies, socioeconomic status, and so on)

- A means-tested (poverty-targeted) C-UCT (PTC-UCT), whereby cash benefits are granted to all individuals in categories (children, the disabled, the elderly, and so on) based on some assessment of their household means

The guaranteed minimum income (GMI) is a widely used social assistance instrument that provides a cash benefit to poor households with some tapering of benefits based on their incomes in relation to eligibility thresholds.

A conditional cash transfer (CCT) is a widely used social assistance instrument that typically provides a cash benefit to poor households with expected coresponsibilities in terms of the participation of household members in work activities (workfare), the utilization of health care (regular visits to a health clinic), or school attendance.

Source: Lindert 2018.

fulfillment of coresponsibilities by beneficiaries.[3] The second column of the table outlines schemes of the UBI type, along with variations. The UBI, though untested, is currently being widely discussed as an instrument to promote many differing policy objectives, including preventing poverty and combating insecurity and uncertainty. A UBI would meet five broad criteria, as follows: (1) it is universal and is paid out irrespective of income or employment status; (2) it is provided in cash; (3) it is paid on a regular basis in uniform amounts to everyone; (4) it is rendered without any condition to carry out activities, such as training, work requirements, and so on; and (5) it is meant for individuals, not households or communities. There can be many variants of a UBI, and the table describes a few variants, such as a UBI with an explicit path for progressive realization (a PRUBI) and a UBI tapered toward the top of the distribution (a TUBI) so the rich receive no benefits. The third column of the table highlights the associated negative income tax instruments. Although most of the features of a UBI can be realized through the redesign of the tax system and through a refundable tax credit, the negative income tax differs from a PUBI along several dimensions. Not everyone will receive a cash transfer through a negative income tax. Benefit amounts may also vary in the case of a negative income tax. The poor might thus receive a much larger benefit relative to the less poor. The permanent duration of the benefit is one of the main ways in which a UBI differs from other cash transfer instruments and one of the features that people count on because it provides them with insurance and stability in the face of change. The current debate is whether a UBI-type transfer or a related instrument such as a negative income tax is necessary as part of the guaranteed minimum core of the revamped social protection policy package.

While GMI or PT-UCT programs cost little and have been effective in reducing poverty, there could be incentive issues associated with the means testing. Many programs in the eastern part of the region are designed as flat-rate benefits for the eligible. Households that are slightly above the eligibility threshold receive

TABLE 5.2 Comparing Cash Transfer Instruments, by Key Design Features

Features	UBI with variations: PRUBI, PUBI, PUBI-AO, TUBI	Negative income tax	UCT	GMI, a type of PT-UCT	CCT
Description, objectives	Provision of a minimum monetary benefit for all individuals to (a) give them basic minimum income support and (b) help cushion them from labor market trends and fluctuations	Provision of a monetary benefit to people below the tax liability threshold; the main objective is to supply a minimum monetary benefit to all (poor) individuals	Provision of monetary support to specific groups	Provision of monetary support to poor households to bring their incomes up to a minimum level	Income support tied in with beneficiary participatory tasks (coresponsibilities). The goal is to (a) reduce poverty in the short run through cash assistance, (b) address the underlying structural causes of poverty in the long run, and (c) narrow the intergenerational transmission of poverty through incentives so households invest in education and health care
Intended population, target group	What does universal mean? PRUBI: everyone, but, first, the poor and vulnerable; PUBI: everyone; PUBI-AO: all adults; TUBI: all, though possibly excluding the rich	All individuals with incomes below the tax liability threshold	Varies: C-UCT: categorical groups, such as children, the disabled, or the unemployed; PTC-UCT: categorical, plus needs based; PT-UCT: the poor and vulnerable, needs based (poverty targeted)	Poor households: needs based (poverty targeted)	Poor households: needs based (poverty targeted)
Benefit amounts	PRUBI and PUBI-AO: flat universal cash benefit for all individuals; TUBI: tapered benefits: higher for poorer households, lower for richer households; possible zero benefits for the richest	Tapered benefit: higher for poorer households, lower for richer households; zero benefits for households above an income threshold	Varies depending on design: flat allowance or stacked benefit amounts	Tapered benefit: higher for poorer households, lower for richer households; zero benefits for households above an income threshold	Varies depending on design, sometimes with a menu: flat benefits, stacked benefits (higher for poorer households), and variable benefits for specific household members (such as children)
Assistance unit: individual or household	PUBI: the individual; TUBI: may be the household	Same as tax filing unit	C-UCT: the individual; PTC-UCT or PT-UCT: usually the household because eligibility is based on household incomes or means test	Household	Household
Conditions	None	None	None	Adults able to work may have to prove they are searching for a job or enrolled in training	Beneficiary coresponsibilities involve the use of health services, school attendance, other education, or other accompanying measures with varying monitoring and enforcement
Duration of benefit	Depends on design. If the UBI is only for adults, then the duration of benefits is for all adulthood. If UBI payments are also assigned for children, the benefits are for life	As long as the assistance unit (individual or household) remains below the tax liability threshold	C-UCT: until the life-cycle period ends—the child becomes an adult; the disability is resolved; the older person passes away. PT-UCT: usually time limited	Usually time limited or recertification is required	Duration varies across programs and countries: some are not time limited as long as households qualify because the structural aspects of poverty and human capital require time; others have time limits

Source: Adapted from Lindert 2018.
CCT = conditional cash transfer; C-UCT = categorical UCT; GMI = guaranteed minimum income; PRUBI = progressive realization; PT-UCT = poverty-targeted UCT; PUBI = pure UBI; PUBI-AO = PUBI for adults only; TUBI = UBI tapered; UBI = universal basic income; UCT = unconditional cash transfers.

no benefits. If taking a seasonal job were to place current beneficiaries a little above the eligibility threshold, they could lose all benefits and thus become less well off. Such a design is not incentive-compatible at some points along the income distribution. The GMI programs in the European Union (EU) offer benefits that are continuously tapered, that is, beneficiary households receive the difference between the eligibility threshold or maximum benefit and the income of the households. While avoiding sharp discontinuities, this design imposes a 100 percent marginal effective tax rate. Thus, a worker who earns an additional euro while remaining eligible will have the entire euro taxed away as part of the continuous taper. Implementing this design also requires enormous information capacity. Observing income as accurately as the GMI designs assume is not possible. An important caveat is that, although the design of GMI programs is conceptually loaded with disincentives, these may not deter work significantly in practice (Tesliuc et al. 2014). Moreover, the eligibility threshold is sometimes sufficiently low that GMI-recipient families are not likely to be earners. Design improvements have attempted to correct for incentive issues with income disregards, base benefit disregards, and so on. In-work benefits have enhanced the monetary benefits of working, but have also increased administrative complexity.

Raising the income support thresholds of a GMI and not finely means-testing the benefit may be one way to protect people in the face of emerging distributional tensions. If the eligibility threshold for assistance is set well below the poverty line and at points at which the distribution of income is dense, this may result in arbitrarily different treatments of otherwise quite similar households that are close to the threshold. Small informational or decision-making inaccuracies might then generate numerous errors of inclusion or exclusion. Many GMI programs in Eastern Europe have become marginalized over the last 15 years and are covering smaller and smaller populations. For instance, spending on the monthly monetary benefit for low-income households, Bulgaria's last resort social protection program, fell from 0.28 percent of gross domestic product (GDP) in 2003 to 0.07 percent in 2010, and the number of households covered declined from 144,000 to 44,000. Only 1 or 2 percent of the population was receiving benefits through the program in 2010. In Poland, the number of recipients of means-tested household benefits dropped from 3.8 million in 2008 to about 2.3 million in 2013 partly because the income threshold was not indexed to inflation (World Bank 2015). Raising the income support threshold would expand the coverage of programs and provide more meaningful protection against economic insecurity. With higher thresholds, the difference in the treatment across similar individuals at the margin remains, but, because it would affect the more affluent segments of the distribution, it may not have catastrophic consequences and may be considered fairer. Depending on where such a higher threshold is set, it might also help avoid the incentive not to take employment at the lower end of the wage scale.

An enhanced GMI (similar to a TUBI) could alleviate some of the burdens associated with means testing and with conditionalities. The current emphasis on narrowly means-testing GMI eligibility may create a significant burden on poor households as they wait to be approved to receive benefits. This may lead to potential beneficiaries becoming homeless because they have fallen behind in paying rent and cause children to cease attending school. In recent years, the emergence of an emphasis on employment activation has generated new conditions, such as the requirement to search actively for a job or enroll in a training program, if households are to continue to be eligible for the GMI. Household members may thus become obliged to prove they have met the conditions. Shifting the emphasis of the program on excluding the rich, while continuing to provide support for the poor and the vulnerable, can alter the dynamics of the determination of eligibility and can significantly ease the burden on the extreme poor. Raising the threshold of a GMI program so that the poor and middle class are included and mainly the rich are excluded would transform the GMI instrument into a sort of TUBI. If such a design is to be seriously considered, estimates ought to be developed on the potential impacts of incentives on second and third earners within the household. Unlike in the case of current poverty targeted programs, a GMI with a significantly higher threshold would be available for many earners along the wage spectrum who are members of eligible households.

A UBI-type instrument can address issues associated with means testing. Because the UBI benefit is not reduced if earnings rise, universal income support does not encourage the underreporting of income or discourage taking a job because of the potential loss in benefits. It eliminates targeting errors that exclude recipients who should be eligible. The take-up of universal programs is much higher than the take-up of means-tested programs. So, a UBI may achieve universal coverage of the poor more easily compared with a means-tested program even if the latter has a high threshold (Bargain, Immervoll, and Viitamäki 2012; Hernanz, Malherbet, and Pellizzari 2004; Immervoll, Jenkins, and Königs 2015). However, a UBI also introduces challenges. The impact of a UBI on work incentives may differ. A high UBI could shrink labor supply if it reduces the willingness to accept a low-paying job. A UBI could also improve incentives for work among the poor by eliminating the threat of benefit withdrawal that is associated with means-tested benefits. Depending on the design, the replacement of all social assistance programs by a UBI may produce unintended consequences. For instance, if a UBI is provided to all adults, then poor families with many children who formerly benefited from the significant child-related benefits in EU member countries would experience a decline in assistance and increases in child poverty. A UBI accompanied by programs that provide targeted support for the most needy could achieve the goal of preventing poverty, while providing protection against insecurity and uncertainty. This implies targeting systems would still need to be developed and maintained to identify individuals who require more assistance than the UBI can provide. Such a system would be expensive.

Some effects of a UBI are difficult to anticipate. While the impact on vertical inequality of a UBI can be calculated in principle, inequality also would be affected by the way the UBI is financed. If the UBI involves higher expenditures financed by a rise in regressive taxation, any improvement in vertical inequality would be limited. Indeed, the greatest beneficiaries could be households with relatively high incomes that otherwise would not receive assistance from the government, while poor households simply experience a substitution or even a reduction in social assistance payments. This underlines the importance of considering carefully whether a UBI should replace other benefits and which benefits this might be and linking the adoption of the UBI to expansion of the progressivity of the tax system (box 5.5). The impact on horizontal inequality (such as across generations, occupational categories, or types of households) depends on the same factors: replaced benefits and shifts in taxation. When concerned groups are concentrated in a specific part of the distribution, for example when all individuals of younger cohorts are poor, the impact can be like that on vertical inequality. However, in other cases, the impact may be quite different and more complex. A debate on how to restore a stable social contract should thus include a careful assessment of the implications of a universal approach for both vertical and horizontal inequality.

BOX 5.5 **Distributional and Fiscal Effects of a UBI, Selected EU Countries**

Simulations of the impact of a universal basic income (UBI) program in selected European countries—Bulgaria, France, Germany, and Hungary—reveal a wide range of impacts on income distribution and fiscal expenditures, largely depending on the amount of the transfer.[a] These scenarios do not include any changes in taxes that might be necessary to finance expenditures under a UBI. It is assumed that the UBI entirely replaces all current nonpension benefit programs, whether means-tested or not, including social pensions.

Total UBI expenditures could be set equal to current benefit expenditures (on all means-tested and non–means-tested income-support programs, including social pensions), so that the fiscal budget is unaffected (the budget neutral scenario). Each individual would receive a UBI equal to this amount, divided by the number of beneficiaries. This would involve a sharp reduction in transfers to lower-income households because a much larger share of the total available benefits would be shared with higher-income households. The Gini would rise slightly in the countries considered (figure B5.5.1, panel a), although this could be offset by a more progressive tax structure (not examined here). However, this approach would clearly lower the benefits going to the most vulnerable.

This underlines the importance of establishing a UBI that replaces current benefits adequately. One view of adequacy might involve providing a transfer equal to the national poverty line (the poverty line scenario), which would provide everyone with insurance against poverty.[b] The benefit amount would be roughly the same as the disposable income enjoyed by single individuals without children who used to earn 50 percent of the average wage, but lost their jobs. This UBI would improve income distribution by between 8 and 13 Gini points in the four countries considered. It would also result in a sharp rise in fiscal expenditures, which, without complementary steps to increase taxation, would amount to a net expenditure (cost minus tax inflows) of an additional 30 percent of gross domestic product (GDP) in Bulgaria, 25 percent in France, 15 percent in Germany, and 15 percent in Hungary (see figure B5.5.1, panel b), amounts which are likely to be fiscally unsustainable. To maintain the improvement in income distribution obtained through the provision of the UBI, a substantial expansion of the progressivity of the tax structure would have to accompany any boost in taxes to finance the greater expenditure.

An intermediate scenario can also be envisaged. The benefit amount under the UBI could be set at the average amount of means-tested and non–means-tested benefits (including social pensions) paid to each recipient under current programs. This scenario would result in a moderate enhancement in income distribution in the four countries.

(Continued)

BOX 5.5 **Distributional and Fiscal Effects of a UBI, Selected EU Countries** *(continued)*

FIGURE B5.5.1 The costs of a UBI and the various effects of a UBI on income distribution

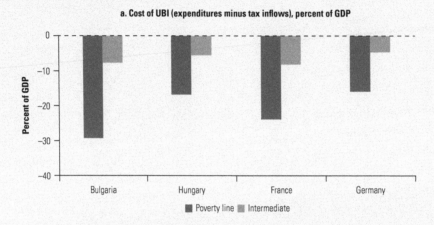

a. Cost of UBI (expenditures minus tax inflows), percent of GDP

Poverty line ■ Intermediate

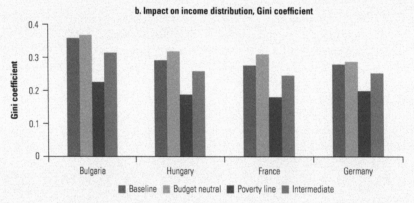

b. Impact on income distribution, Gini coefficient

■ Baseline ■ Budget neutral ■ Poverty line ■ Intermediate

Sources: Calculations based on data on 2017 tax-benefit systems in EUROMOD H1.0+ (Tax-Benefit Microsimulation Model for the European Union) (database), Institute for Social and Economic Research, University of Essex, Colchester, UK, https://www.euromod.ac.uk/2017/12/13/euromod-h10-released; 2015 data of EU-SILC (European Union Statistics on Income and Living Conditions) (database), Eurostat, European Commission, Luxembourg, http://ec.europa.eu/eurostat/web/microdata/european-union-statistics-on-income-and-living-conditions.
Note: All scenarios assume no changes in the tax structure. The budget neutral scenario has no effect on the fiscal deficit.

Current beneficiaries would receive the same benefits on average, but individual households could experience significant changes in benefits. The fiscal cost would be far less than the cost under the poverty line scenario, but would remain close to or somewhat above 5 percent of GDP in the four countries (see figure B5.5.1).

Other design choices would affect the impact on distribution and on the fiscal deficit. The scenarios above assume that the UBI is paid equally to every individual in the population. Alternative assumptions under which the UBI is paid only to adults have also been considered, whereby each child under 18 years of age receives 50 percent of

(Continued)

BOX 5.5 **Distributional and Fiscal Effects of a UBI, Selected EU Countries** (continued)

the payment to adults, but the UBI is paid only to the poorest 80 percent of the population. There are some differences between the impact of these alternatives on income distribution and the fiscal deficit relative to the scenarios presented in figure B5.5.1. For instance, eliminating payments to children or cutting them by half would reduce the fiscal cost somewhat and would reduce the improvement in income distribution. However, given the importance of child-related benefits in current EU welfare systems, limiting the benefits to children would penalize poor households with children and could result in higher child poverty rates. Eliminating payments to the top 20 percent of the income distribution would result in a smaller fiscal cost and a greater improvement in income distribution relative to the provision of benefits to everyone.

Thus, a UBI that substantially enhances income distribution is likely to require greater fiscal expenditures, although design choices influence these effects significantly.

a. These simulations are based on the tax-benefit microsimulation model EUROMOD (version H1.0+) and use the most recent tax-benefit systems available (2017) as a baseline. Under all scenarios, the UBI benefit is assumed to be taxable, following Browne and Immervoll (2017). For EUROMOD, see EUROMOD H1.0+ (Tax-Benefit Microsimulation Model for the European Union) (database), Institute for Social and Economic Research, University of Essex, Colchester, UK, https://www.euromod.ac .uk/2017/12/13/euromod-h10-released.
b. This is based on each country's relative poverty line, which is set equal to 60 percent of median equivalized household disposable income (the standard EUROSTAT definition of income poverty in EU countries), using the modified Organisation for Economic Co-operation and Development (OECD) equivalence scale, which assigns the following weights to household members: 1.0 to the first adult, 0.5 to the second and each subsequent person ages 14 and over, and 0.3 to each child under 14.

More Progressive Taxation

Considering a change in tax policy to improve progressivity in conjunction with the introduction of universal measures of income support is important. More progressive tax systems would help narrow inequality of opportunity and improve equity. Changes in the tax system could ease the increase in vertical income inequality, the heavy tax burden on labor incomes, and the rise in inequality of opportunity.

Increasing the top income tax rates would help dilute the concentration in incomes. The growing share of top earners in total income since the 1990s has coincided with substantial cuts in the highest income tax rates. The lowering of the top rates from the peaks of the 1980s may have improved efficiency. However, optimal tax theory does not supply a convincing rationale for the additional cuts since the 1990s. This is so because (1) there is no evidence of an expansion in income tax elasticity among top earners; (2) the share of income earned by the top income percentiles has not declined, but rather has increased; and (3) changes in social preferences do not seem to support higher welfare weights for the rich (IMF 2017). There is also little evidence that progressive income tax regimes lead to slower economic growth.[4] Indeed, many people are expressing concern about the rising number of billionaires and the increasing influence exerted by elites on government decision making. Raising top income tax rates would be a key signal that governments care about the growing unfairness in the distribution of income.

Shifting more of the tax burden to capital rather than labor would reduce inequality. As a share of GDP and household disposable income, labor income has fallen, and capital income has risen in the countries of Europe and Central Asia and in most other countries since the beginning of the 1990s.[5] Moreover, private wealth is typically much more unequally distributed than income, and the concentration of wealth has increased in the last two decades. These two phenomena have contributed to the widening in income inequality since the early 1990s. Thus, all else unchanged, a shift in taxation from wages to capital income would reduce vertical inequality. It would also lower the intergenerational divide in the western part of Europe and Central Asia: because the oldest generation earns little labor income, but tends to hold a larger share of society's private wealth than younger generations, a shift in taxation to capital would help address the relative decline in income among the younger generations.

Shifting more of the tax burden to capital would reduce inequality of opportunity. Wealth is partly generated by the savings of individuals and partly transmitted by transfers either inter vivos or through bequests. Transfers are a major channel of the intergenerational persistence of wealth and economic status. Therefore, increasing taxes on transfers inter vivos and bequests would reduce the unequal access to economic opportunity by compensating for the unequal endowments of birth (Atkinson 2016; Piketty 2015).

Shifting taxes from labor income to capital would also affect efficiency for both good and ill. The high taxation of labor income can reduce labor supply and raise the costs incurred by firms. Easing taxes on labor income could thus have a positive impact on employment. Reducing taxes on labor income might also encourage greater investment in human capital by both firms and workers. It is often argued, however, that the taxation of capital decreases investment and savings and lowers the incentives for entrepreneurship and risk taking. Yet, recent studies find that the imposition of a tax on wealth has limited effects on behavior, although it does affect the reporting of asset holdings (Brülhart et al. 2017; Seim 2017; Zoutman 2015).

The feasibility of raising the taxes on capital is open to question. Capital is much more mobile than labor. So, increasing taxes on capital may be met by a rapid drop in the tax base. Competition among jurisdictions to attract capital is doubtless one of the drivers of the decline in capital taxation and the relative rise in taxation of labor income in recent decades. Achieving more substantial taxation on capital likely requires coordination across countries to establish uniform or similar tax rates and administrative procedures. Thus, Atkinson (2016) and Piketty (2014) propose global taxation schemes. A less ambitious proposal would involve a uniform tax on capital throughout the EU (Atkinson 2016). The recent effort to share information among tax administrations is a promising step. Whether a shift toward capital taxation should take the form of higher taxes on capital income or a tax on wealth is an issue much discussed (box 5.6).

Overall, there is a strong case for increasing capital taxation. A mix of more progressivity in the inheritance tax, a capital endowment for all adults, and greater progressivity in capital income taxation would promote equality of opportunity, fair redistribution, and enhanced efficiency.

BOX 5.6 Should Taxes Be Higher on Capital Income or on Wealth?

A recent report argues that, in tackling widening wealth inequality and inheritance inequality, greater progressivity in capital income taxation and inheritance taxes is more efficient and equitable than taxes on the stock of wealth (OECD 2018).

A wealth tax is prone to several problems. Unlike a tax on capital income, a wealth tax is imposed on accumulated assets irrespective of the return on the assets. It may therefore distort the investment decisions of private agents and encourage taxpayers to invest in highly productive assets. It is not clear whether this would generate efficiency gains or losses because it might also discourage socially profitable investments. A wealth tax is procyclical, that is, during an economic downturn, the income from capital may decline sharply, while, despite any decline in asset valuations, the wealth tax is unlikely to fall by as much. Thus, taxes rise as a share of income in a downturn, potentially deepening a recession because of falling demand. Moreover, a wealth tax might be a source of inequality because the middle class tends to hold low-return assets, while wealthier taxpayers are often more well placed to manage high-risk assets. This favors a tax with a high wealth threshold or a progressive tax schedule. A wealth tax may involve substantial administrative costs, including a recurrent and costly valuation of assets. In addition, individuals with low income, but substantial wealth may face difficulty in acquiring liquid assets to pay taxes.

There is little theoretical difference between an inheritance tax and a wealth tax (Piketty and Saez 2012). However, unlike a wealth tax, an inheritance tax provides incentives to spread the wealth among the next generations. Also, an inheritance tax may be more acceptable politically because the link to the promotion of equality of opportunity is clearer.

To modernize inheritance taxes, Atkinson (2014) proposes instituting a lifetime capital receipts tax or integrating a tax on capital receipts into the personal income tax, which would raise the revenues from and the progressivity of the personal income tax. Under the former proposal, every gift or legacy received would be recorded as of the date of the initiation of the tax, and the tax payable would be determined by the sum received to date. All gifts inter vivos above a modest annual exemption would be included. The rate structure of the lifetime capital receipts tax would be progressive, and the tax would be imposed on the receiver, not on the donor, which, combined with the progressivity, would provide incentives to spread wealth around more widely.

Atkinson (2014) proposes that the revenue from the lifetime capital receipts tax be used to pay a minimum inheritance to each individual when they become an adult. This is related to an approach proposed by Ackerman and Alstott (1999) in the United States involving the payment of US$80,000 financed through a 2 percent tax on personal wealth and the proposal of Julian Le Grand (2003) to supply a start-up grant to young people in the United Kingdom. A minimum inheritance program might be more acceptable and perhaps more effective in improving the prospects of recipients if restrictions on its use were imposed to avoid wasteful spending. Investment in human capital could be a good use of these funds from an efficiency and equity perspective. Whether the entire endowment should be given at once or over time (as in the universal basic income program) is another important question.

Reducing Inequality of Opportunity through Improved Services

Strengthening access to services would complement reforms in labor markets, social protection, and tax regimes to address the distributional tensions that threaten the social contract. Ensuring that everyone, including rural residents and people in poor communities, has equal access to high-quality education and expanding the provision of lifelong learning so that workers can upgrade their skills in response to technological change would improve access to economic opportunities and reduce the widespread resentment over the perception that the rules of the game have been fixed.

Efforts to improve equity and equality of opportunity also depend on timely early childhood development. The first 1,000 days, from conception to age 2, are critical in the development of the neural pathways that promote the linguistic, cognitive, and socioemotional capacities that influence labor market outcomes later in life (Atinc and Gustafsson-Wright 2013). Poor health in early childhood, including poor nutrition, limits the development of physical, cognitive, and socio-emotional skills. Children who are healthy and living in a safe and nurturing environment perform better in school, attain higher educational degrees, and enjoy better chances of succeeding in the labor market later (OECD 2017). Heckman and Carneiro (2003) find that the returns to early interventions are much greater than the returns to remedial or compensatory interventions later in life. Children ages 15 who have attended at least one year of preprimary education have higher mathematics scores, and the gap with their peers without preprimary education is almost one year of formal schooling after one controls for socioeconomic status (OECD 2013).

Despite the importance of early interventions, the access to childhood services during the first three years of the lives of their children and the access to preschool education, which contributes to equality of opportunity later in life, are limited among disadvantaged groups in Europe and Central Asia. Increasing the supply and quality of early childhood education, ensuring adequate pre-, peri-, and post-natal nutrition, health care, and a safe physical environment, and strengthening the ability of parents and other caregivers to support healthy development among their children can mitigate inequalities that accumulate throughout a person's life (Arias and Bendini 2006). Sustaining the gains in early childhood education requires the development of benchmarks to measure quality and the integration within formal education systems of the content, budget, and capacity of providers in preschool programs.

Ensuring access to equal quality foundational, that is, basic and compulsory, education is also critical in narrowing inequality of opportunity. While the ECA region performs well in educational coverage and attainment relative to other regions, education systems in some post-transition economies have not adjusted following the significant economic transformations of the last couple of decades. Many students in disadvantaged regions and many sociodemographic groups still leave school without the skills they need to lead productive lives. This perpetuates the inequality of opportunity across generations.

Key steps in enhancing the educational experience among disadvantaged students include addressing the policy drivers of school segregation (for example, school assignment, school financing, and lack of information on school performance); improving community outreach; promoting cross-learning between leading and lagging schools; delaying tracking; addressing early school leaving; and providing support to deal with mental health or substance abuse issues. Investments in teachers and management capacity in schools and across education systems serving disadvantaged groups can promote better student performance. Expanding accountability for results, including by monitoring the performance of schools serving disadvantaged communities, is crucial to confronting deficiencies and inequalities in education systems. Standardized tests are important in promoting reform and accountability and should be implemented across the region.

The ongoing expansion of tertiary education in the region would make a greater contribution to productivity if greater effort were applied to tying curricula to labor market demand. One approach involves providing students with access to information about employment and earning prospects, including the collection and distribution of data on employment and earnings linked to tertiary institutions. This has already been done in several countries in the region, particularly in the EU, including Bulgaria, the Czech Republic, Hungary, Italy, the Netherlands, Poland, Romania, and the United Kingdom. The greater use of performance-based financing and performance contracts can support quality enhancements.

Population aging and the critical role of rapid technological change in determining the demand for skills underlines the importance of lifelong learning. Developing education and training services for adults that foster workforce upskilling and reskilling and that involve the private sector in defining the skills taught and in the supply of training initiatives would help ease the distributional tensions arising from job polarization and the inability of many workers to sustain a middle-class lifestyle. Given recent technological changes, focusing on the tasks workers carry out in their jobs everyday, rather than on traditional skills training, could be more effective in helping workers gain access to more economic opportunity. For instance, Generation—a training program for youth run by McKinsey Social Initiative in India, Kenya, Mexico, Spain, and the United States—designs training sessions around imparting the skills needed to master critical job tasks.

Conclusion

A more universal approach to the provision of social assistance, social insurance, and key services, in conjunction with more progressive taxation, has the potential to raise the welfare of the vulnerable households that are losing out because of the economic changes affecting Europe and Central Asia. In many countries, the adoption of more universal approaches could be more effective than current institutional arrangements in addressing the distributional tensions that threaten the sustainability of the social contact.

Providing universal access to social insurance—essentially decoupling access and employment—could provide younger generations in the western part of the region with the levels of protection enjoyed by older generations. Workers in non-standard employment, many of whom are young, could gain protection similar to that of workers with regular contracts. In the eastern part of the region, the access of informal workers to basic social insurance would improve. Among all workers, financing minimum social insurance through the tax system would reduce the taxes on labor and thus boost the demand for labor by firms.

Low-income households that eke out a living by relying on social assistance and a hodgepodge of temporary jobs could benefit from a more universal approach to social assistance. Their benefits would not decline as earnings increased, allowing them to accept all types of jobs, including temporary or seasonal work, without fear of losing benefits. This has the potential to improve their welfare and increase their labor supply.

Policy reforms could contribute to reducing inequality of opportunity in the region. Greater taxation of top incomes and of capital income, along with increased taxation of bequests and other transfers, would narrow vertical inequality and help curtail the perpetuation of economic privilege across generations. Using a portion of the higher revenues to expand key services to rural areas and disadvantaged communities would expand economic opportunity. Services focused on the youngest children should be broadened.

Universal approaches have the potential to enhance economic security, opportunity, and growth. Institutions and conditions differ considerably across the region. So, the appropriate policies will differ as well. Nonetheless, many people across the region share a belief in the value of equity and social cohesion. They also face a common challenge: adapting institutional arrangements to economic change is a struggle. This highlights the potential benefits of a serious debate over the pitfalls and virtues of universal approaches in the region. The goal of this publication has been to contribute to the resolution of this debate.

Notes

1. The discussion on active labor market programs borrows from World Bank (2018).
2. This section borrows from the White Paper developed for the World Bank's Forward Look 2030 strategy (see World Bank 2018). It also borrows from *World Development Report 2019: The Changing Nature of Work* (World Bank 2019).
3. The comparison of the various dimensions of cash transfer instruments is adapted from Lindert (2018).
4. There is evidence that extreme tax rates on top incomes may have negative growth effects; however, the evidence is inconclusive in the case of the current rates in the countries of the Organisation for Economic Co-operation and Development (OECD).
5. For a summary of the literature arguing for a rise in the taxation of capital relative to labor, see Atkinson (2016); OECD (2018).

References

Ackerman, Bruce, and Anne Alstott. 1999. *The Stakeholder Society*. New Haven, CT: Yale University Press.

Arias, Omar S., and Maria Magdalena Bendini. 2006. "Bolivia Poverty Assessment: Establishing the Basis for Pro-Poor Growth." En Breve 89 (May), World Bank, Washington, DC.

Atinc, Tamar Manuelyan, and Emily Gustafsson-Wright. 2013. "Early Childhood Development: The Promise, the Problem, and the Path Forward." *Costing Early Childhood Development* (blog), November 25, Brookings Institution, Washington, DC. https://www.brookings.edu/articles/early-childhood-development-the-promise-the -problem-and-the-path-forward/.

Atkinson, Anthony B. 2014. "After Piketty?" *British Journal of Sociology* 65 (4): 619–38.

———. 2015. *Inequality: What Can Be Done?* Cambridge, MA: Harvard University Press.

———. 2016. "How to Spread the Wealth: Practical Policies for Reducing Inequality." *Foreign Affairs* 95 (1): 29–33.

Bargain, Olivier, Herwig Immervoll, and Heikki Viitamäki. 2012. "No Claim, No Pain: Measuring the Non-Take-Up of Social Assistance." *Journal of Economic Inequality* 10 (3): 375–95.

Browne, James, and Herwig Immervoll. 2017. "Mechanics of Replacing Benefit Systems with a Basic Income: Comparative Results from a Microsimulation Approach." IZA Discussion Papers 11192 (December), Institute of Labor Economics, Bonn, Germany.

Brülhart, Marius, Jonathan Gruber, Matthias Krapf, and Kurt Schmidheiny. 2017. "The Elasticity of Taxable Wealth: Evidence from Switzerland." Working paper (January), Department of Economics, Faculty of Business and Economics, University of Lausanne, Lausanne, Switzerland.

Caliendo, Marco. Steffen Künn, and Robert Mahlstedt. 2017. "Mobility Assistance Programmes for Unemployed Workers, Job Search Behaviour, and Labour Market Outcomes." IZA Discussion Paper 11169 (November), Institute of Labor Economics, Bonn, Germany.

Dares (Direction de l'animation de la recherche, des études et des statistiques). 2012. "Les mouvements de main-d'œuvre en 2011: une rotation élevée dans le tertiaire." Dares Analyses 056 (September), Dares, Ministry of Labor, Paris.

Diedrich, Andreas, and Ole Bergström. 2006. "The Job Security Councils in Sweden." IMIT Report (October 5), Institute for Management of Innovation and Technology, Gothenburg, Sweden.

Eurofound (European Foundation for the Improvement of Living and Working Conditions). 2018. "Industrial Relations, Sweden: Developments in Working Life 2017." Working paper, Publications Office of the European Union, Luxembourg.

Heckman, James J., and Pedro Carneiro. 2003. "Human Capital Policy." NBER Working Paper 9495 (February), National Bureau of Economic Research, Cambridge, MA.

Hernanz, Virginia, Franck Malherbet, and Michele Pellizzari. 2004. "Take-Up of Welfare Benefits in OECD Countries: A Review of the Evidence." OECD Social, Employment and Migration Working Papers 17, Organisation for Economic Co-operation and Development, Paris.

IMF (International Monetary Fund). 2017. "Tackling Inequality." Fiscal Monitor (October), World Economic and Financial Surveys, IMF, Washington, DC.

Immervoll, Herwig, Stephen P. Jenkins, and Sebastian Königs. 2015. "Are Recipients of Social Assistance 'Benefit Dependent'? Concepts, Measurement, and Results for Selected Countries." OECD Social, Employment and Migration Working Papers 162, Organisation for Economic Co-operation and Development, Paris.

Le Grand, Julian. 2003. *Motivation, Agency, and Public Policy: Of Knights and Knaves, Pawns and Queens.* New York: Oxford University Press.

Lindert, Kathy. 2018. "Some Reflections on UBI as an Unconditional Cash Transfer." Working paper, World Bank, Washington, DC.

OECD (Organisation for Economic Co-operation and Development). 2013. *OECD Skills Outlook 2013: First Results from the Survey of Adult Skills.* November. Paris: OECD.

———. 2017. *Preventing Ageing Unequally.* Paris: OECD.

———. 2018. "The Role and Design of Net Wealth Taxes in the OECD." OECD Tax Policy Studies 26 (April 12), OECD, Paris.

Piketty, Thomas. 2014. *Capital in the Twenty-First Century.* Cambridge, MA: Belknap Press.

———. 2015. *The Economics of Inequality.* Translated by Arthur Goldhammer. Cambridge, MA: Harvard University Press.

Piketty, Thomas, and Emmanuel Saez. 2012. "A Theory of Optimal Capital Taxation." NBER Working Paper 17989 (April), National Bureau of Economic Research, Cambridge, MA.

Rodríguez-Planas, Núria, and Jacob Benus. 2010. "Evaluating Active Labor Market Programs in Romania." *Empirical Economics* 38 (1): 65–84.

Seim, David. 2017. "Behavioral Responses to Wealth Taxes: Evidence from Sweden." *American Economic Journal: Economic Policy* 9 (4): 395–421.

Tesliuc, Emil D., Lucian Pop, Margaret E. Grosh, and Ruslan Yemtsov. 2014. *Income Support for the Poorest: A Review of Experience in Eastern Europe and Central Asia.* Directions in Development: Human Development Series. Washington, DC: World Bank.

Winter-Ebmer, Rudolf. 2001. "Evaluating an Innovative Redundancy-Retraining Project: The Austrian Steel Foundation." IZA Discussion Paper 277 (March), Institute of Labor Economics, Bonn, Germany.

World Bank. 2005. *World Development Report 2006: Equity and Development.* Washington, DC: World Bank; New York: Oxford University Press.

———. 2015. "Sustaining Recovery, Improving Living Standards." EU Regular Economic Report 2 (Fall), World Bank, Washington, DC.

———. 2018. "On Risk-Sharing Policy for a Diverse and Diversifying World of Work." World Bank, Washington, DC.

———. 2019. *World Development Report 2019: The Changing Nature of Work.* Washington, DC: World Bank.

Zoutman, Floris T. 2015. "The Effect of Capital Taxation on Household Savings." Working paper, Norwegian School of Economics, Bergen, Norway.